ONE MAN'S
MEDICINE

ONE MAN'S MEDICINE

MORRIS GIBSON

*Foreword
by James Herriot*

A TOTEM BOOK
TORONTO

First published 1981
by Collins Publishers
100 Lesmill Road, Don Mills, Ontario

This edition published 1984
by TOTEM BOOKS
a division of Collins Publishers

Canadian Cataloguing in Publication Data

Gibson, Morris.
  One man's medicine

ISBN 0-00-217125-2

1. Morris, Gibson. 2. Physicians—England—
Biography. I. Title.

R489.G43A3 1984   610.69'52'0924   C82-094961-2

Printed in Canada

In the text the names and descriptions of characters have been fictionalized except for those physicians and public figures whose identities it would be impossible to conceal.

Acknowledgements

The Yorkshire winds and snow blew against the window as James Herriot said, "Don't just *tell* stories; write them." My first acknowledgement is to him for his encouragement, and for so generously offering to write the foreword.

My next is to Fred and Helen Wooding who advised and listened wisely and sensitively; to Derek Cassels, editor of *The Medical Post*; Stan Gibson and other friends who over the years encouraged me to write; to Margaret Paull of Collins for her confidence in *One Man's Medicine*.

Skipper Tom Nielsen, secretary of the Hull Trawler Officers' Guild advised me. Mr. Saltiel of the Fishermen's Mission and Mr. Sharp, editor of *The Hull and East Yorkshire Times* kindly supplied information as did Miss Jefferson, formerly Head of "Tranby" School for Girls, and Miss Fallucco, archivist, the American Medical Association.

Thanks go to my friend, Squadron Leader Cy Goodwin, who typed much of the manuscript so impeccably. To Mary and Doug, my enthusiastic supporters, and above all to Janet, who throughout has advised, gently driven, and constantly sustained me with patience and infinite good humour.

ONE MAN'S
MEDICINE

Foreword

It may seem a little odd for a veterinarian to be writing a foreword for a book about human medicine. But the healing art holds a general fascination – for the lay public and for people like Morris Gibson and me.

There are all kinds of doctors but even among the very good ones like Morris there are those who regard their calling in the light of cold science. Fortunately for mankind and for literature there are the many to whom the medical profession is an endlessly unfolding rich panorama to be savoured anew each day. There is the drama, the grief, tragedy and humour of human life and there is also the deep satisfaction which the truly dedicated doctor finds in the practice of his skills, in the exercise of his hard won knowledge.

My enjoyment of *One Man's Medicine* was mingled with an eerie feeling that I was reading about James Herriot, because the careers of Morris Gibson and myself seem to have followed almost parallel lines. Quite unknown to each other, we grew up in the west of Scotland, were educated in Glasgow and rejoiced in exploring and camping in the glorious countryside around that city. And it all took part in the shadow of the impending war. We did our war service then settled in Yorkshire where we fell in love with the beautiful Dales. Yorkshire is a big county and we were many miles apart, but when he was fighting to build a practice in Hull I was doing the same in Darrowby.

The similarity goes deeper than mere geography because though Morris was treating people and I was treating animals we responded in the same way to the laconic, sometimes grim, but utterly genuine Yorkshire folk.

Then, as though this were not enough, we both, at an age when most professional men are happily embedded in their own particular rut, seized hold of a pen and decided to become authors.

I don't know what actually sparked off Morris's writing activities but with me it was a sudden flash of pique. I have been married – again like Morris – for nearly forty years to a woman whom I love deeply and who has battled alongside me through every step of the way and it is from such a wife that a man often catches an unexpected gleam of self-knowledge.

Being utterly absorbed in my job with its excitement, humour and occasional sadness I fell into the habit of recounting to my wife, Helen, little anecdotes from the day's work. I used to do this regularly at meal times or at spare moments in the evening and Helen was a good listener. And apart from telling her the stories, I often announced that I would write a book one day and this nebulous concept developed over the years into "my book" as though it were an accomplished fact.

It was over tea one summer afternoon that the blow fell. I had been happily burbling about something amusing which had happened that day and I finished my account as I always did with, "I'll put that in my book."

Helen usually accepted this remark without comment but this time she put down her cup and looked at me steadily.

"Jim," she said, "You're never going to write a book."

I was aghast. "Whatever do you mean?"

"Well, don't you remember?" She gave me a quizzical smile. "We celebrated our silver wedding last week. You've been telling me for twenty-five years about this book, but nothing has happened yet. And you're fifty years old now."

I tried to point out to her that I was not an impulsive type and that naturally I needed a little time to work things out before I started, but she was not impressed. Women can be so unreasonable.

She must have seen that I was taken aback by her attitude because she reached across the table and rested her hand on mine.

"Don't be upset, Jim," she said. "Thousands of people have had the same idea as you. In fact, nearly everybody has a sneaking feeling that they can write a book, but very few do."

"But that doesn't apply to me," I declared stoutly. "I definitely will do so one day."

She shook her head slowly and though her expression was kind her words were like a knell. "Old vets of fifty don't suddenly start writing books."

That did it. I rushed out, purchased a large quantity of paper, and began immediately.

I have no knowledge of how Morris Gibson was launched on his literary career but I wonder if he needed some sort of a push. It is just possible.

The opening chapters of *One Man's Medicine* take us through the doctor's student days and here, among the struggles and the laughter, I recognized the authentic whiff of Glasgow; the toughness, the squalor and the beauty which lies so close at hand.

One of the fascinations of the book is that it deals with the period when the new drugs – the sulphonamides and antibiotics – burst upon the medical scene. I can remember the days when "blood poisoning" was a constant hazard and I could relate to Morris's joy and thankfulness when his armoury of therapeutics was magically revolutionized and he was able to benefit his patients as never before.

Like the best kind of doctor, he is intoxicated by the great spectrum of medical science. Everything absorbs him; not just the physical side but psychiatry, hypnosis, the nature of pain. And through it all there is the deep appreciation of human nature.

This is not simply a recital of a doctor's cases, vivid and exciting though they are; it is a warm, funny, touching book. Episodic in character and filled with lovely punch lines it dips into the lives of shepherds, soldiers, hardy fishermen and countless ordinary people.

Throughout it all the character of the author emerges with increasing clarity. So many virtues are here. Compassion, courage, integrity and a vulnerability which enlists our sympathy and understanding. Dr. Gibson is not afraid to describe his failures and bafflements – things which I know so well myself.

But there is something else in the book which intrigued me greatly – a delightful paradox. I thought I had him summed up pretty thoroughly. His strict, almost Calvinistic upbringing in Scotland, with its rigid values and its shrewd approach to the practical and commercial problems of the world must surely have produced the archetypal canny Scot; a man of sober judgement and cautious action. Indeed, he mentions in one chapter the advisability of young doctors gaining an early knowledge of investment and the handling of money.

But what do I find as I read on? After he and his wife, the pretty little red-head about whom he writes so fondly, had managed after years of labour and sheer hardship to scrape together a thousand pounds – what does he do? He invests it in a pig farm and he doesn't know anything about pigs nor does his new partner in the venture.

I know from my experiences in my veterinary work that this

is the classical scenario for financial ruin and.I almost shuddered as I turned the pages. But he did it and he got away with it. I realized that here was a complete man and I warmed to him as I did to little red-headed Janet who on receipt of the news of her husband's decision responded only with "Oh, crumbs!"

As I finished the last page it was a comforting thought that though this was the end of *One Man's Medicine* it merely completed the first chapter in a fascinating career. There is so much to come in other books and I for one eagerly anticipate them because I found Dr. Gibson's medicine very easy to take.

JAMES HERRIOT

Chapter
One

Walter Kerr's gray stone cottage stood in the low field of the hill, a mile or so back from the highway. It was difficult to see the place from the red-topped main road as it wound its way through Lanarkshire to the south, along the beautiful valley of the Clyde, miles away from Glasgow with its industry and pollution. Here the air was fresh and the hill country just beginning, those bare, windswept hills of the Scottish lowlands.

Automobiles were seldom encountered. Hikers tended to head north to the Highlands. This country was still relatively unknown to them, and nighttime accommodation hard to come by. The occasional seasoned walkers, clad in flannels and sports jacket, raincoat shoulder-slung, might pass and bid a curt good day, as might some countryman townward bent on an ancient bicycle; but that was about all. One could walk for miles, alone.

In this country, on one of the bicycling trips I enjoyed so much in my student days, I was caught early one summer evening by a sudden change in the weather. The red sandstone road had gradually lost its brilliance. The drystone walls that flanked it no longer reflected the delicate golds and greens of the mosses that clung to them. They became a dull, uniform gray. Intermittently the sun retreated behind advancing clouds. A cold wind swept down the glen, bringing with it an occasional drop of rain, the merest hint of what was to come. It was very still. Even the birds, paying homage to the gathering storm, had stopped their singing. Suddenly, high above a hill, the first storm clouds began to gather and swirl in the sky. I decided to stop at the nearest farmhouse and ask permission to set up my tent in the lee of a drystone dyke.

And so I had come upon Walter Kerr's cottage.

I slept that night, not in the flimsy shelter of my little tent, but in the security of Walter's barn, snuggled into the soft hay, oblivious to the wind and rain that raged outside.

In the morning the storm was gone and a friendship begun. The Kerrs gave me breakfast, waved aside my offer of payment and invited me to come back. Since then Wattie's place had

1

been my *Shangri-la* for years, as I tramped the hills with him. He knew that with my bicycle, bivouac tent and haversack, I needed little in the way of shelter. He knew when I'd arrive, and he would be there at the junction, leaning on his crook, waiting, Prince and Queenie at his heels, their intelligent eyes taking in every move as I dismounted.

This time Queenie indicated her suspicion that introductions and gossip might take some time. She settled her forelegs along the ground in front of her and rested her chin on them. Prince hadn't forgotten an old friend and his black bush of a tail told me so as it swept the red gravel of the side road. But today he didn't leap forward as he would have done the previous summer, or come and plead to be spoken to. He had learned his place.

Walter, like most of his kind, was not given to idle talk, and Queenie's reverie was broken as we turned and walked towards the cottage. Walter was a tall, broad-shouldered man in his early fifties, handsome in a rugged way; his height and dark moustache made him look more like a Highland laird than a Lowland hill shepherd. Steady blue eyes looked at the world from under the peak of his cloth bonnet, often pulled low on his forehead to shield his eyes from the sun as he scanned a hillside for sheep.

In winter his old raincoat was worn with a piece of twine for a belt. In summer the same twine kept the coat strapped over his shoulder like a soldier's bandolier. He always dressed in heavy gray tweeds, in summer without the jacket, his shirt, collarless, open at the neck. He paid winter the compliment of donning the jacket and wearing a scarf that in a storm could mask his face like an Arab's burnous. An old sack might sometime protect his back against the winter downpour.

Dogs at heel, he would take to the hill at first light to tend his herd. For weeks each summer my tent was my home, set up in the field behind his cottage, sheltered by the low drystone dyke. At night I could lie and read by my lantern until, lulled by the symphony of the soft wind over the heather and the quiet bleating of distant sheep, I would drift into sleep. Minutes later, so it seemed, the heavy "thwack" of Wattie's staff on the canvas would signal the dawn of a new day. "First light, lad," he'd cry. "Breakfast's ready."

An old, brown stained photograph on the mantelpiece showed a younger, thinner Wattie and a laughing girl. Bessie had once been pretty, perhaps even vivacious, although now with her gray hair and plain face it was difficult to imagine.

She would place breakfast on the table – well-turned eggs and toast with steaming tea – her only remark to ask if it would be enough.

Their's was a quiet partnership seldom disturbed by philosophical or economic crises. Their needs were few. Walter's job was assured, and though by today's standards they lived below the statistical poverty line, they were content. To Bessie, Walter was the "Maister," a mark of rank it never occurred to either of them to question.

An ancient bicycle provided transport in any emergency or when Walter went to the village some miles away to report to the boss, who bore the name of Mr. Lamb. A grocery van called once a week. Like most hill shepherds, their contacts with neighbours were few.

They never read a newspaper. In the evening the Maister would switch on an antique wireless set, listen to the news headlines, switch the set off with a quiet "Well, that's that," and the rest of the evening would be spent in silence. Bessie would sit on a wooden chair beside the kitchen table, her knitting spread before her, while Walter, from the comfort of the Maister's chair, silently smoked his pipe. If Walter rose to his feet to do some chore, Queenie was instantly beside him. "Aye, Queenie," he'd mutter, and they'd be off together.

In the previous summer I had often been invited to spend the evenings with them, and that was when I first met Prince, a lolloping affectionate bundle of fur, all tail and wet nose. Like his mother, he was a border collie. And then I found that Walter and Bessie were not at all a dour couple. Bessie wanted to know all the news from "the Wishy," my home town, and Walter, though he had little time for idle conversation, also wanted to talk.

"They bliddy Jairmans are goin' tae hae anither go at us, lad – eh? An' this felly Hitler – he must be clean oot o' his mind? Mind you, it'll be the Somme and Arras a' ower again afore we hae him licked – an' then it'll be they dam't Amerrykins say they did it!" He gave a sour grin as he sucked his moustache with his lower lip, a little habit he had when troubled.

Prince had been a puppy when I first met him, loose-jointed, craving an affection that was all too easy to give. When a little whimpering at the flap of my tent door announced the arrival of my friend, I never refused him entry, a wet nose thrust into my face being ample reward. Walter, disapproving though he probably was, indulged us both, and though he knew the

3

truant's whereabouts, he never objected. Only once in all the years of our friendship did Walter rebuke me, and then gently. One evening, seeing Prince sitting at my feet, his eyes fixed on my face, one ear cocked ridiculously upright, I picked him up, a gesture Prince greeted with obvious delight.

"Pit him doon, lad," said Wattie gently. "He's a working dug, no' a pet."

A week or so later I had seen Prince begin his education. In the early morning light, with the red sky still throwing a reflection on the lower field, we quietly approached a group of sheep. Warily, they sidled away from us. Queenie was a few paces behind her master. Prince, lolloping along behind us all, was exploring every rabbit hole in sight, and setting up his territorial rights with a vigour, thoroughness and frequency that made me wonder if he was mostly made of bladder.

"Here, Prince!"

Walter waited patiently while His Highness lifted his leg one final time against a briar bush and then, deciding that this command might have something in it for him, approached, tail wagging his bottom almost off balance. In the process he stepped joyously all over his mother, who paid him no attention whatsoever. "Doon lad!" Little lessons had had their effect and Prince plumped his bottom on the heather.

My friend never struck his dogs. That would have been self-confessed failure. Rebukes were given and known by his tone of voice, and that was never harsh. He never showed them open affection, yet their devotion to him was implicit. Taking a piece of twine several feet long, and an old cloth from his pocket, he wrapped the cloth round Prince's collar, fastened it down with the twine, and attached the other end to Queenie's collar.

"Noo, lad," he addressed Prince in one of his rare moments of elocutionary extravagance, "ye're goin' tae the university this day. Only I'm going tae be yer professor, an' yer mother's goin' tae keep an eye on ye. More, I daresay, than your friend has tae put up with."

He tested the knots, hitched his raincoat over his shoulder, and turned to me. "Noo then, lad, we'll see if he's got it in him." Prince came of good stock. To my unqualified eyes he was bright, intelligent and above all, a lovable puppy. To Walter he was still unproven. The sheep had moved away, munching the grass, but keeping a sidelong watch on our movements.

"Oot bye," muttered Wattie, raising his crook to the left.

4

Queenie was off, slipping through the grass to her quarry. She moved quietly, deliberately, tugging her bewildered son along behind her.

"Slow, noo, slow," urged the shepherd. Queenie, receptive to every gesture and tone of voice, moved slowly, bunching the sheep together. They were suspicious by now. They had stopped feeding and were watching the dogs. Queenie, belly to the ground, was motionless. The sheep had bunched together.

"Noo! Queenie, noo!" The collie ran forward, weaving to keep her quarry in a group, a very puzzled puppy pulled in her wake.

"Doon!"

Immediately she stopped in her tracks, but Prince, full of enthusiasm for this strange game, sailed on, until at the end of the rope he turned an almost complete somersault. I couldn't suppress a guffaw, but there was no answering mirth from my friend.

"Ye see, lad," he said, sober-faced, "that's what I mean. If he's got it in him he'll no' let that happen verra often."

Within a few days Prince had learned, and within weeks he was off like a streak at Queenie's heels, quivering with alertness, following her every move, listening to his master's voice. In fact, he passed his "finals" a year before I passed mine!

Walter and I had cleared the hill together many a time, and sometimes he let me take a section on my own, paying me the great compliment of sending Prince with me. One day I met him on the hill, cap pulled over his eyes, staff raised like a teacher's pointer as he counted his charges. Queenie was sitting on the heather a few feet away.

"Forty twa, forty three, forty four ... "

"What's up, Wattie?"

"Queenie'll no come off the hill. She ken's there's one missing. Ah thocht I had them all, but she'll no budge."

"She must count them, Wattie," I scoffed.

"By gor, I sometimes think she does," he grinned, unstrapping the well-worn binoculars he always carried and scanning the hillside, outcrop by outcrop.

"Canna see a dam't thing," he muttered. "But she ken's there's ane somewhere. Lad – d'ye see yon hummock?" He pointed to a mound half a mile or so away on the steep slope.

"I see it, Wattie."

"Weel, your young legs are better than my auld yins. Go on ower and hae a look."

5

"What makes you so sure it'll be there?" I asked.

"Man," he said, to the heather in general, "and I suppose one of these days he'll be a big professor up in Glasgow! Because lad, that's where they aye get coupit. Off we' ye, and ye can take yer pal wi' ye."

Prince and I were off at a run. He found the sheep, overturned in a gully just as Walter had said. Sheep are surprisingly unstable creatures on their feet, especially if their coats are heavy, and once overturned, have difficulty in righting themselves. Then lacerations or bruises become infested by maggots, and unless these sores are dealt with, they become enormous, the flesh filled with hundreds of squirming larvae. Our patient had suffered no injury and Prince sent her on her way.

But months had passed since then, and my friend no longer crept under the canvas and shoved his nose at my face. He had all the dignity of a graduate and didn't associate with mere students. One morning, however, it was Bessie's gentle tapping on the canvas that wakened me.

"Walter's no' goin' up the hill the day. He's no' weel."

I was awake and dressed in a moment. "What's the matter Bessie?"

"Oh, he says it's the flu. He's fevered and coughing, and for once I hae laid doon the law," she finished with great firmness.

"Good for you, Bessie. Let's look at him."

Walter was sitting up in bed. Shamefaced, he pushed a bowl of porridge away as I came near. "It's naethin. The flu, that's all. I'll be up by the morrow."

But as a medical student I had spent three years watching pneumonia kill strong men under the best of care, and I was taking no chances. "Let me examine you, Wattie, and if I'm not happy I'll go for the doctor."

He looked at me, then nodded. "If that's whit ye think best." So I tapped out his thorax for the tell-tale dullness that would suggest pneumonia, and, at least, if I had no medical equipment, I could put my ear to his chest and listen for the moist bubbling of fluid. In those days, before the sulphas and other antibiotics, pneumonia killed thousands in the prime of life.

"A couple of days in bed for you, Wattie!" And then I remembered his vocation. "The sheep, Walter, what'll you do?"

"I'll be up by the morrow. Maybe they'll manage the day without me."

"Walter," I said hesitantly, "let me go up the hill. Maybe Prince would still work with me." I could see my friend was turning the idea over in his mind as he started to finger the blankets.

Suddenly he nodded, his mind made up. "By gor, he just might at that, and it'd save me frae sending for Tamson o' Langdale."

"Here, Prince," I said, in a way that brought the dog to my side like a flash. Queenie settled down beside Walter's bed.

"The twa rookies, that's what I'll hae to call ye," grunted Walter, "the two rookies." He looked at us both, relieved, yet I do believe a little put out that his recent graduate could attach himself, however temporarily, to another "chief."

Prince and I set off. A few yards from the cottage my companion hesitated and looked back, but I spoke to him, stroked him, and, his doubts seeming to be resolved, he followed me. I couldn't have dealt with any real problems of the shepherd's craft, but together we cleared the hill. When we got down to the low field, Walter stood waiting for us. I proudly indicated my flock.

"Ay, but hae ye counted them?"

"Me? No, Walter, I left the counting to Prince!" That worthy, just out of hearing, had moved too close to a lamb and with alacrity and skill was dodging the mother's charge.

The next day I left. Walter and the dogs accompanied me to the main road. Just as I was about to mount my bike he reached into his pocket and produced a packet, covered in newspaper. The jam was already seeping through the paper. "Here," he said, "frae Bessie. A jelly piece to keep ye frae getting hungry." The thoughtfulness was typical of them. Settling myself in the saddle I reached over to shake his hand.

"Man," he said, "it's an awful pity ye have to go back to the university. With a bit of training doon here lad, ye'd be gey near as good as another dog to me."

Chapter Two

"Come here, boy," commanded Miss Shirlaw. "Come here and let me look at you. And tell me what mischief you've been up to these days. For if you're not up to mischief at your time of life, you're too good for the Lord to let live. Besides," she added with her deep laugh, "I want to know all about it."

Miss Shirlaw had played bridge with my parents for years, and my early return from medical school that day had upset a "three-handed" game. My father looked at me quizzically; my mother, a matriarch in the often matriarchal Scottish society, gazed upon me with blind and proprietorial pride.

"Look at that dreadful eye," Miss Shirlaw exclaimed. "It was the other one last month. And your nose is beginning to look bulbous. We will simply have to find you a girl before all this boxing ruins your face forever, then no girl will ever look at you! So what are you doing with yourself apart from ruining your looks?"

I had to confess that I was leading a life of irreproachable virtue. I did not confess that I had begun to look upon a little red-headed lady medical student with distinct, if distant desire. Had not Sir William Osler, that great Canadian doctor, advised all aspiring physicians to lay their emotions behind them until they reached their thirties? Had not my parents, secure in the traditions of middle-class Scottish Calvinism, indicated that marriage must be based on an ability to support one's wife appropriately? Anything less than this was, by tradition, irresponsible.

It was the spring of 1939. I was twenty-two. I didn't see how I could continue my present monastic existence until I was thirty. I felt it might be possible until I obtained my burning ambition and achieved the degrees of Bachelor of Medicine and Surgery of Glasgow University, with a little bit of luck, that September.

Beyond that I could not see. Very few of us tried. Behind us, and hovering over us still, was the depression. Few of us believed Mr. Chamberlain's unctuous reassurances of "peace in our time," or Hitler's promises. We had little optimism for

8

the future. All we wanted to do was get our degrees before the axe fell.

There I was, a final-year medical student, one of 180 in our year, and for all of us the next six months would be crucial. At the end of that period we would spend three gruelling weeks facing the examiners each day, clinically, orally, and in our "writtens," reproducing all that we might have learned in the past few years. With luck we would emerge from the final examinations qualified, at least on paper, as doctors.

Scottish medical students have traditionally been portrayed as a licentious and riotous lot. It is a lie, but one the adolescent student body has jealously fostered. The slander was probably initiated by the divinity students anxious to divert public attention from their own activities. Most of us were callow youths, straight from school at eighteen. We had satisfied our high school principals (or rectors, as headmasters are more grandly called in Scotland) as to our academic qualifications. The university entrance committees believed us to be upright and moral young people. And so we entered upon the study of medicine at Glasgow's ancient university.

In my wanderings I have seldom found Glasgow revered as one of the world's centres of high culture. Even by its expatriate children it seems to be associated with shipbuilding, sea-going engineers and the comic songs of Harry Lauder. Yet the university, founded in 1450 by Papal decree at the request of James II, King of Scots, became renowned throughout Europe as a centre of learning.

Adam Smith, the father of modern economics, had held the Chair of Moral Philosophy. James Watt, inventor of the steam engine, had been an instructor. Tobias Smollett and James Boswell, the writers, studied there and so did Jamie Graham, the great Marquis of Montrose, soldier and poet. While a professor there, William Thomson, later Lord Kelvin, perhaps the world's foremost physicist, carried out his research into thermodynamics.

The medical school is a distinguished one. Lister, the founder of modern aseptic surgery taught there. The great Sir William MacEwan, god-like, strode the surgical wards. When I was a student his name was still spoken with reverence. Perhaps the most renowned surgeon in Europe, he was famous for his manual dexterity. Legend has it that he could tie a surgeon's knot with a spider's thread.

Thus is mythology born.

In my year, there were a dozen or so girls and it was generally and condescendingly accepted that they were there on sufferance. They sat in a body in the front two rows of the great steeply-sloping lecture amphitheatres, for to have "sat among the boys" would have been tantamount to relinquishing one's reputation, and was seldom, if ever, attempted. It was the self-imposed and happy duty of a number of lecturers to make their collective life if not as miserable, certainly as embarrassing as possible, and they rose to this duty with pride. The delighted plaudits of the male chauvinist and frequently juvenile audience were all the rewards they asked.

"Ay, well now, today we'll be discussing the question of abortion," began one preceptor in a broad Glasgow accent.

"Not just abortion," he paused, a slight inclination of the head acknowledging the feminine occupants of the two front rows, "but septic abortion, a verra different kettle of fish, indeed. A matter of great interest to criminologists and moralists alike."

Somehow, managing to combine tones of academic omniscience with the suggestion of a leer, he scanned their faces as they sat primly in place, pencils poised over paper.

"Septic abortion, ladies. An unpleasant but verra necessary subject for this morning's lecture. But then," he paused again, revelation having descended upon him, "but then, you may know all about it already! Not yourselves, of course, but a friend or two perhaps?" And with the howls of male applause ringing in his ears, he proceeded with the business in hand.

Indeed it was a serious business. Abortion was a criminal offence. The doctor who took pity on some hapless girl would be disbarred and jailed if discovered. He was no less a criminal than the back-street abortionist. Every year women were admitted to hospital with acute pelvic infections. Barred by law from obtaining abortions from qualified doctors, they had resorted to the dangerous help of so-called "abortionists." The results were often catastrophic. With eventual recovery, after weeks of illness, went the strong possibility that further childbearing was impossible because of the damage that had been done. And death from such criminal abortions was common.

But the male chauvinism of the time in medical schools was not as dreadful as it sounded. A good deal of it was mischievously humorous, a tradition rather than a threat, and while the majority of teachers eschewed such frivolity, those who deemed themselves practitioners of the art of tormenting the women were specialists in the craft. Sometimes the barbs were blunt, even sadistic, occasionally poisonous and not infrequently coarse. But the women students survived it all and came to little harm. Indeed, a few years later, experience having triumphed over shyness, some could recall with a grin some particularly juicy insult.

The young women, of course, were very bright. They had to be, to find themselves there at all. They were formidable academic opposition and none of us took them lightly. Today's soft anonymity in the way of marks and competition was unthought of. There was no general "Pass," or polite oblivion if you failed. Class standings were published and certificates of distinction given, and the women took their fair share of these. Some of them were very pretty, too, including "my" red-head.

The years of clinical medicine were hard going, and most of us, living at home with our own folks, subject to parental scrutiny, financially and morally, worked very hard. Summer jobs were the exception rather than the rule, and licentious living was, to say the least, difficult. Our noses were kept hard to the grindstone. It was an exacting discipline. There was no formal instruction in how to deal with people. As students, busy taking careful history notes, pumelling abdomens or thumping out chests, we moved in and out of people's lives so frequently and so impersonally that faces and personalities became blurred. Though we might remember every detail of the acute leukemia case in bed 22, the patient's personality and background too often remained an enigma.

Patients were case histories rather than people. This was not deliberate callousness. It was perhaps the end of an era, when the great hospitals had been charity institutions. When we interviewed patients we were interested in blood corpuscles, the involvement of disease, the "feel" of an abdomen, the character of the heart sounds, and sometimes we were interested in the clinical process of dying. We were often too young to discern behind those composed and polite faces in hospital beds the courage that we should have admired, the fears that we might have allayed, the despair we could have comforted.

Fortunately there were some wonderful teachers who were also warm human beings, and from these we learned by example. Dr. Milne MacIntyre, Clinical Professor of Surgery at the Glasgow Royal Infirmary was such a man. A stern old Scot, he insisted that every patient in his public wards "had a handle to his name." The use of a surname in addressing patients, however humble their station in life, was forbidden, from surgical specialists to medical students. His morning

11

rounds were examples of "professional manners" as he used to put it, and the patients looked forward to his coming as if he were some kind of god.

He had a handshake for each patient and a touch on the shoulder for many, especially those fresh from surgery. The quiet, "You're going to get better, Mr. Baird," was worth a dozen of today's tranquillizers.

Milne MacIntyre gave hope. Where there was no hope he would sit with the patient behind those white hospital screens in the ominous privacy allowed patients towards the end, and when he left, he left behind him some kind of acceptance, even serenity.

Of course, there were the others – the comics (and hard-bitten comics they sometimes were) treating life as rather a jest, if sometimes a harsh one. For before the arrival of today's wonder drugs, life for the sick, the acutely infected, was often cruel, harsh and brutally short. The sense of useless tragedy was not lost upon our profession, and each doctor reacted to it in his own personal way.

One eminent gentleman, disguised as a specialist in general medicine, was in fact one of Glasgow's best known experts in venereal diseases. Apart from his university and public hospital commitments he had, in that long row of elegant Georgian houses that was the consultant's enclave, "rooms" for his private practice. There he once, with feigned humility and hardly concealed glee, announced to his select little following of students that he believed he made more money than any other specialist in the city.

"Ye wouldn't think it, of course, to look at my rooms," he grinned wickedly. "Nobody ever parks outside my door y'know. They all go round the corner and park outside Professor So and So's" (naming his arch enemy in university politics and a specialist in a 'respectable' branch of medicine), "but, ach, well we all know they're walking round to see me!" He owned a Rolls Royce, and had inscribed on the bonnet in small, elegant, but eminently readable letters, the legend, "The Wages of Sin."

It was very difficult to maintain an attitude of constant solemnity or pristine purity in the face of several years of this kind of experience, but we were still, mostly, a very green lot. This was about to be rectified by our compulsory rotation as student midwives in the East End of Glasgow.

Chapter Three

Tommy Starkey and I were to be partners for the next few weeks, when for the first time we would be turned loose upon the public as student midwives.

It was an academic requirement of our final year that we deliver a prescribed number of babies over a period of a month or so, during which time we would live in groups of a dozen or two in the spartan student residence at Rotten Row, close to the Royal Infirmary. We worked in pairs, but *never* in mixed pairs. That would have been too much for the tender susceptibilities of the university authorities. The women were cloistered elsewhere.

The area we served was a rough one. Grim rows of tenements flanked the dirty streets where the rain, which seemed to fall almost constantly, pelted the blowing tramcar tickets and discarded newspapers until they ended up in soggy masses drifting along with the gutter water. When the cloud ceiling was low, spots of soot would drift idly down.

It was a forbidding place, the east end of Glasgow. Poverty was everywhere. There were few middle-class homes, no terrace houses. Mostly our clientele lived in tenements. In some of these the homes were places of warmth and love, despite the age and decrepitude of the buildings, the surrounding squalor, and the lavatories on open landings that had to serve several families.

The depression had brought working people to their knees. The middle-class knew deprivation. For them it was a struggle to maintain appearances. Threadbare clothes were carefully pressed and kept in service. They still had their pride although to the unemployed pride was a luxury. In the tenements there might be one man in a dozen who worked and brought home a wage packet. On Fridays his door could be plagued by neighbours asking desperately for a loan that in today's terms would be paltry.

It was often a dangerous part of the city. Gang warfare was bitter and though these youths fought mostly amongst themselves their very presence brought fear to whole neighbour-

13

hoods. Their loyalties were based on religious affiliations, though the love of Christ was notably absent from both sides. The ''Billy Boys,'' admirers of King William of Orange (though few of them knew anything about him) were supporters of the largely Protestant ''Glasgow Rangers'' football team, while their opponents, papal delegates to a man and mostly Irish Catholic, put their weight behind the Catholic ''Glasgow Celtic.''

Games between these two teams, attended by huge crowds, were signals for open warfare. Law-abiding, or merely cautious people moved as far away from the potential contenders as they could.

At the end of the game, players and referee headed for the safety of the dressing rooms under police protection. Their partisan supporters, marshalled at opposite ends of the field, wearing opposing team colours, now surged forward, a ragged horde, waving scarves and banners, breaking beer bottles on the benches as they ran. The jagged edges became dreadful weapons. Fingering their cloth bonnets, they would make sure the razor blades concealed in the borders were exposed. They would uncoil the sharpened bicycle chains and whirl them around their heads as they made for their hated opponents.

The Glasgow police, overwhelmingly Highland and overwhelmingly huge in stature, had been standing on the sidelines waiting just for this moment.

When the signal was given they moved in. Police capes and batons wielded with a fine lack of partisanship always won the day, but not before injuries had been suffered by all sides. The policeman who slipped and fell on the wet grass would be surrounded and kicked by shrieking savages before he could regain his feet, or his comrades could get to him. Faces were lacerated, skulls cracked, groaning bodies lay scattered on the field.

Meantime the players, under police protection, had reached the dressing rooms. The crowds were streaming home, getting away as far and as fast as they could, boarding the waiting tramcars or, if they were foolhardy, lingering on the terraces to see the aftermath of war.

The Casualty Department at the Royal Infirmary dealt with many such injuries, but the opposing sides never needed a football match to inflict them. A Catholic youth who looked with favour upon a Protestant lass was likely to be thrashed mercilessly. The wrong answer to the question ''are ye a Protestant or a Catholic'' could be catastrophic. Shopkeepers feared for their premises, and decent folk that their bairns would be drawn into violence.

It was in this area that we delivered our first babies. I never heard of students being molested. The women students were given no favours for, like the men, they had to walk to their cases. The medical bags we carried were known by everybody. "Dr. McGregor and His Wee Black Bag" was a favourite song sung in Glasgow music halls. Little ones were often told that the doctor would be bringing the new baby in his "wee black bag" and it certainly was our passport to safety.

In these surroundings Tommy and I gained practical experience in obstetrics. Our hospital training bore little resemblance to what was in store. The mothers-to-be had already been examined at clinics and were classified as normal pregnancies. There were, however, the exceptions.

Two of the girls (my little red-head being one of them) had been called to deliver a woman of her eighth child. When they arrived at her home they found her lying in a pool of blood, the baby already delivered.

It had come into the world suddenly after one contraction of the womb. Despite frantic efforts to stop the haemorrhaging, there was little that could be done. The mother was what is technically known as a "grand multipara." Women who have had six children should always be delivered in a hospital where emergencies can be dealt with. Uterine muscles in such cases are weak, and patients are often serious risks. This woman should have been in hospital, but someone had decided otherwise. She died.

Two inexperienced and badly shaken girls had witnessed an avoidable tragedy and had been left to deal with a stricken father, seven motherless children, and a new-born infant.

The first obstetrical case assigned to Tommy and me was quite different to that experienced by the two girl students. There was no tragedy involved, and the only casualty was our dignity.

Swan Lane was a badly-lit cul-de-sac of small brick houses opening on to the pavement, newspapers blown by the wind, flattened against the walls. The door handle refused to answer to my polite push.

"Shove it," I was advised from inside. I shoved. No response.

"For God's sake," whispered Tommy, "shove the bloody thing or let *me* shove it."

Giving him a withering look, I put my shoulder to the door

and with lightning speed was inside flat on my face, the door beneath me. Tommy, behind me, retained his stance and composure.

"Ach, the bliddy door," said a large and cheerful lady advancing upon me and effortlessly hoisting me to my feet. "It's aye aff its hinges." The rain and fog swirled into the room as she cried, "Come on, fellas, gie's a hand tae get it back in place."

That task accomplished we were free to take in our surroundings, drab and dimly lit by a single naked guttering gas lamp suspended by a pipe from the middle of the ceiling. A ragged piece of cloth was pinned across the only window, looking as if it had been placed there recently, and hurriedly.

The wooden floor was unswept, and thanks to my thunderous arrival, every crack had thrown up a cloud of dust. The bed was in an alcove in the single room that was a home, and the patient, alarmed, had poked her head round the side of the wall to observe the cause of all the commotion.

The walls were patched with remnants of what might once have been cheerful paper, and the blankets were worn and soiled. In the middle of the room stood a wooden table and two old kitchen chairs. But there was a good fire in the grate. Apart from the most basic of kitchen sinks and a tap for cold water, there were no toilet facilities. The lavatory, somewhere in the yard at the back, we later found, was shared by the surrounding families.

On the floor near the bed sat an earthen chamber pot half full of urine. This my welcomer kept calling "the chanty," and so indeed was this ubiquitous receptacle known to half the city's population.

The patient, a buxom lass in her early thirties, had watched these proceedings from her bed, her face registering a variety of emotions. Apprehension was now one of them.

I had seen babies delivered but in the efficient, impersonal atmosphere of hospital sterility. I had, euphemistically speaking, assisted at deliveries, directed here and there by nursing sisters who regarded doctors and students alike as a bar to the efficiency of their wards. This was my first house visit, my first attendance at a "domiciliary delivery." I later did a thousand of them and developed strong views on the subject, but wher the lady who had so casually lifted me to my feet said, "Noo! If you two fellas 'll jist stand ower there out o' the road we'll show you whit this is a' aboot." I thought for a moment that women must naturally dominate the baby-delivery business and might have done as I was bid.

Tommy, however, was made of less compliant stuff.

"What d'ye mean 'stand over there?' I'll have you know I'm in charge here."

"Oh, doctor," with elaborate obsequiousness, "Ah widnae for a minute dream o' interferin wi' ye in yer duties. It's jist, ye ken, that we've all been through this togither afore. I've got five a'ready, Chrissie there has four o'her ain, an' Jeannie's goin' tae be upsides we'me afore the night's oot. That's right, Jeannie, isn't it?" delivering a friendly and none too gentle slap on the patient's exposed rump.

The other woman who had stood silently by the bedside smiled and said in what Glaswegians would call a "polite" voice, "I'm Mrs. MacKenzie from next door."

"Oh aye, an' I'm Mrs. Brogan," agreed the Amazon with imitative politeness, "frae the next door but one. Ye see, we're a kind o' team," she went on, "just like the 'Celtic,' or," she added as an afterthought and in kindly deference to our probable Protestantism, "the Rangers, of course."

But this little piece of repartee soon came to an end.

"It's comin' again, pet?" she queried, as the patient reached for a towel tied to the bedrail just above her head, and nodded grimly.

Immediately the women each seized one of the patient's legs – Mrs. MacKenzie, the younger, climbing on to the far side of the bed and seizing the patient's left knee, while Mrs. Brogan standing on the floor, flexed her right. To the timed urgings of Mrs. MacKenzie to "push, pet, push," they braced her legs almost against her abdomen. Jeannie, silent, her reddened face showing her effort, pushed against them, the perineum beginning to bulge with pressure from the downcoming head.

It was obvious even to our unpractised eyes that something was going to happen soon, and swiftly, so I helped Tommy into his sterile gown and gloves, poured hot water into one of the three available kitchen bowls and generally made quick preparations. Another bowl was needed, and in my best hospital manner I asked that one be procured.

Mrs. Brogan with cheerful impatience let me know the culinary facts of life in Swan Lane.

"That's all there is, doctor. Atween the three o' us we hae three bowls. But we hae some cups. Would a cup no' do ye?"

It did me.

I had never seen anything like this before. It was a far cry from the cool impersonality of the maternity ward. Tommy, no doubt intent on the technical details of his task, had his gloved hands in the antiseptic bowl, steeping them, keeping them sterile for the sacred moment when he would usher a new life into this world. He wasn't watching the drama before him. He looked deep in thought. I felt he might be praying. He may have been.

Mrs. MacKenzie, gently wiping Jeannie's sweating forehead, assured her it would all be over soon.

"One good push and it'll be here."

"Aye, darlin'," agreed the redoutable Mrs. Brogan. "Yin guid push an' we'll hae yer wean, Jeannie."

The sequence began again. This might be the final team effort, for at the vulva there appeared a small but rapidly growing transparent bag, full, not of baby, but of fluid. I had never seen this either, not such a huge birth sac, anyway. I was transfixed by its growing enormity. Suddenly, I saw the beginnings of a little head within the sac.

"Tommy," I cried, "Quick! It's almost here!"

The ladies, triumphant, stood aside, courteously awaiting the arrival of the obstetrician.

Tommy, resplendent in hospital gown, gloves held up before him, turned and seeing this sudden change in the state of affairs, to which, he later informed me, his attention might have been drawn earlier, dashed to his duties.

Unfortunately, in the excitement of events, I had forgotten to remove the chamber pot.

Tommy put his foot in it. With a reflex speed I question he could produce nowadays, he fought to maintain his balance. His spine arched backwards with a grace that would have excited Nureyev himself, arms outstretched to the heavens in a plea that would have done credit to a Greek god, and then with the speed of a bird his body described a parabola that landed him, sterile gown and all, across Jeannie. At that moment, not surprisingly, the sac burst and the baby arrived.

When we left, with what dignity we could muster, Jeannie was crooning away to her infant, already cuddling it. It had all been ridiculously easy. We needn't have been there at all, and well the ladies knew it. Still, they were nice about it. The cups were being washed, the tea already made. Would we stay?

Regrettably, urgent matters called us away.

"Aye, weel, lads," said Mrs. Brogan, as she removed the

door for us. "I suppose it's yer first time oot, but ye've no' tae worry, ye've done just fine. Especially you, doctor," to Tommy as she handed him the bag. "Jeannie's real pleased wi' yer attention. Besides, she hasna' had a man jump at her like that in years!"

Chapter Four

We were moving through our stint as student obstetricians. Tommy and I, more or less without problems, had delivered half the required number of babies. Gone was the awful sense of inadequacy both of us had presented in the face of the formidable Mrs. Brogan at Swan Lane. There was even a certain jauntiness in our approach to the whole business.

"Fifteen Parnell Street? A first baby? Yes, certainly. Right away." Donning our raincoats and picking up the "wee black bag," we'd descend on the required household, where we might see love, indifference, cheerfulness, fear, apprehension, joy, or sometimes despair. But we learned something from all of them. We visited comfortable working-class homes and we shivered with cold in hovels.

Once in a rat-ridden and filthy garret I wrapped a baby in newspaper and sacking while Tommy sent for the parish priest. He found coal for a fire in a fireplace that had not been used in months, except as a garbage repository, judging by its contents of rotten banana skins and smelly refuse. The rat holes were plain to see in the corners of the room, where splintered and rotting floorboards had been eaten through. A filthy mattress on the floor, probably lifted from some rubbish dump, was the bed for mother and child. The hopelessness written on the husband's face, the lines of hunger and pain on his wife's, have never left me.

We were learning, perhaps the rough way, but steadily and surely we were beginning to see how people live, think, and act. The doctor's visit has been largely replaced in North America by the sterile atmosphere of the hospital emergency room. Patients have to haul themselves out of warm beds (where they'd be better off to stay, many a time) and present themselves to some brusque, if efficient, stranger in a hospital. There are occasions when a fast trip to the emergency room is the right course of action, others where it is wrong, but even in the harsh conditions of my youth the doctor's visit had something to commend it in terms of reassurance for the patient, the reward of gratitude and knowledge for the doctor.

That summer of 1939 was a golden lesson in public relations and sociology for Tommy and me. Our partnership was pretty good, all things considered. Tommy was a serious-minded chap, a year or so older than I was. I was much more volatile, hurt by the misery I saw around me, the depths of which I had never quite believed existed. Tommy saw it all, took it in his stride, and cursed a system that allowed it to happen.

We quarreled, of course. Most of us did, I afterwards discovered. We quarreled as to who should deliver the next baby, as to whether our techniques were correct or not. If the baby arrived before we got to the house and without our help, we were required to report the matter, and the case didn't count towards our total. Then there would be words about one culprit or other not getting out of bed fast enough. The truth was that our "finals" were only months away, an ordeal that would return to some of us in our dreams for years to come, and this compulsory rotation, on top of it all, made us edgy.

So we were tense that spring and summer, and the edginess sometimes led to trouble.

It was a Saturday afternoon. There must have been a dozen or so of us in the residence. It was warm and muggy for once, and the sun, even the smog-filtered sun of Glasgow was outside, and we were inside, compulsorily, until the phones began to ring. Then, two by two we'd move into the streets, bound for some tiny little episode in what is called a lifetime. But this afternoon nothing was happening. Some fellows sat by their bedside tables, studying. Others wrote letters, or sat around talking. Then some junior specialist or other put his head round the corner of the door and announced that things were quiet: few "bookings" were due that night, and we could all relax a bit.

It was an invitation to disaster. Some joker vanished and quickly returned with a couple of cases of beer and a bottle of Scotch. I naively confessed that I had never tasted whisky.

"He's never tasted whisky," proclaimed one of my fellow

students to the assembly, his Johannesburg accent becoming a dreadful sing-song falsetto Scottish burr for the occasion. "Well, little fellow, now's the time to start," and handed me a generous glassful.

Some of the students quietly moved out of the room, but I had been caught, an innocent unawares. Whisky is an acquired taste. I downed the contents of the glass, trying not to grimace, knowing I was being watched.

"And now the chaser." It was the Scottish custom — a whisky followed by a glass of beer. The beer mug was thrust upon me. The day was warm, and the beer got rid of the taste of Scotch. I welcomed it.

"Have another!"

"No, thanks."

"Oh! Yourr Sunday school teacherr would rraise objections perhaps? Orr yourr mummy?" Some diagnostic possibilities regarding my personality followed, none of them flattering, and there were a few snickers at my expense.

Hours had passed since a sparse lunch. The alcohol was flooding my system, and Glasgow — or what I could see of it — began to follow the city's unofficial anthem, a song I have heard sung wistfully and sometimes, it must be admitted, drunkenly, from Australia to the Yukon border. Glasgow *was* going round and round.

My tormentor was what is technically known in pugilistic circles as a "long drink of water," and I, full of Scottish spirit in more ways than one, took the only course possible. I punched him in the abdomen. When he rose from the floor clutching his middle and threatening me with immediate annihilation, I was measuring him for another right (for was not I, chronically lacking in aggression, the flea-weight champion of the University?) when the gathered moralists demanded a stop to the violence.

What they wanted to do was organize it! A three-round, bare-fisted contest, the contestants to be stripped to the waist, was agreed upon. Some entrepreneur immediately set up a book and began a thriving betting shop. Furniture was pushed to the wall, seconds elected, and the two gladiators prepared for the fray.

Flushed by the libation my opponent had forced upon me, my linguistic exactitude had departed along with my inhibitions, and I told him a thing or two. My ring sense began to tell me, on the other hand, that my adversary was by this time a little reluctant to continue.

On no account, I was told by the self-elected chairman, was I to call him an unmentionable Colonial. The term was derogatory. Besides that's what the English sometimes call us. Any other swear words would be acceptable, I was told.

The bout was short, sharp, decisive. The flow of blood from my opponent's nose quickly rendered him *hors de combat*. I was judged the victor, except by two fellows who had lost their bets and felt that with a little encouragement my South African friend might still slaughter me. He did not seem to appreciate the confidence they placed in him, and I helped lower him into a hot bath, one arm round my shoulder, the other up to his face where his fingers and thumb pinched his bleeding nose. He was swearing eternal friendship for me when I left the bathroom.

By now I was in top form. The flush of victory was upon me. If only that little red-head had seen me in action! If she'd been around I'd have asked her for a date on the spot! Alas, such moments of triumph are short-lived, I have discovered.

"You're drunk."

It was Tommy, glowering, all the contained and righteous rage of his Presbyterian forefathers showing in his face.

"Good God, look at you! You look as if you've been on the bash for weeks. What good are you to anybody in that state?"

"I've done *him* some good."

The point was not well received.

"Get to bed and pray to God we're not called tonight. If you can't hold liquor and your temper you shouldn't drink."

"I have no temper, Tommy," I smirked wickedly, patting him on the shoulder, "My mummy says so." But I went to bed all the same, secure in the knowledge of a night's sleep.

In about two minutes it seemed, I was caught in a hurricane. Blankets were being thrown through the air and my limbs exposed to the cold of the night.

"Get up. The bell's gone. It's for us. I thought I'd never get you awake."

"Where is everybody?"

It was obvious that they weren't in bed, and Tommy didn't spend time on much explanation.

"All out, the whole boiling lot. I even swapped with MacCallum to keep you in bed. They're gone. Now it's us. Get moving, for God's sake, man."

I fumbled my way into my clothes, tired, but still glowing with the success of my recent endeavours. Even Tommy's grumpiness failed to dampen my spirits. I seemed to make things worse by insisting on carrying the bag.

"Don't kid yourself you're going to deliver this baby, even if it is your turn," declared Tommy. "You're in no fit state to deliver a bloody newspaper. Just because you're carrying the bag doesn't mean you're going anywhere, you remember that!"

The night air was like wine. Certainly it seemed to have an effect upon me, for while I was cheerful, Tommy, I felt, was a trifle morose. Our destination was on the fourth floor of a Glasgow tenement. On the third landing of the stone stairway Tommy stopped, turned to me, and held out his hand.

"The case," he said peremptorily, "the case. I'm delivering this baby."

I had an overwhelming desire to please. Aggression, always short-lived, had vanished. I was happy. I wanted to see others happy, and if having the bag would make Tommy happy I was delighted to cooperate. He took it.

"The next thing," he said, "keep quiet. Just keep out of the road. Understand? You smell like a brewery. Ugh! If you have to say anything, hold your breath while you're talking."

With a look of disgust he knocked on the door. It was opened by a stocky, sturdily built man in his mid-forties. His collarless shirt was open at the neck, displaying a brawny, hairy chest, the rolled-up sleeves revealing tattooed arms that rippled with muscle. His unsmiling face was hardly welcoming.

"You the doctors? In there." He jerked his head to the right. We had opened the door into the kitchen, but there was a front bedroom down a short passageway. The whole atmosphere was one of utter cleanliness. Here was somebody's home. A good coal fire burned in the polished grate. Spotless horse brasses festooned the mantelpiece, and a large black kettle fizzled and sang on the cheerfully dancing flames. The shining linoleum of the floor was partly covered by a carpet, old, but meticulously mended. This was not the home of someone on the dole, half their possessions pawned to keep going, that was easy to see.

On one side of the kitchen grate sat a beshawled old crone, her witch-like figure leaning forward to the fire, skinny hands out-stretched to the warmth, while on the other side a vacant chair showed the low shelves of a well-filled book case. The usual bed, built into an alcove in the wall was scrupulously made and spotless to look at.

Having given his directions, our unsmiling host returned to

his chair, knocked his pipe on the polished oven top, and stared into the fire, paying us no more attention. Tommy led the way into the bedroom. It was a tiny place but there was privacy. We were met at the door by a buxom woman of about forty, her pleasant face showing signs of concern, a white apron obviously donned for the occasion. Her hands nervously folded in the apron kept clasping and unclasping, but she managed a smile for us.

"Here's the patient, gentlemen." She waved us over to a girl, a younger replica of herself, lying in the bed. She was only a child, her huge frightened eyes enhancing her youth. She was in the throes of labour. Tommy, whose responsibilities were, I felt, bothering him, was solemn. He was very much the doctor. I, on the other hand, with all the exuberance of youth (not to mention anything else); felt it my duty to lighten the prevailing atmosphere, and I hastened to assure our young patient that we were probably the most capable emissaries the university could have sent. My brilliant companion favoured me with a malevolent look, but the girl smiled, and her mother's hands lost their nervous grip on her apron.

"Would you gentlemen like a cup of tea?" she asked. Tommy said that this would be most kind and suggested that I might go through to the kitchen and procure some hot water, a task I undertook willingly and immediately.

In the kitchen, I enquired as to any relevant history in the case.

"And the husband?" I enquired.

"There's nae husband." It was a harsh and angry face that confronted me as the man at the fireplace turned and faced me.

"Oh, doctor," his wife hastily interjected, "it's a love child." She moved almost deliberately to block out her husband's glowering face. "That's *our* bairn in there," she went on, half pleadingly, speaking more to her man than to me. "She's our girl, and doctor, it's a love child." Again her hands were intertwined, nervously folding the towel she carried.

"Love child be damned," growled the man, "it's a bastard."

"Have you got that water for me, doctor?" an overly polite voice called from the bedroom, and excusing myself, I hastened to comply with orders. Tommy, I felt contritely, seemed to be a little out of patience with me tonight, and I determined that my enthusiasm for my work would win him around – that optimism and cheerfulness would prevail, despite the unhappiness around us. I hurried to my partner's aid but he seemed very self-sufficient, though he did suggest I ensure a steady supply of hot water. This meant a return trip to the kitchen, and this time Mr. McGuffie was waiting for me.

"I'm sorry I let mysel' go like that. It's no' like me. I love that wee lass o' ours wi' a' my heart. She's a' we've got. The faither o' that bairn has run awa' and joined the Scots Greys. He's off tae Palestine, an' if he ever comes back I'll kill him wi' my ain bare hands."

His anger was easy to understand. "Aye up here, he was. Aye after her. Now who's goin' tae want her wi' another man's bairn tae bring up? Answer me that, doctor! She'll hae tae live wi' us. That's a' right, but I canna stand to see that wean livin' in this hoose."

Choking down his anger and suddenly silent, he nodded his dismissal to me and resumed his seat by the fireplace, his ancient companion as silent as the grave, swaying back and forth in her rocking chair.

It was a long labour, but first babies often take a long time to arrive and all seemed normal enough. Tommy's care was meticulous, but when the baby did arrive it didn't shudder and cry and protest and clench its little fists like the others. It lay marble-white and motionless. Our own anxiety quickly communicated itself to the girl and her mother.

The delivery of a baby, any baby, is an event fraught with the possibility of emergencies, from simple, almost routinely easy, to disastrous, and the wise obstetrician thinks ahead. When one thing goes wrong in a maternity case one should anticipate the next possibility. In our efforts to get the infant to breathe we had failed to see the steady flow of blood from the mother, spreading ominously over the bed sheet. She, heedless of her own plight, had eyes only for her infant.

"It's not all right, is it, doctor?" she cried, her arms outstretched to the little waif, limp in my grasp. Tommy had speedily turned his attention to the mother, while I had grabbed the suction tube we carried to deal with such emergencies. I thrust it down the infant's throat, and was sucking any mucus that it might have inhaled, into my mouth. This was the likely diagnosis – some obstruction to the baby's airway caused by fluid suddenly inhaled in the birth passage, and usually suction would deal with the problem.

Instinct more than tuition told Tommy to reassure his patient.

"Get that kid out of here," he whispered to me. Turning to the mother he said, soothingly, "The babe's all right. This is common. Doctor'll have to work on it, that's all."

I fled to the kitchen, followed by the lady of the house, who stood agitatedly beside me.

"It's deid isn't it, doctor?" The old creature in the corner, hearing part of this statement, stopped her rocking chair as if by magic, threw her shawl over her head and face, and in a piping shriek, wailed, "The wean's deid! The wean's deid!" Then she began to rock the chair again in time with her dirge.

"I'm doing all I can, missus," I said to my anxious companion, between breaths. Her husband moved over, put his arm round his wife's shoulder, and quietly asked me, "There's nothing mair ye want, doctor. Anything I could do?" I looked at him. "Yes. Two basins of water, one hot, one cold.

It was an old remedy, worth a try, and quickly the basins were on the table. The babe was thrust unceremoniously from one to the other while I sucked and blew and compressed the infant's chest in a desperate effort to get air moving. Suddenly Tommy was beside me, his white gown soaked in blood.

"It's stopped," he said quietly, "bleeding's a trickle now. Uterus firm and hard. How's the kid?" One glance was enough. "Keep going!" And he was off.

The wails from the corner would have raised John Knox from his centuries of sleep. I could stand it no longer. "Shut up, will you!" I roared in a voice like thunder, "the wean's no' deid yet."

The wailing stopped and the shawl was removed. For the first time the toothless mouth, between nose and chin that almost met, voiced intelligible words. "Ah thocht ye tell't me the wean was deid! Is it no' deid after all?"

I resumed my by now frantic efforts. A few more moments of this and all would be lost. Suddenly, a convulsive little jerk of the chest, the white skin turning slowly to pink, the chest movements, convulsive at first, becoming jerky, shallow, then steady. The couple stood beside me, the husband's arm around his wife's shoulder.

"Ye hae done it, man," he grunted. The old fiend in the corner sat silent. The day had been won. Soon our patient was reunited with her baby and lay crooning to it, just as nature intended. It was only then I noticed it was a boy. We left a grateful household, and trudged home. By now I was contrite and subdued.

"Sorry about that, Tommy. I wasn't really drunk, was I?"

"Forget it. You smelled like a brewery. God, she bled though. Frightening, something like that." But he had handled things well, and he was quietly delighted.

"I thought the kid was a goner," I remarked as we neared the residence, the first light of dawn around us. "I kept going as if I were possessed – couldn't believe we could lose a baby, just like that. Maybe it was the whisky kept me going," I grinned, "maybe the whisky in my breath started him breathing, Tommy! Never again, though. What ghastly stuff whisky is!"

Tommy did that day's visit to the McGuffies, and the next, and the one after that. I wouldn't go back. "I was tight," I protested. "And they must have known it. You go. You do the visits Tommy. Tell them I'm ill or something."

On the tenth and almost our final day of caring for mother and baby he would indulge me no longer. "You've simply got to go. They ask for you every day. I can't put them off any longer, and I said you'd be out there this afternoon." So I went, climbing the tenement stairs with feet that dragged themselves from step to step. The door was opened and a beaming grandmother led me in. A smiling mother between spotless sheets lifted her little one for me to admire.

I was reassured. I was welcome. I had not disgraced my calling in the infancy of my career after all. A brawny figure stood beside me. Mr. McGuffie's craggy face creased in a half smile as his hand gently stroked his daughter's fair hair.

"Into the kitchen wi' ye, doctor, if ye please," he said. I was finished with my chores and I followed him. It was obvious that there had been a reconciliation. "It's a fine wee lad we've got there." And then Mrs. McGuffie joined in. She wanted to know if I had been to see the film of A.J. Cronin's novel, *The Citadel*, playing at the time, with Robert Donat as the doctor-hero. I hadn't? It was Mrs. McGuffie's opportunity. She herself had not seen the film, but Mrs. MacTavish from next door had, and had come home full of it. Indeed, she had insisted on giving Mrs. McGuffie a lengthy resumé of one particular scene, where Robert Donat, the handsome young doctor, had revived a new-born infant by plunging it into bowls of alternate hot and cold water. It was too much for Mrs. McGuffie. She interrupted her neighbour.

"That," she cried, "was naethin' tae what our young doctor did in our hoose the verra nicht ye were at that picture. He did a' that an' mair than that. Our wean was born deid, just like the one in the picture, an' oor young doctor put a tube down our wean's throat, an' he blew, an' he sookit, an' he sookit an' he blew, an' he blew his air breath intae oor wean's chest.

An' the doctor in the picture, Mrs. MacTavish,'' she finished breathlessly triumphant, "never did that!"

"Aye well, that's just fine," said her man soothingly, "but ye ken doctor, we dinnae even know yer name, yer first name, like."

"William."

"William." He nodded. "Wullie, tae yer pals, I suppose? Well, we've all thought aboot this, an' if it's a' right wi' you, doctor, that'll be wee Wullie McGuffie in next door. He'll hae my name an yours for the rest o' his life." I was flabbergasted. "Aye, weel then," he concluded, "that'll be that. We thocht ye were no goin' tae come back. Seein' we're kind of related like, we'll just hae a wee celebration."

He reached into a cupboard, and placed a bottle of Scotch and two glasses on the kitchen table. "For, ach, man," he concluded, nudging me in the side with his elbow, "weel we all know ye like a bit dram tae yersel!"

Chapter Five

"The diagnosis, gentlemen?"

Dr. Alexander Glen looked up from his bedside chair to the little group around him. Dr. Glen, a soft-spoken, dedicated scholar, was Professor of Clinical Medicine at Glasgow's Victoria Infirmary, and we were lucky to work as "dressers," or senior medical students, in his wards, for his breadth of knowledge and thought far transcended the bounds of clinical medicine. He admonished us young people to retain enquiring and open minds for the rest of our lives: the open mind, he said, is an essential for any good doctor.

That morning his question was all too easy to answer, and all too tragic. The child's fixed and desperately anxious stare, the motionless neck, rigid and arched, the high fever, proclaimed the diagnosis – spinal meningitis.

Spinal meningitis!

There were two common varieties of this acute infection: bacterial and tuberculous. The symptoms and signs were similar, the diagnosis being made by withdrawing some fluid from the patient's spinal canal, using the technique widely called a "spinal tap," easily enough done in most cases with training. A hollow needle, the bore fitted with a fine cylinder, would be inserted into the lower spine at a specified level, and once in place the cylinder withdrawn slowly, so that some spinal fluid could escape through the bore. This fluid was collected in sterile vials for microscopic examination. At the same time, some was sent for culture, so that any bacteria in the fluid would multiply and be identified.

Diagnosis was usually relatively simple: treatment was another matter. No effective cure was available. The mortality rate was a frightful 80 to 90 percent, and the long-term complications were often disastrous.

Yet it was a commonplace infection, as were many other diseases. The onset of an epidemic of diphtheria in a community meant terror for parents for weeks to come. Scarlet fever, another everyday killer, left such a trail of death and complications behind it that its onset was equally dreaded. Tuberculosis still killed whole families, though with the development of preventive medicine its incidence was already declining. Blood poisoning – acute infection caused by the germ streptococcus invading a simple and apparently trivial scratch, could lay a victim at death's door within a few days.

Today, these infections have become relatively rare. A medical student might go through his entire academic education without seeing a single case of any of them, and even a lifetime without seeing diphtheria. I remember hearing a young colleague twenty-five years ago describe the case of a child he had seen earlier that day.

"Sore throat," he remarked. "Didn't look much on examination considering how ill the youngster seemed. It was the smell though, absolutely foul, as if there were something rotten in the room."

"Diphtheria," I said at once, and I was right.

There was nothing clever about my diagnosis. I had smelled that fetid odour only too often, and would never forget it. In diphtheria, trivial signs of a mild sore throat can precede devastatingly serious complications. Death results if the case is untreated. My friend, only ten years younger than I, had never come upon a case.

And so it goes. Infections are vanquished, but the vast armies of man's deadliest enemies, the bacteria, and now the viruses, are constantly regrouping, attacking in new ways, from different directions, and in different guises. Their rate of evolution and change can be astoundingly fast, and Dr. Glen's admonitions always to be on the watch, always ready to face new developments, to assess them when unproven, accept them when proven, were wise and prophetic, for disease patterns are constantly changing. And sometimes they change with an almost invincible rapidity.

On that morning long ago, however, in the long bare ward of the hospital, with perhaps twenty beds to each side, and privacy only for the dying, or the essential functions of living, he had little to offer for the future of our patient. He talked to us about the routes by which the child might have picked up the infection. He raised the possibility of epidemic infection by carriers, who unknowingly might harbour the germs in their noses and throats, infecting those who were susceptible by a simple sneeze or cough while passing by. He discussed the question of lack of hygiene and over-crowding in homes. He talked about the differential diagnosis, how we might recognize one type of spinal meningitis from another, and finally, an almost useless synopsis of the methods of treatment then available to us. Without some miracle, our little girl would die within a few days.

The hours wore on, and I went about my duties taking notes, examining new arrivals, and discussing older cases with my mentor, the house physician, a doctor a few years older than myself. I noticed that "the Chief" seemed to be spending a good deal of his time behind the screens that surrounded the little girl's bed, or talking to her parents. They, desperate with anxiety, stayed around the corridor just outside the ward, trays of food brought to them by a kindly nursing sister, untouched. It is strange how members of a unit, nurses and junior doctors, will emulate their chiefs. Dr. Glen's concern for his patients and for the grief-stricken relatives was not lost upon his staff.

Early the next morning when I returned to the hospital, for some unusual reason I reached the ward before my colleagues – unusual, because all my life I have been teased as "the late Dr. Gibson."

The nursing supervisor met me at the door of the ward with an urgent message: "You're to go straight up to the meningitis case," and then whispered, "The Chief's been there practically the whole of the night."

Dr. Glen was a man getting on in life, in his early sixties,

30

and the hospital employed younger, more junior specialists to attend to emergencies. Why should the professor himself spend the night on his feet? I hurried to the end of the ward and slipped behind the curtain to join him. He looked up, put a finger to his lip and motioned me to leave, following me, walking a few yards down the ward, there to meet one of my fellow seniors hurrying towards us.

"She's just fallen asleep," said Dr. Glen. "Quite astounding to watch. Temperature has fallen. Still there, but great improvement since yesterday. Rigidity of the neck has decreased. Clinically there is a great improvement."

He looked at us.

"I believe she'll recover," he said in apparent wonder. "Quite astounding."

"It's a miracle, sir," said my colleague, "considering the mortality rate."

"No," said 'the Chief.' "It's no miracle. It's a new drug. Something I've been given to experiment with in acute infections. That child was a hopeless case yesterday. That's why I used the stuff. It's called ... let me see ... yes ... sulphonamide."

He looked at us both. "Perhaps," he said, "you haven't seen a miracle, but you have seen one thing today – the passing of the future of medicine from us physicians to the biochemists!"

Chapter Six

It was a Saturday night when I first saw her. Sitting forlornly in a booth of the emergency department, she was clutching at her forearm which was wrapped in a towel that would no longer contain the bleeding, for a steady drip of blood was beginning to form a little pool on the floor.

She was beautiful, I thought, as I introduced myself. Her face had the pallor and sharpness of an El Greco portrait, and dark hair cascaded over the smooth contours of her shoulders. The flimsy dress, tight across her shapely breasts, showed a rounded figure that contrasted with the almost ascetic cast of her features.

We students used to hang around the emergency departments, hoping that someone would give us some "stitching" to do, or that we might see some unusual cases. The emergency departments were kaleidoscopes of Glasgow life: rich and poor, the good and bad received competent care without favour. The choice of which case should be seen first depended solely on its urgency.

In contrast to North American city hospitals, where emergency departments have become the evening and nighttime venue for all kinds of illnesses that could be dealt with by the family doctor, minor illnesses were not seen there. In Glasgow, minor illnesses at all hours of the day and night were attended to by house calls. The emergency departments dealt with street accidents, heart attacks, stabbings and catastrophic illnesses of all kinds.

That night a cheerful "charge nurse," taking pity on me, had whispered, "there's one in there for you – better grab it before somebody else does." And so I met Maureen Connolly.

While the nurse laid out a tray of instruments I quickly examined the laceration. It was inches long, and ragged, a steady welling of dark red blood indicating that a vein was bleeding. There was no sign that an artery was damaged. Indeed, no really serious damage appeared to have been done, but the edges of the wound were lying out in lumpy, bloody triangles of skin and superficial fat. My new patient had lost a fair amount of blood and her fear showed in her huge violet-blue eyes.

Having anaesthetized the area I carefully cut away tags of useless tissue, and inspected the wound, cleansing it preparatory to suturing it.

"Will it hurt?"

"No, not any longer, I hope. All we have to do now is pull the edges together and sew it up. That shouldn't take long, and you won't mind, will you? You won't faint or anything, will you?"

"Me? Faint? No. On you go doctor, I'll not faint."

I talked to her as I worked away. It could have been done much more efficiently by a better qualified man. She would always have a scar. Yet that was how we learned, under the supervision of the casualty officers. The jigsaw began to come together, and soon I was able to inspect my completed handiwork.

"See," I said in triumph, "it's not too bad after all, is it?"

"It's no' sae bad," she agreed, and smiled at me. Her face had regained some colour and the sharpness of fear and shock was disappearing. She was about my own age, and her smile through her tears was warm and grateful.

"It disna' even hurt any longer, and it looks a lot better than it did to begin wi'. Hae ye been a doctor long?" she asked curiously.

Diplomatically I let the question pass, and asked impersonally, "How did it happen?"

"It was nothing really," she said. "Just an accident at my place o' work, that's all, and if you're finished, I'll be going."

"Not just yet. The doctor in charge wants to see it."

I departed to find the casualty officer. That personage displayed all the glowing charm of a Scottish emergency surgeon on a Glasgow Saturday night, but after a brief inspection he told me to bandage the wound.

"It'll have to do," he grunted. "Tell her what to watch for. If there's the least sign of redness or swelling she's to report back here. If all's well, you can take the stitches out in a week." He was off, hurrying to the next booth, a short-tempered angel of mercy.

I warned Maureen to come back immediately should the wound become painful or swollen. Nurse would watch it for any sign of infection when she put on new bandages, for before the advent of "sulpha" drugs and antibiotics, blood poisoning was a serious complication of any kind of wound. The only defences against infection were rigid standards of cleanliness and hygiene, and the patients' own immunity. Blood poisoning was a dreaded complication, even of trivial injuries. The surgeon who nicked his finger during an operation was very much at risk, but so was the gardener pricking a finger in a rose bush.

Today we deal with infections of this type almost casually. The trouble is that we have been too casual. We use antibiotics when we don't really need them, and when we do use them we sometimes don't use them long enough to kill bacteria. We half-kill them, and they develop immunity to the antibiotic. We have used antibiotics without due care. Used to combat viral infections, they are quite useless. We have used them in trivial infections, especially perhaps in children on the insistence of anxious parents, and so we weaken the body's natural immunity.

Thirty years ago I saw a clinical demonstration of a lady suffering from orbital cellulitis. In the thirties she would have died. As it was, in 1949 she was dreadfully ill. The infection had pushed the eye forward in its socket until it bulged out in a hideously inflamed mass. Accompanied by high fever, a rapid spread of infection to the brain was inevitable without the use of penicillin. Death would speedily have occurred.

Treatment with penicillin was initiated. Photographs of the face were taken daily. A dreadful gargoyle of a face became gradually human, and in ten days the photograph showed a smiling, pretty woman.

Her treatment had consisted of a mere 20,000 units of penicillin given by injection every four hours for six days. Today probably millions of units of penicillin would be needed to achieve the same result: indeed, penicillin might, in a similar case, now be ineffective. Bacteria, like their human hosts, are international travellers in this jet age, and half-killed germs can quickly move about the world.

But when I saw Maureen Connolly, all that was in the future, and as she left the cubicle after my little operation she turned to me and said, "Will you be taking the stitches out yourself, or will it be somebody else?"

"Oh," I smiled at her, "it'll be me, all right, a week tonight at about the same time."

"Could I ask tae see you, or is that too much tae expect – just in case they send me to somebody else?"

"No, Miss Connolly, I'll be here, all right."

Her smile had struck a responsive chord to say the least. If somebody dressed her well, they could make a beauty out of this Glasgow working girl, I thought, as I watched her leave. I wasn't the only one to do that, I noticed. She had quite a figure. However, business was brisk, and I had little time for idle thoughts.

The week passed quickly. On Saturday night I found myself back in the emergency department, and there she was, sitting on a bench with a dozen others.

"I hope everything's well!"

"Och!" she replied, "it could nae be better, and I've come back to get the stitches out, if you remember?"

"Of course I do. Come along."

I followed her into the cubicle. It was difficult not to notice the long, shapely legs, the seductive lift of her hips. She walked

34

well, straight-backed, head held high, as if she didn't care a scrap for anyone in this world. She had something about her, confidence, presence.

The sutures were removed. Of course, there would be a scar. It was unsightly, the angry-red scar tissue contrasting with the surrounding skin, but she was satisfied and laughed at my apologies.

"How much dae I owe ye', doctor?"

"Oh, there's no charge. This is the Royal Infirmary you know, and nobody is ever charged for whatever is done here. But there's a box for donations at the door over there."

"But that's charity, and charity is something I'll no hae." She opened her bag, and looked at me directly. "Tell me, what dae I owe ye?"

"Nothing, Maureen. You see, it's a tradition here. No doctor charges. It's not even allowed. Besides," I added, "it's really been a pleasure to look after you."

"Well," she replied, "if ye'll no' tak money, I'd like to pay ye in kind. Here's my card, and that's my place of work." She handed me a business card.

"Card," I repeated bemusedly, "in kind?"

"Aye, that's right," and laying her hand gently on my forearm she gave me a look that would have melted snow.

"Oh, lad," she exclaimed in tones of patient exasperation, "hae ye no' put two and two together yet? I'm a whore!"

Whore or not, she was a lady of some taste. Her business card was engraved!

Chapter Seven

It was September, 1939. War had been declared the previous week. Over the years I had heard my parents speak of the First World War, and how, after terrible battles, the local newspapers would appear, edged in black, their only news the columns upon columns of names – the dead.

Now, hardly a generation later, people seemed stunned by

35

the sense of impending tragedy. Must Europe once again endure this madness?

To those of us facing our "finals" it hardly mattered. For the next few weeks – whatever might happen thereafter – only "the finals" would matter. The climax of five years of intense study was upon us. Those of us who passed the examinations would normally face one to two years of internship before venturing into practice; the degrees of Bachelor of Medicine and Bachelor of Surgery would be the prelude to hard hospital work, but at least the main hurdle would be behind us.

We stood, nearly two hundred of us, on the wide stone steps of Bute Hall, waiting for the stroke of nine when the great doors would be opened and we would pour into the vast hall, make for our allotted desks, to begin our "finals." The first paper would be our written examination in general medicine. As we stood, in groups, or singly, there was a quiet buzz of conversation; but some stood silent, desperately going over some last points in their minds. The Head of Medicine was a specialist on liver disease. A sudden rumour had it that diseases of that organ would figure prominently in the examination. Rumour was a false jade again.

There was already a smattering of uniforms, and one of our number was fated to go down with his destroyer in a few weeks. There was some loud, too loud, laughter but overall hung the low murmur of voices as the crowd edged slowly towards the doors. I saw my little red-head in the midst of a group of fellow students who, to my eyes, looked supremely confident of themselves, judging by the occasional light-hearted laughter. She saw me, waved sedately, and I felt the better for it.

Promptly on the hour, the doors swung open, and like runners poised for a race, adrenalin coursing, we quickly dispersed to our desks to open the folded examination papers and sigh with relief, or groan with despair. For the next few hours we would lose ourselves in pouring out, or dragging out, the knowledge we had gained these past few years.

The next three weeks were to be a nightmare for many of us. At its end we were exhausted, drained almost of ability to think clearly. In middle age, in conversation with two old colleagues, I confessed that a dream a few nights previously had wakened me in a cold sweat. I had been deprived of my licence to practise, I dreamed, and must go back to Glasgow and re-sit my "finals." To our amusement, all of us had a some time had the same dream, with variations.

In North America today, students accepted for medical training are usually older and more mature than their Scottish counterparts of forty years ago. They have already proven themselves academically. Many already possess university degrees, generally in one of the sciences. Consequently the "drop-out" rate is low, and the chances of finishing final year are excellent. In Scottish medical schools forty or fifty years ago, a few students dropped out in the first year, but the second year with its grindingly hard courses in anatomy and physiology disposed of still more. Once through "the seconds" it was usually assumed that students would finish their "finals" – but not necessarily within the prescribed five years.

The "plough," or fail rate, was considerable even then, and many an excellent student was failed, or "referred for further study" into a sixth year of hard work because of some error in fact or judgement. Appeals were almost unthought of. I never heard of review committees of professors and one's student peers prepared to pore over past records and work, make reassessments or recommendations to Executive Councils of Faculty. Yet many years later when I sat on such committees I admired the sense of democracy that initiated them and the benefits students received from them, even in the sense of impartial, helpful discussion of weaknesses in their academic performance.

But in my time a "referral" was almost always final. It meant six months or a year of repeat studies in one or other, or all subjects, and we dreaded the word. On the other hand, there were no restrictions. There were none of today's ultimatums to "get on or get out." Some happy souls, chronic students, took defeat after defeat with the greatest of good humour.

Written examinations were interspersed with clinical ones. In the latter we would interview selected patients in hospital and listen to their "histories," the details of onset of their illness. Then we would examine them, present a "differential diagnosis" or list of diagnostic possibilities, followed by our own final diagnosis or opinion. Our examiners, standing over us, watching our techniques, were then free to question us in detail. The examiners had their own techniques! They might be polite, easy-going or openly disapproving, and some of them were dreaded, sometimes quite unjustifiably, by the student body.

Most were fair, but all the same, when a gray-haired expert in medicine pushes across to you a treasured glass jar from the depths of the pathology department and says, "Mr. So and So. As you can see, this is a human heart. What disease did this patient suffer from? How would you have diagnosed it, and how would you treat it?"... it is no wonder that students could break out in cold sweats.

"Sick kids," or pediatrics, were generally considered to be a menace. For one thing the little-horrors were apt to howl at the very sight of a stethoscope. For another, they couldn't tell you anything. Many a lucky student has been saved from the gong by some wizened old patient whispering when the examiner has momentarily turned his back, "it's ma hert," or conversely, and sometimes urgently, "it's no' ma hert, it's ma chist."

But the examinations came to an end. The three weeks had seemed an eternity, but another three weeks of eternity lay before us while the examiners compiled their findings. The results were then posted on an open-air noticeboard, sheet after sheet of typed paper thumb-tacked on the board, the supervising official surrounded by a tense, silent crowd, turning, twisting, manoeuvering, elbowing to get a glimpse of the names.

I had never been a brilliant student. Not for me the golden words of commendation reserved for the chosen few. However, I had been accepted as one of the three "intensive" or final year students in the "flat" or clinic of Professor Sir Archibald Young, Regius Professor of Surgery. "Archie" had the reputation of being a holy terror. In fact, he was a gentle, sincere and kindly chief. It was considered quite something to be an intensive in his flat, but the honour became a little tarnished when a cynical tutor summed up the three new hopefuls.

"You," he said to me, "might one day, with a hell of a lot of work, and more luck, get through."

He turned to the first of my companions, a young gentleman superlatively sure of himself. "You," he said, "though I hate to say anything that will increase your own natural conceit, I believe will make it first time." Turning to the third of our trio, he shook his head. "As for you, my friend, you'll never even *see* your finals."

Had I known that this last outcast was to become a distinguished surgeon it might have helped when the fateful morning arrived. At noon the results were to be posted.

My hopes were anything but high. Rather than join the throng and see them witness my downfall, I would go when the crowd dispersed. My hometown, Wishaw, lay on the edge of Scotland's industrial belt, a brief half-hour's journey by rail from Glasgow's Central Station. That day I selected an empty compartment for the journey. I was in no mood for companionship.

As if in a dream I looked at the great steelworks, after years of idleness, already belching smoke from their high chimneys; at the huge slag heaps topped by smouldering ash. Row upon row, the gray stone houses slipped by, one industrial town after another. At each station there were men in uniform, heaving kitbags aboard the train, tearful women clinging to them, fathers, grim-faced, giving their sons last handshakes.

The journey seemed interminable. The train stopped at every station. And then, at long last, the terminus. My heart was leaden, but by now my feet were winged as I hurried into the thronged city streets and boarded a tramcar bound for the university. If the train had stopped at every station, the streetcar crawled like a snail.

The last few hundred yards on foot were an eternity.

The first final year man I met walking towards me needed no words to proclaim his news. His face was set and grim. He barely nodded as he passed. And then another, who a few days before told me he confidently expected an 80 percent in medicine. "Ploughed," he grunted as he trudged past. My heart sank to my boots.

For several years the failure rate in "the finals" had been alarming – at least to the candidates.

A year or so before, in the Spanish Civil War, the commander of Toledo's fortress, the Alcazar, had become famous by issuing the edict, "They shall not pass." The cynical students said the examiners had decided to apply the slogan to the final year examinations.

Was this to be another "monumental plough?"

Then, running towards me, a girl, auburn hair shining in the autumn sun, was waving, calling out: "You've passed, you've passed! We both passed!"

But over a third of us had failed.

It was a momentous, euphoric occasion for the two of us. For a few hours even the war ceased to matter. Then came reaction. All we wanted to do was sit in a coffee shop and quietly talk. We had talked a lot in the past few months. Quickly we had discovered we shared opinions, ambitions and ideals.

We had met that spring, though our paths had crossed occasionally and briefly throughout our student days, when I had assumed I was quite beneath the notice of such a popular, vivacious girl.

People sometimes say our meeting must have been *so* romantic, and my answering smile requires explanation.

We met over a cadaver in surgical anatomy. Four students – Janet, myself and two other men, in alphabetical order according to our surnames – were assigned to the same surgical table. There we would carry out allocated dissections on the preserved remains of an elderly man. This involved working on the subject's limbs or neck, exposing muscles, nerves or blood vessels for the inspection of our teachers, or "demonstrators" as they were called. It was tedious, exacting work.

It was also spring, and on that fateful day it was hot. The sun streamed into the dissecting room through the skylights above, tightly sealed against the possibility of any pollution from the fresh air. Formalin, the chemical used to preserve cadavers, has a very pungent smell, and there was no air-conditioning in those days.

I completed my assignment quickly. Janet Grant was working on the opposite side of the table. With her white laboratory coat emphasizing the brilliance of her auburn hair, she looked glamorous even in those surroundings. She was working smoothly and quickly at her dissection.

"I've finished." I announced after a final assault with forceps and scalpel. "Anyone for coffee?"

"Finished?" exclaimed Gibb. "You must have been given an easy dissection to do." Scalpel poised in mid-air, he leaned over to examine my handiwork.

"Call that shambles a dissection?" he scoffed. "Just wait till the demonstrator sees it." Then, leaning over to Janet's side of the table, he said approvingly, "now Janet's *really* done a job."

Ignoring this remark, I repeated my question.

"No," said Gibb. "You're a nuisance. Buzz off."

But Janet was smiling at me.

"I'm ready for some coffee." she said.

Spring
When lovers' fancy takes its wing.

It was more than lovers' fancy that made us take flight that day to the banks of Loch Lomond, a short bus ride from the smog of Glasgow. With text books and a few apples to sustain us, we discovered that studying for the finals was really more delightful than we had ever dreamed of.

And on that September afternoon in 1939, our flight took us to Ferguson's Tea Shop.

"Well, doctor," said my fellow physician, as she sipped her coffee. "This is the most important day of our lives. I just wonder what's ahead for us?"

Chapter Eight

The customary "turnover" of junior hospital doctors did not take place that September. A few young doctors moved on, either into the forces or to take more senior positions. The majority of departmental chiefs in hospitals took no chances. Afraid that if their existing junior medical staff left, they would not be replaced, they kept them on. Indeed, in some cases "house doctors" or interns were forbidden to leave. The result was that very few hospital jobs were available for the new graduates. Hospital experience is essential before going into practice. It was accepted that all of us would undertake at least one, but usually two years of further training. This was not mandatory, however strongly recommended, but few recently qualified graduates entered practice without further training.

It was a strange time for all of us. The declaration of war had sped rumours that "the finals" would be a "piece of cake." The need for doctors would be so great that most of us would be pushed through. Instead, nearly 40 percent of the class failed. Then those of us who had our degrees couldn't find work. Hospital administration had been disrupted by the war. Some hospitals were closed altogether, to be held ready for the expected air-raid casualties. Others were transferred to the military, who produced their own doctors and nurses.

Expecting hostilities to take place immediately, I had joined the reserve and became liable for "call-up" at very short notice. My old chief in medicine had offered me his junior internship, but when he learned of my commitment to the Services he gave me a lecture on the impetuosity of youth. A year or so of training would have made me a more useful army doctor, he said, and added that my decision was one I would always regret. He had joined up in 1914, a young and inexperienced doctor, and he knew what he was talking about. There was no point in taking someone who was liable for call-up on a couple of days notice. He let me go, but insisted on giving me a letter of reference. I still have it.

However, there were no air-raid casualties. The "phony war" intervened. Nothing happened. Instead of being in uniform I had to look for some kind of temporary work. The man Janet had expected to replace was kept on, and she was in the same position as myself, as were dozens of the others. Bewildered and anxious, we phoned medical agencies for possibilities of work, or knocked at the doors of hospital directors. We asked advice from older physicians who themselves were at a loss to explain the situation.

I was lucky enough to get a temporary job and within six weeks of graduating was working as assistant to a general practitioner in a Lancashire mill town called Wass.

The one point on which Janet and I did not agree was the war. I had become belligerent; Janet was a confirmed pacifist. Our arguments were often heated. But all the same, when the express for Manchester pulled out of Glasgow Central Station, she stood on the platform beside my parents and waved until the train rolled out of sight.

It would be nice to say that Wass nestled in a valley of the Lancashire moors. Wass never nestled. It was not that kind of town. Its grim surroundings and its own colourless facade did not encourage any sense of being cozy. The narrow, cobbled streets were lined by rows of small barrack-like houses, each one a replica of the next. The streets ran from the town centre to the low, bare hills that surrounded the place. Wass looked not so much as if it had grown, as having been dumped there in a take-it-or-leave-it phase of the Industrial Revolution.

The immensely high stacks of the mill chimneys dominated the area. Many of them had been smokeless since the depression and the decline in the Lancashire cotton trade, but those still in use seemed to make up for the rest. Every day masses of dense black smoke slowly uncoiled at the top of the stacks, hour after hour, rolling in thick clouds across the town and over to the Yorkshire moors not far away. There the smoke was presumed to vanish into thin air.

Miles out of town, tramping across the moors, I could pick up a handful of grass and find soot on my fingers. When the cloud ceiling was low, and it was sometimes difficult to differentiate between cloud and smoke, the soot would fall like snow. To add to the general cheerlessness of my surroundings, a strict blackout had been imposed.

But the people were perky, whimsical, warm-hearted, ignoring the grayness around them. They lived for "Wakes Week," the annual Lancashire holiday period. The town would pretty well close down and empty into that fairyland, Blackpool, the large seaside holiday resort on the northwest coast of England. The mill girls, dressed in their best, and lads, in their blue serge suits, would have a heyday in what must have seemed to them, with the sea and the bright lights, a different world. "Ec lad," they'd say with fondly reminiscent relish, "that were a great Wakes Week, that one," and then they'd come back to the reality of Wass, and another fifty weeks of steaming, sweating labour in the mills.

The mills dominated their lives. They were huge blocks of buildings, the rows of dirty windows, gray and cold, staring down at the town like the eyes of nameless, faceless monsters. Glasgow with its sordid tenements could be harsh and cruel, but beautiful country, and the sea, the glorious estuary of the Clyde, lay a bicycle ride away. Glasgow's life had some variety to it.

In Wass, where whole families, the women as well as the men, worked long, exhausting shifts in the mills, even their meals were prepared "outside." There was often no time for home cooking, except at weekends. Fresh fruit and vegetables were beyond the reach of most. Small corner shops prepared food daily. It was adequate enough. I can see them still, the white bowls with the blue bands around them, waiting on the stone slab counters. The whole street would eat the same food that day: tripe and onions on Mondays, pigs' trotters on Tuesdays, jellied eel on Wednesdays, and invariably, fish on Fridays.

When the shifts changed at the mills the cobbles would ring with the clatter of wooden clogs as the women ran to pick up that day's food. It was quickly done, and however basic the sustenance, the service was fast, efficient and very personal.

"Mornin' Ada," "Ta love," and "Day Bill." "Take care o' yerself." And so it went, until the queue had vanished as quickly as it had formed.

People were poor. I have often wondered whether they could

afford alarm clocks. Perhaps the invention had passed them by. Or perhaps they kept the "knocker-up" going because it afforded some older man, no longer fit for mill work, a little badly needed money. Before dawn, he walked through the streets, carrying a long pole. Periodically he stopped and with the pole, knocked gently on an upper floor window. He would continue gently tapping until he got some kind of response, a hoarse "A right, Alf," or a candle shining in the glass. Then he would move on to waken his next client, leaving behind him a growing number of people hastily dressing in the cold attic rooms in order to get to the mill on time. As far as I know, this was a Lancashire institution.

After we came to Canada one evening at a party Janet described this quaint job, convulsing everyone by describing this functionary as the "knocker upper." Oblivious to the growing hysteria around her, she finished everybody off by saying, "Oh! but it's an official trade in Lancashire."

In poor homes in Glasgow it was often possible to pick up some book and thumb through it: the Bible often, Robert Burns almost always, Karl Marx not infrequently. In Wass the steady literary diet was the weekly magazine *John Bull*. Old copies were to be found in every household, heaped high on shelves. Very few of my patients showed any interest in being drawn into political discussion.

In Glasgow, one struggled to avoid it.

Chapter Nine

Our "suite of offices" in Wass consisted of two rooms and a long dark corridor which served as the waiting room. A backless wooden bench was nailed to the floor along one side of the corridor, while the other side provided standing room. When the place was full, which was most nights, any other patients waited outside. Each time the door was opened, the rain came in on the people nearest to it. Since on wet nights they were usually soaked anyway, this last inconvenience may not have mattered much to them. It mattered to me, for the cold wind swept in on my feet under the ill-fitting door. The tiny gas fire at the end of the corridor was symbolic of better things.

My "surgery" was sparsely furnished. The only decoration was a calendar on the wall bearing the Christian admonition that we should love our fellows. The lack of decent lighting and the absence of any kind of examining couch precluded putting the calendar's teaching to any practical purpose as far as I could see.

Anything approaching a proper physical examination was almost impossible to carry out. Indeed, complete physical examinations were neither expected nor encouraged. A number of times I had to ask patients to lie on the floor while I examined them to exclude the possibility of acute appendicitis and the like. One lady, complaining of fever and a cough, protested volubly when I asked her to strip to the waist while I examined her chest.

"Ee! Boot I 'aven't coom *prepared* for that, and," she exploded, "Dr. MacRoberts would need owt like an *examination* t' tell what's wrong wi' me. 'E'd know just by lookin'."

None too graciously she permitted me to place my stethoscope on the area around her collar bones, decently covered by her blouse; that, she told me, was how she was usually examined. My impression was that she considered me not only a very forward young man, but probably a lecherous one as well.

It was rapidly being brought home to me that the practice of medicine in the industrial north was a little different from learning it in medical school.

I had been an assistant doctor for nearly a month, and was beginning to know my way about the town and its sidestreets, but night calls were difficult. The blackout left the place in stygian darkness. The moon and stars were hardly ever visible and the upward directed beam of a flashlight to confirm a street name was enough to draw a rebuke from air-raid wardens, even passersby. I was responsible for all night work in the practice. My bicycle was useless in the snow and dark, so I walked. I was allowed a full half-day once a week. It usually began when the morning office session was over and house calls had been completed. At midnight I must phone in, and announce my return to duty.

My lodgings were comfortable, and my landlady, an elderly

widow, did all she could to make me feel at home. But morning after morning, still tired from the physical work of the day before, as well as the mental concentration I found necessary because of my inexperience, I would be awake before dawn.

Subconsciously, it seemed, I would hear the clogs in the distance. It was always the same. I would waken and listen to those distant footsteps, a sharp clatter on the cobbled street, far away at first, then rapidly approaching, passing my window, and fading into remoteness. They were a woman's footsteps, fast and purposeful. It was always the same person, and I used to wonder what she was like, and why she was so far ahead of the rest. Was she young and pretty? Or middle-aged perhaps, glad to leave a lonely home and go to work? Did she have a special job to do?

There would be a period of silence and I would drift into sleep, but soon, in twos and threes, talking cheerfully, the mill girls would begin to go by. In the end they were a throng, the wooden shoes clattering out a deafening cacophony as they made their way to the mills, those gaunt, cavernous places that shaped their existence.

It was early morning. My half-day had not long ended. The persistent knocking at the door dragged me back from sleep. Pulling on my dressing gown, I stumbled downstairs, anxious lest my landlady should rush to the door herself. When I opened it a man, soaking from head to foot, stepped inside. He quickly closed the door behind him, oblivious to the pool of water that had already begun to form on Mrs. Stauffer's spotless linoleum.

"Can ye coom at once, doctor? It's Bill Kettlewell, the sewerman. 'E's 'ad an accident, 'as Bill, an' 'e doesn't look none too good. Jack Oates an' me' 'as got 'im 'ome. Ah'll take ye reet now if you'll come."

"What happened?"

"Well, d'ye see, wi' a' this snow an' rain like, one o' t' sewers blocked up, an' we 'ad t' free it. Bill took a bit o' a tumble. Laid isself out for a minute. If ye'd coom, Jack an' me'd be mooch obliged." He fingered his cloth cap as he watched me, polite yet anxious.

I nodded. "Of course I'll come. But you'll have to take me, and you must be freezing yourself!"

"Aye, it's reet cold, an' I was in t' water oop to you know where," he half laughed. "We had to get Bill out."

In seconds I was in my bedroom, struggling into my clothes, my mind working furiously. Blows on the head, even minor

46

ones causing seemingly trivial concussion, are insidious, dangerous injuries. Concussion always warrants admission to hospital for twenty-four hours of "neurological watch." A year or so ahead of me at university a brilliant student fell from his bicycle, hitting his head on the pavement. For a moment he was stunned, but picking himself up, he went on his way to classes. He reported the injury, his skull was X-rayed but there was no fracture to be seen. The next morning he failed to appear at his class. His friends, anxious, found him unconscious in bed: he was in an irreversible coma owing to bleeding within his skull. This can happen in the absence of any fracture. This tragedy was impressed on all of us, together with the need for constant watch in such injuries.

I needed help. I phoned my chief and told him the circumstances. How should I deal with this problem? The nearest hospital was miles away in another town. "Deal with it as you think fit," was his answer and the phone was replaced.

To refuse to do a house call was a disgrace. I should, of course, have phoned the police, let them get the ambulance and have the man removed. Instead, we faced into the winter night, my companion's teeth chattering as the wind tore into his soaking clothes. After walking through alleys and across what seemed like open ground we arrived at the patient's home.

Jack Oates opened the door. Like my guide, he was drenched, but had managed to get Kettlewell into bed. A heap of sodden, foul-smelling clothing lay on the bare wooden floor. It was a cold, comfortless room, but as the patient was at least in bed, and looking no worse than I expected, I sent his companions home lest they end up with pneumonia.

An examination assured me that pulse and heart sounds were good. Despite his tumble he had no headache. The pupils of his eyes were equal in size and reacted to stimulation. He had no bleeding from his nose, throat or ears. So far, so good. But he was shivering with cold, and shocked, and in a man in his fifties that is not very good. The first essential was to get him warm, so I lit a fire, gave him a hot drink, heaped his meagre blankets on the bed and reinforced them with a threadbare top coat I found. Then I asked which of his neighbours I should rouse to fetch the police. Like most folks in Wass, he had no telephone.

"I 'ave no neighbours. I live alone. There isn't a soul wi'in shoutin' distance. You'd maybe notice I live a bit oop t'hill? But ah'm all right. I'm warmer and I feel mooch better. Thee'd better get thas'en back to bed, doctor!"

47

Leaving him alone was out of the question. So I sat beside him all night, making endless cups of tea, and even dozing on the kitchen chair. He, too, now and then dozed but we talked a little, and Bill Kettlewell was an intelligent, thoughtful man. We talked and dozed the night away.

At dawn I checked his vital signs again. He was feeling fine, he assured me, and it was time I went home, he said. I could find nothing amiss when I re-examined him. I was amazed to find how mistaken I'd been as to the whereabouts of his little cottage as I looked out at the moor. We were at the very edge of town, with the morning mists swirling down the gullies, and the great mill chimneys looming through the gloom.

Promising I'd be back in a couple of hours after a bath and breakfast, I found my way to my lodgings. In those two hours Bill Kettlewell died. There was no autopsy, and as far as I know, no inquest. I was grateful for that. An unexplained death within one month of qualifying as a doctor! I have never been able to explain his death. I can only conjecture. A sudden, massive, delayed haemorrhage into the brain? A heart attack? Embolism? There were many possibilities.

There was no *official* enquiry, but there was an unofficial one – *my own*, into my own conduct of the case. No coroner could have been any more harsh in his reprimand than I was on myself. Kettlewell should have been transferred to hospital at first light. He should never have been left alone, even in the face of apparent improvement.

Cases like this still happen, when "trivial concussions" are sent home. A few days after Kettlewell's death, walking between house visits, I passed two housewives leaning on their brushes beside their front doors, flush with the pavement. "Oo's 'e?" one asked, and the other replied, "Don't ye know? That's 'im as killed Bill Kettlewell."

My face taut with pain and humiliation, I walked on, knowing that the carefree days of studenthood were gone forever.

Chapter Ten

I had arranged to meet Nurse Midley at the Graingers, so that while she dressed the varicose ulcer on Mrs. Tidswell's leg I could inspect it, and being fresh from my studies at a great university, perhaps give expert advice.

The Graingers were a nice couple in their early forties. Bert, a quiet self-effacing chap, worked in the city nearby. Elsie, his wife, looked after the home. Old Mrs. Tidswell had lived with her daughter, Elsie, for years, I had been told, but as a newcomer to Wass I knew little about the family. Bert was not, like the majority of townspeople, a mill worker, and he had more schooling than most. He was reading D.H. Lawrence, I observed.

Nurse Midley was in her early sixties, old enough to be my mother; close to retirement, her dedication to her calling and her patients was undimmed. The district nurses, like the district midwives, were, and surely still are, unsung heroines. Perhaps nowadays they all have cars, but not so long ago in the foulest of winter nights, with the North Sea gales sweeping across the moors and cities, they would uncomplainingly turn out of bed for their patients, wheel their bicycles into sheets of rain, and be off, cycling sedately on some errand of mercy.

Our work done, I suggested a new type of bandage involving a medicated paste, and prescribed that it be changed at less frequent intervals than previously. This procedure would keep the ulcer covered, away from possibly contaminated air, and at the same time the medication would continue its work. It was a theory of the time. I had seen it work, and had little hesitation in trying it.

"So there you are," I said finally, for Mrs. Tidswell was charming and had treated me with great deference. "Any problems, be sure to let me know."

I had left my little car in a nearby street, for I had several calls clustered together. Between such visits I walked, thus helping the war effort by conserving gasoline and satisfying my Scottish instinct to save money.

Nurse Midley wheeled her bicycle off the pavement and

walked beside me, a sturdy figure in her blue nurse's raincoat, cap perched rakishly on the back of her head as she must have worn it when a young girl. But now the rebellious hair that edged from under it was snow white. She looked at me sideways, balancing the bicycle with an ease born of long practice.

"You like old people, doctor."

It was a statement rather than a question.

"Yes, as a matter of fact, I do. They're often interesting, and I don't just mean medically. Take old Mrs. Tidswell now," I went on, "charming old lady."

"She's a wicked old schemer," said my companion matter-of-factly and with great cheerfulness.

I stopped in my tracks, and looked at her in amazement.

She laughed. "You brought up her name yourself. It was a great relief, for it saved me bringing the subject up. You see," she went on, "you have just issued an invitation to more sleepless nights than you already get."

She tipped the bicycle pedal forward with her foot so she could mount more easily, and laughed, again.

"Well, there you are. I felt I had to warn you. It's not easy to talk like that to a doctor y' know." She smiled apologetically. "Some of them are a bit standoffish when you tell them anything – even when it's for their own good!"

Perched on the saddle by now, she hitched her cap out of the danger zone. It looked as if it might stay on for the next few hundred yards.

"Nurse, thanks. I will say, I'm always learning."

"Well," she finished, "don't change your ways. Old folks can be fun. Many of them have been through a lot, and have plenty to teach us. Just learn to be selective. After all, becoming old doesn't *always* mean becoming nice," and with a wave she was on her way.

It was my first lesson in geriatrics, and far from my last.

Great Britain is probably still a relatively static society, where whole families, grandparents, sons, daughters, aunts and uncles have lived in the same city or village, even the same close neighbourhood, for generations. Many of our patients in England talked of London as if it were on another planet. Even a visit to Leeds or Manchester, less than a hundred miles away, was a great event. This restricted sociological picture had one benefit – the old lived near to their kith and kin, and with luck they received care and affection from their

own. However well-intentioned, however devoted and dedicated, few professional agencies can equal the love of one's
family.

But sometimes that is non-existent. Once in the early fifties
at the request of his neighbours, I visited an old widower, sick
and alone in his home. It was midwinter. Probably he had
struggled out to get his groceries and been caught in a downpour. Now he had acute bronchitis and obviously was de-
pressed. But he was not seriously ill. With care, I was
cautiously confident, he would recover. With old people one
can never be too sure, however. Quite unexpectedly they can
"take a turn for the worse." And so I asked about relatives,
for hospital beds, always at a premium, were reserved for the
seriously ill. Perhaps, I suggested, someone could come and
stay with him?

The neighbours, all willing to take turns at looking after my
old patient, told me that his son lived on the other side of the
city. He had done well for himself and had a house in a pleasant
suburb.

" 'E 'asn't been near 'is dad i' months," remarked one of
the ladies as she showed me to the door. "But maybe," she
went on, "if you phoned 'im, doctor, 'e'd pay heed."

I phoned. Half-way through my explanation of his father's
predicament the son interrupted me. "What do you think this
National Health Service is for, doctor? It's the state's job now
to look after my father, and you're being paid to see to that
kind of thing. So just you go and look to it."

North America is a mobile society. The elderly widower
still working his farm may speak fondly of his son "in oil,"
thousands of miles away. Charming old ladies in Alberta,
phone their daughters in California, but they are often at risk,
however well-to-do. They may fall victim to possibly the greatest social evil of our affluent modern life – loneliness. Later,
as country G.P.'s in western Canada, Janet and I saw little of
this; the prairies may be lonely places but the pioneering spirit
of neighbourliness is a tradition and few old people are neglected. But the impersonality of the cities can be another
matter.

It was a few days after my consultation with Nurse Midley
that Mr. Stainforth walked into my office. He was a little old
man, spry as a sparrow and just as cocky.

"Stainforth, William D.," he announced when I asked for
his name. "I've had a sore knee for two weeks," he said, and

before I could ask any questions he rolled up his trouser leg and presented a knobbly old joint for my inspection. "I want t' know what yore goin' to do aboot this," he said in tones that implied he hoped for much but expected little from the looks of me.

"You've had trouble with it before?" I asked. "The look of the joint suggests you've had rheumatism for some time." It also suggested that he'd had arthritis for years. But there are some people you feel instinctively you're better off with when they aren't argumentative. I felt Stainforth, Wm. D., was one of these.

"Aye, a bit," was all the answer he gave.

He obviously felt this was information enough for me, and he waited impatiently while I carefully palpated and moved the knee about. It creaked like an old mill wheel. He must recently, I told him, either have wrenched it, or had a flare-up of his rheumatism. However, I encouraged him. He was pretty smart on his feet despite the knee problem, and didn't even need a walking stick.

"It's hardly a catastrophe, Mr. Stainforth, but we'll see what can be done," I concluded cheerily.

Obviously, he had disapproved of my slow, painstaking appraisal of his problem, and this final levity was not appreciated either. Had I been smarter, I would have been a sight quicker in making a diagnosis, he implied, letting me know that he had only condescended to see me because my boss had temporarily stepped outside.

Nodding appreciatively and remembering the saying that some are born with humility, some achieve it, and some have humility thrust upon them, I drew the prescription pad towards me.

I needn't give him any ointment, he said. Lancashire's favourite remedy, goose grease, would suffice. He didn't want tablets either – full of sugar and either rubbish or dangerous new-fangled chemicals. Medicine in a bottle would be acceptable. I had more sense than to debate the point with him.

Nodding learnedly, I placed the prescription pad firmly on the desk before me and with great deliberation wrote the following mystic formula:

Ac. Ac. Sal.   gr X

Tinct Camph Co.   m VIII

Aq. ad.   ℥ss

Mitte   ℥ VIII

Sig ℥ss t.i.d. p.c.

He perused the symbols and for a moment I thought he was going to challenge them too, but grumpily acquiescent, he retired to obtain his bitter mixture of liquid aspirin, to be taken three times per day, after food, for the next two weeks.

In four days, however, he was back.

"No better," he snapped, "and change the medicine." I switched to the very latest medication in tablet form. Reluctantly and with obvious suspicion, he agreed to try it. Within a few days he had given me his opinion of that, too. Predictably, it was useless. His final visit demonstrated the limit of his patience.

"Stainforth," he announced, as he sat down.

"Yes, Mr. Stainforth, I remember."

It would be difficult to forget by now, but my patient's attitude suggested that my mental processes were none too bright.

"It's no better."

"Yes, I understand."

"You understand! You understand what? Do you realize I'm no better than when I walked in here two weeks ago?"

I, too, had reached the limit, not so much of my patience (though that was wearing thin) but of my knowledge of pharmacological treatment. Even his goose grease wasn't helping, and that was Lancashire's very own therapy. I decided to appeal to my patient's sense of justice. He was, after all, getting on a bit in life.

"You see, Mr. Stainforth," I soothed him, "after all, you're not any youngster, are you? Joints get worn, you know, and it's sometimes difficult to get results when you get to your age."

His belligerent old face was turned on mine, but I just had to remind him. "After all, how old exactly are you?" I queried innocently.

"I'm ninety-seven," he snapped. "What's that to do with it? Am I to stay a cripple the rest of my life because you don't know your job?"

Chapter Eleven

As the months passed, so did the pain of Bill Kettlewell's death. People still sought my advice. There wasn't much else they could do. Apart from my boss and myself there was only one other doctor in Wass.

I had never met Dr. Acey. He was "the opposition" and my employer didn't like him, When Dr. MacRoberts decided to take a couple of weeks holiday it was no surprise to be told that in case of emergency, I *must* call Dr. Wilson from the next town. I had met Dr. Wilson and had not been impressed. He was cherubically rotund, and with it, ill-tempered, if one scratched the surface of his prejudices.

Not that there would be any emergencies, said Dr. Mac-Roberts, for everything was taken care of. The district mid-wives could handle anything within reason, and in any case no deliveries were due till he got back. If I got in any trouble, I should simply admit the patient to hospital. It was easy, he said, cheerfully bidding me adieu.

I had bought my first motor car not long before. It cost me twenty pounds – less than a hundred dollars. It was very old, and the offside rear wheel, I discovered after I'd bought it, had a tendency to come off. It was all right if you noticed the wobble in time; otherwise a wheel careening down the road in front of you was an indication that the car was going to tilt badly in just a second or two. It never did any damage. I carried spare screws and bolts, and when the wheel came off I would retrieve it and bolt it back on.

These days I was no longer lonely or alone. I had persuaded Janet to apply for a "house job" in a nearby hospital, and there in the doctor's quarters I was made welcome, and could share my problems with her. It was in these few months that we got to know one another. I have sometimes told Janet that I wooed and won her because I took her away from the dreadful hospital food and saw that she was decently fed. "Meals out" were more than she could afford. For the privilege of working a steady eighty hours a week she was paid a little over three pounds per month (with board; less laundry costs). On the other hand, while I worked as hard, I received five pounds per week, a princely sum, indeed.

Not that our courtship was a smooth affair. For one thing Janet could not believe that Germany, the country of humanism and giants among men such as Beethoven, could behave with the brutality ascribed to it. For me the "phony war" was the quiet before the storm. For Janet it was, at least, the absence of senseless killing. We quarrelled, more than once we parted forever, but after a few days one or the other of us would recant, drawn together by affection, physical attraction and, in old-fashioned terms, respect.

Dr. MacRoberts' practice was to be my responsibility for the next two weeks. Three months had made a great deal of difference, and I had already regained much of the confidence I had lost after Kettlewell's death. All went well for the first week of Dr. MacRoberts' absence and, cautiously perhaps, I felt I had once or twice handled matters well.

Then the axe fell. The persistent ringing of the telephone would not be denied. Sleepily I picked it up. "It's Joe Featherstone here, doctor, 10 Ivy Street, and the midwife needs you. She says to come at once please; it's urgent." Instantly I was awake. "Tell her I'll come." Urgent midwifery was hardly my line. I had delivered a few dozen babies, all of them normal cases, and I had met the local midwives. Between them they must have delivered thousands of babies – and one of them now wanted *my* help!

Until the 1950s, most babies were delivered at home in England. Complicated cases were admitted to hospital. The trained midwives did excellent work and they were backed up by G.P.'s with an interest in obstetrics as well as by specially equipped "flying squads" from local hospitals. But even with organization and varied skills, obstetrical emergencies can occur with frightening speed. There wasn't any flying squad within miles, and as I hurriedly dressed I ran the possibilities through my mind. Haemorrhage? Obstructed birth? These were the likely ones.

The Featherstones lived a few hundred yards away and I walked. The walk, in the shelter of a factory wall, sharpened my wits. "Grow yourself a moustache," Dr. MacRoberts had told me a few weeks before. "You look too young. Nobody wants young doctors – except maybe young nurses. But not patients – they want experience and that comes with age. You've got neither, so let's see that moustache on you." If MacRoberts felt that way, what about the people who came into my consulting room? What about Mrs. Featherstone? The Featherstones were nice young people. She had been in the office a few weeks before, pleased as punch about having the baby, and proud of the shawls she had so carefully knitted during the months of waiting.

Joe Featherstone was standing on the pavement waiting for me. A couple of days before when I passed him in the street he'd looked like a fresh-faced boy. Now, I thought, he's a drawn-faced man. At the top of the narrow stairs stood a sturdy, serious looking woman, the patient's mother.

"This way, doctor. She does look bad. You'll do your best, won't you?"

The midwife stood waiting for me at the foot of the bed. Everything had been arranged with meticulous care. Young Mrs. Featherstone's tasteful little ornaments and lace tray cloths had been swept ruthlessly away from the dressing table top, and replaced by newspapers and enamel basins. The nurse's paraphernalia was laid out on the side table.

A glance at the girl in the bed told me of her exhaustion, and the nurse's concise report confirmed my fears. Worn out after hours of labour, of more recent unavailing effort, she no longer had the strength necessary to expel the baby. She would need to have her infant delivered by instruments. Worse still, the baby was showing ominous signs of distress, one of them being a sudden alteration in the quality of its heart sounds, which could normally be heard through the mother's abdomen. There was no time to be lost if the baby's life was to be saved.

I saw Jill Featherstone's anxious eyes go from the nurse's face to mine as I made my examination. Her great dark eyes, dilated with fear and fatigue, searched my face. I saw the dry lips, the disordered hair, and instinctively, automatically, for my mind was racing ahead of events. I comforted her.

"Nothing's going to go wrong, my dear. You just can't make that final effort, can you? You need help!"

Need help? Yes, indeed. What she needed was an immediate general anaesthetic and the application of obstetrical forceps. The baby's head was low in the pelvis. It was a procedure that required skill – a skill I did not possess. If something wasn't done, and done very quickly, we'd have a dead baby. It could be a catastrophic emergency, for exhaustion, mental or physical, in childbirth is often the forerunner to collapse in the mother, if not corrected.

"Simply move the case to hospital – it's easy," had been MacRoberts' parting words. The hospital was miles away; there was no time. I remembered how old Sir Archie Young, my chief in surgery, once said, "In your lives you will be called upon to make decisions and take action that may cause *you* torment of spirit, and others grief. Never have regrets if, in conscience, you have done the right thing."

The days for heroic decisions in medicine have largely gone. With rapid means of transport and communication, doctors seldom nowadays are "men on their own." Nonetheless I remembered Sir Archie's remark. My conscience was going to be clear all right. It wasn't quite what my old chief had meant, but I was about to cause some grief too – to Dr. MacRoberts when he got home. Portly old Dr. Wilson would take an hour to get over here, and it would be too late. Dr. Acey lived just down the street and was well spoken of. Straightening up, I looked at the nurse. "I'm going for help. I'll be back in a few minutes." She nodded, her relief obvious. In similar emergencies it was commonplace for the doctor, rather than wait for the arrival of an anaesthetist, to give the anaesthetic, hand it over to the nurse, and quickly apply forceps. That would all come later for me. Tonight my one hope was that Acey would be at home.

Telephones in Wass were as scarce as hen's teeth, and I ran to Acey's door. He lived in an imposing Georgian house, heavy with the dignity of generations of occupying physicians. I pulled on the ancient iron door handle, and heard the bell clanging in the darkened house. There was a pause, and suddenly an eerie whistle sounded almost in my ear. Dr. Acey owned a very efficient anachronism – a Victorian speaking tube which allowed him, from the comfort of his bed, to converse with anyone at his door.

Quickly I explained the situation. Lights went on and seconds later the door was thrown open. "The opposition" stood before me, attired in dressing gown. Despite tousled hair and sleepy face, he was a good-looking fellow, middle-aged, tall, and even at that unearthly hour, welcoming.

"Come in, doctor, I won't be a moment." He ushered me into a large room just to the right of the entrance way. A heavy oaken sideboard graced one wall, while in the centre of the room stood a huge old dining table. The matching chairs were distributed around the room and old magazines in neat heaps graced the table top. He smiled at me. "This is the dining room on state occasions, but most of the time it's the waiting room. My study cum surgery is just across the hall. I won't be a second." He was gone, bounding up the wide staircase two steps at a time.

I hardly had time to take in my surroundings when he was back. "The car's at the door. I just want to pick up my sterile drum – we may need it." Hurriedly he grasped the steel container holding gown, masks and surgical equipment and made for the door.

At our destination Acey's experienced eyes took in the situation at a glance. A quick examination confirmed my own previous findings. "You're right," he said, "there isn't any time to lose." Acey turned to the girl and reassured her. "You're going to be all right, lassie. I'm going to put you to sleep, and your own doctor is going to fetch the baby for you. Just breathe this in. Don't be afraid. Just breathe in like a good girl. That's it. Let yourself go to sleep. When you waken it will all be over."

He slipped the mask over her face, and quickly the girl's breathing became deeper and the nervous twitchings were gone.

"And now," said a voice from the other end of the bed, "I'll give you a little demonstration." He was beside me in a trice. "Just watch the airway and keep the chin up." Quickly he set to work. "Adjust the forceps so. Check the position of the head. Is there any palpable abnormality? Above all, make sure the cervix is dilated fully. Now insert blade one. Now blade two."

I saw his forearm muscles hard and tense as he applied himself; the task was no easy one, and a film of sweat appeared on his brow above the mask.

"Never more force than is necessary," he was saying. "Always follow the natural curve of the pelvis."

Quite suddenly it was over and he straightened up, pulled the mask from his face, and grinned, a strangely boyish grin in a man of fifty. "The little blighter's blessed with a powerful pair of lungs too," he murmured.

Mrs. Featherstone was stirring and soon she was awake, staring wide-eyed at the baby. She turned to me, grasped my hands and cried, "Oh doctor, thank God you came! As soon as *you* walked in the door I knew it would be all right!"

Flushing to the roots of my hair, I looked at my benefactor. He might as well not have been in the room. Apparently deaf, he was nonchalantly standing at the door, waiting for me.

"Doctor Acey did ..." I began, but that individual broke in, "Come along, doctor. We do have another appointment. Nurse will handle everything. She always does, isn't that right?" he asked the smiling midwife. Together we walked down the stairs, Acey taking time to congratulate Joe Featherstone on the arrival of his son and heir.

Miserably I climbed into the car. Torn between humiliation, embarrassment and gratitude, my thanks stumbled out. My companion laughed.

"I was twenty-three myself once upon a time, and inexperienced. That is forgiveable, for you will learn. Incompetence, that's another matter altogether. And now," he said as he slipped the car into gear, and we moved down the street, the cobbles glistening in the rain, "that next appointment – will it be port, brandy, or your national beverage?"

I had learned a lesson: to recognize my limitations and seek skilled help in time, for the patient's safety, not the doctor's pride, is all that matters.

Chapter
Twelve

In the spring of 1940, after a winter of ominous calm, the German Army advanced. Within weeks the French were thrashed, the British Army saved by the skin of its teeth at Dunkirk. "Call-up" came peremptorily and I dashed home to see my people and obtain a uniform "off the peg" from one of Glasgow's gents' outfitters. I am not exactly undersized but I could find nothing to fit.

"They didn't used to have officers as wee as this," sniffed one store attendant. I would have to have a uniform tailored and sent on. I joined the depot in plain clothes. There were a couple of dozen doctors. We arrived in dribs and drabs, varying in age from my tender twenty-three to dignified gentlemen in middle life.

For a few days we attended lectures, received injections and reduced the drill-sergeant to near tears of grief and rage. Doctors, especially if they've been their own masters for many years, are difficult people to transform, almost overnight, into well-drilled soldiers. Their discipline tends to be one of self-control. The commands of the barrack square are foreign to them, and the end result of a session of close-order drill can be disheartening for the instructor. On the other hand, some physicians love the panoply of war and become terrifying military men.

The depot didn't fit me up with battledress very well either. The jacket fitted well enough, but the trousers were so short they kept coming out over the top of my gaiters, and when I wore them without gaiters, inches of my lower leg were coyly exposed to public view. I looked as if I'd just been released from a mental hospital.

After a few days of initiation as a subaltern, Royal Army Medical Corps, I joined my regiment in sports jacket and flannels, walking into the adjutant's office and dumping my suitcase on the floor.

"And," demanded Dick West, the adjutant, looking up from his desk, "who the hell might you be?"

I introduced myself. "I'm the new medical officer."

"Ah! The doctor," he corrected me, adding, "and another Irishman, too!"

"Oh no!" I reassured him. "I'm a Scot."

"Is that it!" he murmured, with a wry smile. He tapped on the door of the room behind him, had a few words with the occupant, then ushered me in.

Impeccably uniformed in whipcord khaki, with his height and double row of ribbons, the colonel looked like something out of "The Bengal Lancers" – one of the great films of my youth. Monocle in place, he appraised me from head to foot. "How nice of you to be with us, doctor," he said, and dismissed me to the care of his adjutant, as elegant and distinguished looking an individual as his commander. My military career had begun.

Most of the regiment with which I was to serve for a year were at that time either regulars or regular army reservists ("Seven years with the colours, five with the reserve") with a leavening of territorial or militia men. There were rifles for one man in three, though we quickly received Canadian Ross rifles to supplement the Lee Enfields. There were 60 rounds of ammunition per rifle, and the rest of the armament consisted of Lewis machine guns with 600 rounds per gun, enough for a few minutes of sustained fire.

We were stationed in reserve on the northwest coast of England, about as far away from an enemy landing as we could get, which was just as well, considering the state of the regiment's armament. To my surprise, I later learned that some units of our first line of defence on the east coast were in no better shape than ourselves.

The regiment, or the effective part of it, was constituted as a mobile column, using a motley collection of hastily requisitioned trucks. The officers had some Colt and Webley revolvers, and that was about it. They were mostly Londoners; I was the only Scot. The weapon they did have, and in profusion, was the Mills bomb. They were kept handy; a bit too handy for my still civilian nerves, for occasionally one dropped off to sleep feeling that a very loud bang might herald, not the arrival of the enemy, but our own departure for more celestial quarters.

I speedily found I was not expected to be a soldier. I was the regimental doctor, a butt of jokes from my fellow officers rolling their ghastly "r's" about porridge. I was almost rankless, as much at home in the sergeants' mess as in the more select surroundings of the officers' quarters. In fact. I was spoiled to death.

Within a few weeks I had settled into my new way of life. and if the army is not exactly an academic atmosphere in which to practise medicine. it is an excellent place to learn about human nature. It was an interesting sociological study too. if that's what you could call the military caste system.

The world of blistered feet. bruised shoulders and certain social diseases became my oyster. There was later to be experience in more trying illnesses than those. but I speedily realized that my new vocation was not intellectually demanding.

"There's a medical officer outside. sir. Wants to see you."

This was certainly a break in the routine. I thought. as I looked enquiringly at my sick bay attendant. Lance-Bombardier Wilkin. The lance-bombardier was standing to attention with dignity. Old Wilkin didn't stand to attention like other people. He managed. even in his old-fashioned uniform jacket. brass-buttoned up to the neck. to look like a cross between a butler and a rather bibulous Harley Street specialist. Being the sick bay orderly he regarded himself as a semi-professional man in his own right.

He was of indefinite age. and had been a regular for so long that his long service stripes decorated almost the whole of one arm. They were the size and shape of a sergeant's stripes. but sewn on upside down. and made me think when I first met him that he was some very senior kind of non-commissioned officer. Of medium height and build. his most obvious features were a florid complexion and a bulbous. large. and beery nose. This latter adornment. I would later learn. had been honestly come by. Like a lot of men. he had a complete contempt for the new battledress. "Lacks h'originality. sir" he told me when I asked the reason for his shunning the new uniform.

Somehow or other. he had kept this old service tunic. and wore it with a pair of carefully pressed battle-dress trousers. The trouble was that the tunic and the trousers didn't quite match. The trousers were a distinctly lighter shade of khaki than the jacket. and that flat service cap that topped the lot was a lighter shade still. However. he simply gleamed with polish: his treasured leather belt gave a rather comical military look to the whole ensemble. I suppose nobody in the regiment had the heart to tell him off. He was a bit of an institution. and I never underestimated him. He was standing politely awaiting my command as I looked up.

"Bring him in."

My visitor was Hugh Lauder who had been a year or two ahead of me at Glasgow. We hadn't met since the day, a few months before, when we had pledged our allegiance to king, country and the corps after an interview with an elderly major-general, who took an interest, not in our academic achievements or our medical experience, but our ability to "play games." As Hugh had put it at the time, the interview had been superfluous. "As long as you're still warm and breathing, you're 'in' at this stage."

Hugh was still not a military man. Ignoring the protocol which demands that on entering any officer's place of business, a salute be given whatever the rank, Hugh nodded at me, and threw his forage cap on to my desk. Hooking a chair from under the nearby table with one of his long legs, he sprawled over it, lit a cigarette, and told me he'd heard I was in the brigade area. What about working together, sharing facilities, giving one another some time off, he wanted to know. This excellent idea I at once accepted, to our mutual advantage for months to come. After a few pleasantries mostly devoted to derisive comments on the stupidity of certain military traditions, he uncoiled himself and loped off.

Even if I was in the army I had ideas about how I was going to practise. None of this marching people in and "stand-to-attention-take-y'r-hat-off," stuff for me. I provided a chair for my patients and I used phrases like "would you mind"; very shortly I had a flourishing medical practice.

One morning a battery commander phoned me. Could he please have his battery back, he wanted to know. Puzzled, I asked for some elucidation of this statement.

"I'm training men to fight the enemy, doctor, not to attend your sick parades," he said. Gentlemanly though his tone may have been, even I recognized the underlying threat.

Embarrassed, I promised to rectify matters as quickly as I could, but the answer was beyond me. It was not, however, beyond Lance-Bombardier Wilkin who, standing deferentially beside me, politely silent, had put two and two together. Like a rather disreputable military version of Wodehouse's Jeeves, he leaned over me.

"If I could make a suggestion, sir? Tomorrow, sir, let me take the sick parade."

I stared at him, astounded. "Of course, sir, you would be in charge. Make sure nobody was really sick. I'd suggest, with your permission, sir, that anyone with a temperature of over a hundred would be considered sick, sir. I would personally take their temperature, sir, and send them to see you if necessary, sir. Anybody else, sir, I'll deal with." He paused, "sir."

His expression was bland and respectful, and I was smart enough to sense that he knew what he was up to.

The next morning, when I entered the sick bay, the patient's chair had vanished. My colleague, the lance-bombardier, had already admitted the first half-dozen patients and was inspecting the insides of their mouths as if they contained hidden gold. He then inserted thermometers. I saw one or two patients, but the rest, before they left, halted at the door.

There, on a shelf, the lance-bombardier had placed, for the inspection of all, a large glass Winchester full of clear liquid, boldly labelled "Castor Oil." Beside it was a large box, which bore all the signs of the bombardier's military sense of propriety. It was equally clearly marked "Army issue, tablets no. 9, patients for the use of." With due ceremony each sufferer received one tablet and a dose of castor oil, to be swallowed in my colleague's presence.

I have never, in all my life, known a practice to fail so quickly: sadly, I realized that the British soldier knows a rookie when he sees one.

Chapter Thirteen

Bill Brewer, the regimental captain and quartermaster, taught me the ways of the army, its traditions, the unwritten laws of the mess. Bill had joined up as a boy, and his service as a common soldier, an "other rank," had been comparatively short. In his late twenties he became a sergeant. Now in his early forties, with his body beginning to thicken, he looked, and was, a formidable man.

Much of his service had been spent in India, and he was no stranger to the fabled North-West Frontier, having served there for long periods with Afghan "irregulars." Despite his meticulous attention to military procedure, he was a non-conformist. Perhaps the years he had spent with such unorthodox fighters had made him receptive to the unusual. The British soldier, he said, spent too much time drilling, and not enough perfecting fighting skills.

The army, he said, didn't do enough to encourage individual initiative. For a man of limited education, whose life had been spent in the service, his mind was critical and open, but for all that, as I was to discover, his sense of military discipline was strong but functional. Tradition, according to my friend, was there for a purpose.

The colonel, no conformist either, despite the monocle, asked Bill to teach the regiment the elements of street fighting. We might have to fight the Germans in the streets if they landed. The quartermaster did his job superbly. He seemed to be everywhere. His small group of instructors was keen, and little escaped his eagle eye.

Momentarily, one day, a soldier leaned out of a window to level his rifle at one of "the enemy." "A" battery was defending the street while "B" battery played the part of the invaders. The action was immediately stopped by an irate bellow from my friend, standing beside me.

"You there," he shouted at the surprised rifleman, still silhouetted at the open window. "Your name, gunner?"

"Jones, sir."

"Well, Gunner Jones, you've just been shot dead. You're a professional soldier, aren't you?"

"Yessir."

"Well, act like one. You exposed yourself just now. You gave away your own position an' your mate's with you. A good shot would have picked you off. Shoot from the shadows, man. Never expose your position unless you have to. And remember," Bill concluded in a roar, "you're a professional. It isn't your job to die like a bloody hero for your country. It's your job to make *the other* poor sod die like a 'ero for '*is* country. See?"

With his help I began to learn the military "do's" and "don'ts," though some of them with my liberal upbringing I found hard to accept, and some I ignored – at first.

One evening the mess was empty, and I was alone. My room-mate had departed on some exercise, and even Bill, who spent most of his evenings in the mess, had gone out. Recently

I had come across some interesting cases and, eager to make notes, I took myself off to my room.

The headquarters mess was a large house that had hurriedly been converted to military use, and the walls were thin plasterboard partitions. My room was next to the kitchen, and the only other occupants of the building seemed to be two batmen. Judging by the noise of brushing that was going on, rows of boots would be shining like mirrors by morning.

The two men, like so many of their comrades, were cockneys. Suddenly their conversation, which had been a background buzz of "oos" and "ahs," impinged on my consciousness as I heard my name mentioned.

" 'Ere mate," said one to the other, "wot d' yer think of the new M.O. anyway?"

"Aow, 'e's awright mate, I fink."

"Fink so, mate? D' yer fink 'e's a reg'lar?"

"A regular? Ow, I dunno mate. 'E could be."

"Naw, mate, 'e ain't no reg'lar orficer, 'im, 'e ain't, an' I'll tell yer somefink else, mate, 'e ain't no gentleman neither."

"Ow! Wot makes yer fink that, mate?"

"Garn! Listen to 'im talk. It's 'please' and 'thank you,' an' 'please' and 'thank you.' Yer've never 'eard a reg'lar gentleman speak like that. No," he concluded pontifically, "'e ain't no reg'lar orficer, 'im, mate."

As Robert Burns once wrote:

> Ah! Wad some power the giftie gie us
> To see ourselves, as others see us.

It was a long way from Professor Milne McIntyre's wards, where every man "had a handle to his name," to the "reg'lahs" of the Royal Regiment of Artillery. At the same time Dr. McIntyre's teaching of deductive reasoning had not been lost upon me. I was seeing interesting cases and my curiosity had recently been excited.

London was being bombed, and the East End was suffering badly. When the men went home to see their families they talked ironically about "going up to the Front." One battery sergeant-major went to London on a weekend pass and was two days late in returning to duty. He had been searching frantically for his wife and child. The area in which they lived had been reduced to rubble. His little family was missing. They found them eventually, under the heaps of bricks and masonry, dead. His battery commander asked me to see him, and when he arrived at the sick bay, he told me he had come because he had been ordered to. My awkward condolences seemed almost unwanted.

His face was set and grim, but he was a soldier. He stood there at attention, and when I suggested he sit, he thanked me for my consideration, but continued to stand, although properly at ease. "Thank you," he had said, but he needed no help, and would return at once to duty. He saw no reason not to. He was back to where he had started. He was a trained soldier. This was where he belonged. And with a salute, he was gone.

A few days later I saw him again. He lay on his cot, and he was in agony, beads of cold sweat standing out on his sharp gray face. The muscles of his abdomen were as hard and as rigid as a board, and the pain in his upper abdomen was intense. The diagnosis was simple. He had an acute, perforated duodenal ulcer, and fluid was seeping into his abdominal cavity from his upper bowel, causing inflammation, infection, and severe shock. The case was a surgical emergency. I admitted him to hospital, where he was operated on immediately and the ulcer repaired. I saw him several times during his convalescence. He would appear before a military medical board, and almost certainly be "boarded out" of the service. The regiment would see him no more.

What could have been done for him? His wife and child were lost, and now the army, to which he had given the best years of his life, would reject him. What would become of him? I was convinced that despite his spartan behaviour he had attempted to stand up to more stress than his constitution, both physical and mental, would tolerate. I believed that he had developed an acute duodenal ulcer as the direct result of unresolved mental strain, for he had no previous history of a similar problem.

Confirmation of my suspicion, in the form of a similar case, was not long in coming. One of our sergeants was a regular reservist, recalled to service. He had spent twelve years in the regular army, but was liable to recall when war broke out. He and his wife had bought a little tobacconist's shop in north London and after several years of hard work they were just getting on their feet. With his recall to duty the business began to fail. His wife was writing despairing letters. The sergeant had no complaints: as he put it, he had been "recalled as per agreement," and he was a good man, meaning to do his duty. Perhaps had he talked matters over with a battery officer a solution might have been attained, but he was too proud a man for that.

His self-constraint, his stiff upper-lip doggedness coupled with worry produced. I am convinced, the duodenal ulcer that brought him his discharge from the service. Many a man would have welcomed that solution, but in this N.C.O.'s case he left the army tight-lipped and bitter, believing that he had "let the side down."

Other cases followed, and I began to search the medical records of local military units. A common cause of trouble was infidelity. Girl friends and wives wrote to say that separation was too much. For some strange reason it always seemed to be the sensitive and devoted who received this treatment. They were the ones who reacted by developing acute dyspepsia.

Some of the others, receiving letters of this kind, proceeded home and gave their nearest and dearest all the physical satisfaction needed — some of it with their fists. They came back to their unit leaving a state of married bliss behind them, and "made it" with the local girls for good measure. Such hearty souls probably made the better soldiers. Certainly this type didn't get ulcers — whatever else they had to be treated for.

I became so convinced of my theory that I wrote a paper on mental stress as a cause of acute duodenal ulcers in soldiers. There was evidence to support my contention which, though not revolutionary, was not generally accepted. The paper was rejected, and I was informed that duodenal ulcers were seldom caused by stress. Of course, nowadays it is recognized that unresolved mental strain can cause all kinds of illnesses. Certainly it is a factor that has to be reckoned with in a whole range of diseases, and even today we have not completed the list. But I know few G.P.'s who would deny that unhappiness, unresolved grief, chronic frustration and prolonged resentment are excellent foundations for the development of future physical disease, and not only in our digestive systems.

But the routine work of military medicine had to go on. Attendance at firing practice, sick parades, and the innoculation of "intakes" was a heavy part of our work. The "intakes" were civilians conscripted for military service, and they had to be medically re-examined, then innoculated against typhoid, smallpox and tetanus. Hugh Lauder and I joined forces, and with an increased staff we made an efficient and congenial team.

That presiding light, Lance-Bombardier Wilkin, had gone on leave, and I enlisted the services of a younger gunner, a Territorial. He had had no medical training, but he was intelligent and interested. Hugh, M.O. to the regiment a few miles away, had selected and trained his own right-hand-man, and one day, joining forces and working from morning till night we examined and innoculated several hundred men. We kept the N.C.O.'s busy marching up troop after troop of recruits, and we worked without respite, grabbing sandwiches and the occasional cup of tea where and when we could.

Our two assistants were kept even busier, for they kept the queues moving. The result was that when we had finished, and seen the last troop marched off, they had missed their evening meal. On learning this, Hugh took me aside.

"These chaps'll get no supper now, and they've worked like beavers for us all day. What about taking them downtown and standing them a decent meal?"

I was doubtful of the wisdom of this, however much I appreciated the lads' loyalty.

"Hugh," I said, "they're 'other ranks.' If anybody sees us there could be a bit of trouble."

"Oh, hell," replied my friend. "Who's going to see us? Besides, we're fighting for democracy. We owe it them. No supper, poor chaps. Com'on, let's go."

So we went. Hugh's pay was as meagre as my own, but he walked into the best hotel in town as if he owned the place. The two gunners were at our heels.

I think I felt it before I saw it. A flickering glance took in our little quartet, passed over my face in a bleak unrecognizing appraisal, and drifted out of a window on to the sea. It was my room-mate, Captain Ronald Flush, the garrison provost-marshal.

Commandeering the *maitre d'*, Hugh, oblivious of my developing discomfort, led the way to the most prominent table in the place and courteously drew out a chair for gunner Forbes.

"Hugh," I whispered, "there's Flush."

Hugh, with the benefits of a sound Scottish education, had a nice sense of alliteration. His verbal disposal of Captain Flush was short, pithy, Anglo-Saxon, and specific.

Despite the excellence of the meal I developed indigestion. (My theory on this subject was further hardened.) The provost-marshal left before we did, sauntering out without a glance in our direction. But I had a feeling that I had not heard the last of our little dinner party.

A couple of days later, having forgotten the affair, I arrived for breakfast. The M.T. officer and I were usually the last to put in an appearance, for I was a healthy young animal and enjoyed my sleep. On this occasion as I entered the anteroom the M.T. officer was just leaving. Obviously he was off to attend to matters of some urgency, for the only greeting I received was a hurried nod.

But the morning was bright and cheerful, and so was I. I would breakfast alone for once.

However, when I entered the dining room, the colonel was seated in his usual chair at the head of the table. Bill Brewer, a few seats away, was fiddling with his napkin ring.

"Ah, doc," said the Old Man, "I do trust you are rested."

I never could be sure at times whether he was solicitous or mildly sarcastic, but I assured him I was in excellent health.

"Good," he replied, folding his own napkin, and rising to his feet. "I think 'Q' would like to see you in his office this morning. Nine hundred hours, I think you said, Q?"

Bill had risen to his feet and stood while the colonel adjusted riding tunic and tie to his satisfaction.

"Yessir."

"In that case, gentlemen, good morning to you," and our commander was on his way, to be followed almost immediately by the quartermaster.

I was left to my breakfast – a thoughtful meal.

Within the hour, I had presented myself at Bill's office. Now, we were friends. One of us usually picked the other up half an hour before lunch, and en route to the mess had a beer together in a quiet little tavern Bill had discovered in a back street. The other fellows liked their pink gins, but Bill was a beer man and had no social pretensions.

My morning salute was usually returned with a perfunctory nod towards the quite sumptuous chair that faced his desk, but this morning I saluted the top of his head as he scribbled away at his "indent" forms. I knew better than to sit, uninvited. So I stood there and waited. And waited.

Eventually that heavy head was raised upright, the broad shoulders straight and square as he sat back in his chair. The face that confronted me was grim and unsmiling.

"I've been deputed to give you a tellin' off, doc," he began, "by the Old Man himself," he added weightily. "And," he added, "I agree with 'im."

There was no invitation to make myself comfortable, so I continued to stand.

"What the hell is this I hear about you and that other porridge-eatin' sawbones from next door taking 'other ranks' out to dinner?"

"Next door" was the soubriquet for our sister regiment and I was well used to exotic descriptive terms for the people of North Britain. Usually they were more affectionate than scurrilous.

"Well, Bill," I said, "to begin with, they're nice chaps," and I went on to explain how, working in the interests of the service, our two orderlies had missed their suppers.

"Poor sods," said Bill commiseratingly. "Fancy missin' their suppers like that. You could've given them a chit for food. They'd 've got something. What's the rest of the excuse?"

"Excuse!" I exclaimed. "I'm not making any excuses. We're fighting for democracy aren't we? And if I feel like taking an 'other rank' out to dinner that's precisely what I will do."

Captain Brewer glowered at me, his dark eyes smouldering with contained anger.

"No you won't, doc. Not again. That's an order – from the colonel. Look, if the men get to know, they won't understand. You'll simply lose caste. That's all. And caste is what keeps the army together."

He was no longer angry. Bill was no Prussian disciplinarian.

"Sit down, doc," he nodded towards the chair, "and just listen to me. The men wouldn't understand. I agree with some of your views, but this time you're wrong. We all have caste. Y'know, when I was a sergeant in this regiment, and some gunner wanted to speak to me, he stood *at attention* six paces off, and said, "Sergeant, permission to speak." And I was in '*is* position for years before that. And that's caste. Caste maintains discipline. And officers must never lose caste."

He paused, looked at me hard, and shook his head wonderingly.

"And here you are, doc, two months in the regiment and taking 'other ranks' out to dinner!"

He emphasized his point.

"It *isn't done*, doc. That's all there is to it. It's not to happen again, and that's an order from the Old Man. Understand?"

"Yes, Bill, I understand."

I did, too. My mind was thoughtfully recalling the conversation of those two boot-cleaning batmen only a few nights before as I worked at my little thesis.

I made for the door. My friend's head was already bent over his work, but just as I grasped the door handle, he looked up.

"They were 'nice chaps,' " he said wonderingly, repeating my opening remarks. "Nice chaps! Well, Jesus Christ was a nice chap, and if he was an 'other rank' in this regiment, he wouldn't go out to dinner with any bloody officer."

Chapter Fourteen

The country was in the grip of an epidemic. Senile old ladies with foreign-sounding names who forgot to pull the blackout curtains were reported to the police. Undoubtedly they had left the lights on to guide German bombers to that very spot. The epidemic, of course, was "spy mania." All kinds of people caught it.

Janet was a house surgeon in the heart of Lancashire's industrial area, at Oldham. Even in wartime it was only a few hours train journey from our headquarters, and occasionally we could meet. While she helped to take out appendices and gallbladders, I looked after the blistered feet and social problems of several hundreds of healthy young men. In her hospital were a couple of German refugee doctors. Their command of English wasn't very good, and sometimes when talking on the telephone they would lapse into their native tongue. Their British colleagues were hard put to it to defend their innocence from suspicious busybodies. A lot of this kind of thing was ridiculous, and anybody with a modicum of common-sense was above being caught up in the nonsense.

Still, strange things happen. I had been given a weekend pass, and Janet had managed to snatch a day off. We met in Manchester. Now, Bill Brewer's admonition as to behaviour appropriate to an officer had not been lost upon me. When Janet told me that she meant to buy, on this her treasured day off, some delicate underwear in a shop specializing in that sort of thing, I said I wasn't going to be caught dead in the place. I'd wait outside and it was there, standing on the crowded curb, that I saw coming toward me a formidable-looking man.

I watched him and noted the dinaric skull and nose. He's German, or of German ancestry, I thought. And his clothes – several sizes too small for him. I noted the square shoulders, the military walk. It was very interesting.

Leaving Janet in the shop, I strolled along the crowded pavement after him. Then – the final and most baffling touch of all – *he* was following someone! A very ordinary chap in a cloth cap, a dozen or so yards ahead of him in the busy crowd, kept looking nervously over his shoulder to see if my blond friend was still there.

My surveillance of this strange little procession lasted for several hundred yards, but afraid that Janet might feel that I had deserted her, I went back. But I couldn't get the business out of my mind. I told Janet, and we agreed that there was probably a perfectly rational explanation for the incident.

That night, driving back to Janet's hospital in the decrepit old car we shared, I told her of the beauty of the night sky as seen from the moors and suggested we make our way there, via one of the side roads. A few hundred yards was as far as we got. A couple of figures loomed out of the gloom, a bayonet was thrust under my nose, and I was instructed, uniform or no, to open the trunk of the car for inspection. This procedure was repeated on another road a few miles further on. To use today's terminology, we were, obviously, not going anywhere, and I took my favourite doctor home.

Next day I told my room-mate, the provost marshal, about it.

"There could have been some connection between that chap I followed and those soldiers. They'd blocked the whole area off and they didn't strike me as just being on a night exercise."

Flush had listened impassively to my recital of events. "And why didn't you do something about it?" he asked me. "We're at war: anything's possible. You should have trailed that man until you saw a policeman. All you needed to do was to ask him to check the man's identity. You needn't have been involved. The fellow's either in the clear, or he's not. It's that easy."

He looked at me. "You, a doctor, a trained observer, and you don't do a damn thing. It defeats me. Well, I'll make enquiries, but next time you see something suspicious, *do* something. Get a policeman, even act on your own. You're a serving officer, and there's a war on."

His enquiries produced graphic enough reasons for the road blocks. Parachutes had been found on the moors and the area had been cordoned off. It might, said the provost marshal, be nothing. On the other hand, it was all very suspicious, and let it be a lesson to me. I was contrite, even humiliated. Next time I would do something.

I didn't have long to wait. A few weeks later, having attended a boring course on gas warfare, I was on my way back to the regiment. With all the proprietorial privilege of a man with a free first-class railway ticket, I settled myself in a suitable compartment. Just as the train began to slide out of the station, my peace of mind and dignity were disturbed by the door being swung violently open as a man heaved himself into the compartment at a run. He slammed the door shut, lowered the window, and cautiously watched the station platform before throwing himself into a corner seat.

He was not of first-class railway ticket calibre. Unshaven and dirty, his clothes might have been taken from a scarecrow. His whole demeanour was most suspicious. At every station he inspected the platform.

The stations passed, one by one. Only two remained before the terminal – the south or suburban station, and the central terminus. Perusing my newspaper with feigned interest, I made up my mind: at the terminus I would approach a policeman, civil or military. There were always plenty of Flush's boys around. My duty done, I would make my exodus with dignity. As Flush had said, it was easy.

Easing its way into the south station the train jolted to a stop. Doors slammed. A whistle sounded. Moments later, the engine puffed into activity. The purples and yellows of the carefully tended embankment flower beds began to slide by. My suspect, as usual, had looked the platform over and again hunched in the corner seat. Suddenly, like lightning, he opened the door and in a flash had thrown himself on to the platform. The train was by now moving at quite a clip.

I was dumbfounded. To be outwitted like that? Not on your life! The platform was empty as I took a header on to it, recovering my balance just in time to see a ragged pair of trousers disappear up the station stairs. I reached the ticket collector a yard or so behind my man. There was the usual little queue and someone was fumbling in a coat pocket for a lost ticket stub, so I took advantage of the delay to tap my fellow-passenger on the shoulder. "Sir," I asked, "may I please see your identity card?"

The effect of that simple, courteous question was startling. The little crowd went flying in all directions as my suspect

74

ploughed through it like a bull at a plywood fence. My pursuit was momentarily checked as I tripped over someone's legs and fell sprawled on my face. But I was up again and within a score of yards I had caught him. In a move (not one that would have been approved by the Marquis of Queensbury), I laid my quarry low, then with some difficulty I escorted him to the stationmaster's office.

Could I use the telephone, I asked, to phone the police?

The suspect had so far not uttered a word. Speedily, I was speaking to the desk sergeant.

"Sergeant Littlewood, 'ere. An' wot can I do for you, sir?"

I explained that I was an officer of the local garrison; that I had detained a most suspicious-looking character.

"Oh, ay," said the sergeant. "An wot's 'e like to look at?"

Eyeing my captive while I held the telephone to my ear, I described him in detail.

"That's about it," I concluded.

"Ay, that's about it right enough," said the voice at the other end, adding cheerfully, and in tones of open admiration, "the crafty owd devil!"

"I beg your pardon, sergeant?"

"Oh, no. Beggin' yours, lieutenant, but that's Bert Bloggs you've got there. Ask 'im 'is name."

"What's your name?"

The only reply was a baleful glare.

"Sergeant," I said. "I'm having some difficulty in getting information."

"Well, don't you bother, sir. Joose keep 'im there. Ah'll 'ave t'lads reet round. Broke out o' Liverpool jail just three days ago, did Bert."

It would have been difficult to describe my state of mind.

I looked at the desperado.

"What's he in for, sergeant?"

"This time? Runnin' an illegal gaming establishment."

All I can say for myself is that, miserably, for it was all I possessed till pay day, I pressed a ten-shilling note into my captive's hand, and walked away. I trudged wearily up the station steps, just as two bobbies strode majestically down them.

The epidemic had infected me, too. But my cure was complete.

Chapter Fifteen

In the winter of 1940, with the regiment still staunchly defending the peaceful northwest coast, I was sent for a few weeks to Aldershot to further my military education. Janet, to improve her medical training, had joined the staff of a large hospital in the English Midlands. As a result, our meetings were now few and far between.

Many British towns have garrisons, but Aldershot is *all* garrison, and has memories for thousands of old soldiers of the allied armies. The surrounding countryside is beautiful, with its quaint hamlets, village greens with cricket at the weekends, old pubs and beautiful woodlands. But in wartime, Aldershot was as drab and comfortless as its barracks. The place reeked of military discipline, and had little to commend it except its proximity to London.

The blitz on London was then at its height and we were not supposed to go there. It was one thing to get blown up honourably on the field of battle, quite another to get obliterated in a London night club. That had happened to some, and I daresay it raised problems of military accountancy. However, a lot of us, being young, curious, and just a little rebellious, ignored the advice of our seniors, and found our way to London. Rumour had it that the military police could stop anyone in uniform, ask his business and pack him out of town on the next train, a little note to his commandant to follow. To avoid this, my companions and I got off the London train in the suburbs, and continued into the centre of the city by Underground.

It was there, on our way back to barracks late at night, that we saw the decency, the steady self-discipline of Londoners. Later in the war the underground railway stations were organized as official air-raid shelters with well-built bunks lining the platform walls, and wardens to keep order. They were hardly needed. There was, somehow, "always room for one more." In the early days of the blitz, neighbourhood folk instinctively sought shelter in the depths of the underground stations, taking food and blankets, and sleeping on the bare platforms in quickly organized groups.

Oblivious to the coming and going of trains, the rumbling of explosions far overhead, the muffled barking of anti-aircraft guns, the children slept. Men would sometimes lie awake, quietly watchful. They would even nod and smile at us as we quietly stepped between blankets and over the recumbent bodies. In one sharp raid I saw an old lady, bent and frail, pulling her belongings, tied up in a blanket, behind her as she made her lonely way to the Underground entrance.

"Let me help you, mother," said a cheerful bobby, and hoisting the bundle over his shoulder and picking up its owner bodily, he deposited the old lady and her belongings on the station platform, found someone to take care of "mother" and went back to duty. Even at the end of the war, with the rockets falling, and the shape of things to come revealed, Londoners were a steadfast, self-controlled lot.

When Janet phoned me to say she had twenty-four hours leave of absence and would meet me in London that next day, I was hesitant. It could be dangerous, I said. She countered by saying that it was important to her. Who knew what lay in the future, or how many more meetings we might have, she argued. These hurried dates were precious as they were for countless thousands of young people. Still, I hesitated. The blitz was in full swing.

"It's the only day I'll have off in a whole month," said Janet. "I could catch the early morning train. I'd be in London in time for lunch. I'll catch the four o'clock train back, and we'll both be out of London by tea time."

The daylight raids were over, but the bombings at night were hideous. We made arrangements to meet the next day, and I would be at the station to meet her train.

Resident doctors in hospitals worked crushingly long hours. They still do in many places. In Janet's hospital, a comparatively large one, with over a dozen residents, the hospital bylaws allowed residents one weekend off duty each month, while during their month on duty they were forbidden to leave the hospital premises. Even wives from distant places visiting their on-duty young surgeons or physicians were not allowed to share their husbands' room overnight. They must stay in whatever lodgings they could find, and few of them could afford that luxury. As for a woman resident inviting a man to her room – the scandal would have shaken the hospital to its very foundations! The long hours they worked, over-exposed to infection and under-exposed to fresh air, led sometimes to real trouble for these valuable and highly trained young people.

Tuberculosis, meningitis and a host of minor infections were not uncommon among them.

Next day I was at the London terminal in good time to meet her train. My one concern was to get her out of town before dark. Noon came and went. The afternoon dragged on. With a very heavy heart I saw the four o'clock train for the north, the one on which Janet had said she must leave London, pull out. There was still no sign of Janet and the next train for the Midlands would not leave for several hours, by which time it would be dark and the bombers could be overhead. It was already dusk, and office people were crowding on to trains, hurrying to get home and away from the centre of the city.

Gradually the crowds thinned out and the place was half deserted, except for groups of servicemen. Then a train pulled in and I saw Janet running towards me, waving.

"I've been over half of England," Janet exclaimed. "There was bombing up the line somewhere. We were stopped for ages and when we did get moving we took a route I'd never been on before. I was worried to death about you waiting here, but there wasn't a thing I could do. We were told the diversion was essential."

We were together, and that was all that mattered. Instead of lunch in a fashionable restaurant, we had tea in the ill-lit, frowzy, railway cafeteria. There was no point in going anywhere else: the city was in stygian darkness. Stale buns and hot liquid flatteringly called tea were our repast.

Gradually the crowd of soldiers and airmen in the cafe departed to their trains, and we two were left alone with the waitress. She was cheerful and fatalistic.

"If it's me night to cop it, miss," she said to Janet, "there ain't a blooming thing I can do abaht it." Within seconds the siren's distant warning reached us: an eerie wailing, rising to a crescendo, then ebbing, almost dying to silence before it began again, was all around us.

It was time for Janet's train to leave. I was already in trouble by now, for my absence would have been noted at roll call; but whatever the consequences I was taking Janet back to the Midlands. It was as black as the pit in the huge station and we stumbled almost blindly to where her train should be waiting.

There was no sign of any train. The banshee wailing had begun to die away, though we could hear distant sirens, and soon a foreboding silence replaced the sounds of the air-raid warning. It was as if the whole city, fearful, was listening.

Then came the far-off, distinctive throbbing sound of German bombers. The first crackle of distant anti-aircraft fire began. The planes came closer, and quickly the deep thuds of exploding bombs mingled with the sharper salvos of artillery as battery after battery opened fire. The cloud ceiling was low and the ghostly shadows of the searchlights flickered, swung and focussed in the sky, their pale yellow light becoming almost gray amidst the clouds, soon to be suffused with red from the flames below.

The roof of the great station, built in the time of Queen Victoria, had been made of glass. There was precious little of that left, but what there was began to crash on to the platform. A porter paused beside us.

"It's goin' to be a big one, mate," he grunted.

I asked about our train. Yes, that was it, he said, standing up the line. Could I see its tail lights? It wouldn't dare move into the station now; I should walk up and check with the railway guard.

I put Janet behind a porter's trolley. It was poor shelter, but it was something. I heaped boxes round her and told her to crouch until I returned: it would only take me a minute or two. Setting off at a run, I heard a sudden scream, and raced back. She had vanished. Then, seemingly from the very bowels of the earth came her voice, shaky but reassuring me. She had fallen, not just on to the rails, but into the deep maintenance pit at the terminal buffers. Had she struck her head on the line her skull would have been crushed. In the pitch dark neither of us had seen how close we were to the edge of the platform.

There was a fire already reflected in the clouds, and before it ebbed and died I saw her lying there. My heart in my mouth. I jumped down beside her, but though badly shaken, she was unhurt. "I felt as if I'd never stop falling," she said. With much scrambling we got out, but hardly had we done so when we heard voices and before I could shout a warning two soldiers had walked off the platform and crashed into the pit.

Their fall was a hard one, for they were heavily burdened. The flow of foul language, delivered in broad Scot's accents, became sulphurous. One chap's groans mingled with his swearing, and I could see him rolling about, so back I went into the pit. Janet, tense, began to laugh but quickly controlled it.

"Whit's sae bloody funny aboot this?" roared an irate voice. "When ah get oot o' here, ma lass, ah'll show ye whither it's funny or no!"

"Now then," said I, as I helped the sufferer to his feet, "you mustn't talk to a lady like that." He ventured the opinion that Janet was not a lady.

"That won't do," I reprimanded him. "She's just got out of here. She fell in just before you did. Furthermore," I continued sternly, "you must not talk to me like that. I'll have you know I'm a commissioned officer."

It turned out he didn't think too much of commissioned officers and he told me what I could do with my commission. His instructions were quite specific. There are times and places where one should correct any misapprehensions that common soldiery may have about the king's commission, and with his hobnailed boot about a foot from my nose as I hoisted him up, I felt that this was definitely not the place.

Janet's laughter had subsided, but the noise all around us seemed to be climbing to a crescendo and the clouds, scudding blue and gray across the sky, were reflecting the glowing flames. Our companions, en route for Glasgow, were making for the same train as ourselves. They were not the Scottish soldiers of romantic song. They didn't give one damn about the green hills of home. They were nearer to reality. They were a couple of Glasgow toughs. They now switched their remarks to the immediate cause of their troubles: the London, Midland and Scottish Railway Company was consigned to the depths of every hell that existed. This subject exhausted, they dealt in the same way with London, the Lord Mayor and Corporation, not forgetting the Pope and the Archbishop of Canterbury. But it was the teutonic gentlemen overhead who most enraged them: their language, as they limped up the platform just ahead of us, was lurid enough to light the way.

Not that we needed any illumination by now, for all London seemed to be on fire. Even amid the explosions we could hear the roar of burning buildings and smell the acrid smoke. The sky, a kaleidoscope of red and gray, seemed alive with the searchlights' rays dancing and darting as if controlled by demons.

The four of us had the train to ourselves. Discreetly we let distance grow between us. Eventually the train moved out, and the conflagration slowly receded while Janet and I watched, awestruck. The very sky seemed alive and on fire.

In a few hours we had reached our destination. There were no lingering kisses that night. I thrust her into the warmth of the hospital hallway, turned, and ran to the station as if all Robbie Burns' witches of Ayr were after me. I did not relish my coming interview with the commandant when I got back.

Fortunately, I managed to board a London-bound train almost at once and it was not quite dawn when we reached the city suburbs. A huge pall of smoke, fitfully illuminated by the still burning fires, drifted low in the sky. The guns were silent. The bombers had gone. The train gradually filled, until in my compartment every seat was taken. Gray of face, wan, tired and weary though they were, my fellow travellers, bowler-hatted, carefully dressed, were on their way to "business as usual" in the city. London suburbanites are not a garrulous lot. Not a word was said.

We had a mile or so to go to reach the terminus when the train slid to a stop, and there it stood, the engine a carriage length ahead of us, puffing contentedly. Minutes passed before one passenger, impatiently consulting his watch, decided to look outside. He opened the window on one side of the compartment, closed it, came to my side, repeated the manoeuvre, spent some time inspecting his surroundings, closed the window, walked back to his seat, unfolded the newspaper he was carrying, and resumed his reading. Soon a second man did the same, then a third, to be followed by others.

Finally, wondering what on earth was holding us up, I decided to have a look. Despite the night of terror they had experienced, and the fact that they had probably spent it on their feet on air-raid duties of one kind or another, not a word of conversation had passed between my fellow travellers; presumably they had not been introduced to one another. I wanted to know what was going on, so sliding the window down I leaned out and looked along the line.

Cold though the morning was, I broke into a colder sweat. Not a dozen yards away, around a hole in the ground stood a group of men, including our engine driver. A lantern held by one of them showed the tail fin of an aerial torpedo. The thing, unexploded, had gone unnoticed throughout the night, must just have been discovered, and the train signalled to stop. A few yards to the left, and our engine would have gone over it. Even now, any vibration could activate its mechanism. My Walter Mitty complex didn't work. My mouth parched with fear, I looked at my fellow passengers.

Thoughts flew through my mind like lightning. "Vanished without trace!" "Medical officer deserts." I could just hear the tongues in my home town. If these were my thoughts, what about those of my companions? One man was sitting quietly, head back against the bulkhead, eyes closed, fists clenched on

81

his knees, his knuckles white with the force of his grip. A second stared in front of him, pale, eyes intense with fear. Two or three appeared to be reading newspapers, but to a man they were restrained, distant, outwardly calm.

Pulling up my coat collar and stuffing clammy hands into my pockets, I sat and waited. Minutes passed. The half-light of dawn became day, and still I was surrounded by the silence of the grave, interrupted occasionally by the nervous rustle of a newspaper. It was just then, as I was figuring out who'd get my pension, or if there would be any at all under the circumstances, when the bowler-hatted man opposite, leaned over, touched me on the knee, and said politely, "Soldier, are you prepared to meet your Maker?"

In a cold sweat, I pretended to be asleep. My questioner turned to his neighbour and repeated his remark. He might have been addressing a Sunday school class, so mild was his demeanour. He received a brief, embarrassed reply before he addressed the occupants of the compartment collectively. "Gentlemen," he began, "we should at this time, prepare ourselves to meet our God."

Under the circumstances it wasn't an unreasonable suggestion. There, a dozen yards away, could be oblivion for all of us. A newspaper was lowered, revealing another bowler hat. A pair of frosty blue eyes set above a clipped moustache coldly surveyed our questioner.

"Sir," said the man with the newspaper, "if you persist in creating a disturbance, I shall have you put out *at the next station!*"

Silence descended upon us once again. I often think that in that one incident I saw revealed the English quality of the stiff upper-lip.

Suddenly the engine gave an extra puff or two. Quietly, smoothly, the train slid forward.

"Jerry," I thought, "you may bomb these people, but you will *never* break them."

Chapter Sixteen

"Stand at aaa – a ten shun: That is not how you stand at attention – sir! Stand aat *ease*! That is not the way to stand at ease – sir!"

The days of wine and roses were over. There I stood, momentarily, and sweated. Momentarily, for in two seconds I would be "quick marched" by the regimental sergeant-major himself. I had been posted as a section officer to an armoured division field ambulance. Field ambulances, each unit comprising about 150 men, were highly mobile medical units. Suddenly I found I was expected to be a "leader of men." This, in the army, means an ability to march in step. My new commander, appalled by what he saw before him, had ordained that I would receive the personal attention of the R.S.M. for one hour each morning until I achieved proficiency in foot drill.

Sadly I left captains Brewer, Flush and the rest behind me. The artillery regiment had been my home for a year and sometimes, especially in moments like this, I wished I never had left. My posting had come suddenly. The colonel had arranged for me to have forty-eight hours leave.

He had his ear to the ground, had the colonel. It was his opinion that I would shortly be leaving for a sunnier climate. With that amused guffaw of his he'd suggested that I take myself off to Scotland and "make an honest woman" of that little red-head I was running around with.

Janet accepted my proposal. Her one stipulation was that our marriage would be a partnership of equals. She was not a "woman doctor." She was a doctor, she said. I would have had it no other way. We have remained partners, and later on I was to benefit from her wartime hospital training. She has always been an active doctor, although once after an appendectomy she did take time off. At a cocktail party when asked if she was back in active practice she said innocently, "Oh! I'm just a sleeping partner in the practice," and for a second wondered why everyone laughed.

Our honeymoon was spent in a railway compartment crowded with men travelling south, and a day later I reported to my new unit, stationed in the beautiful, wooded meadowland of Surrey, in the south of England. Janet, for a time, like so many young wives, had become a camp follower. Local doctors were only too pleased to offer her work. But our corps commander, a gentleman by the name of Montgomery, didn't like wives around the place. King Lobengula of the Zulus, so it is said, slaughtered the women before great battles: with no mental diversions, the men fought better. Monty merely ordered our women home.

But Janet didn't go home. I hid her. We found a delightful hamlet called Friday Street, where the window of her hotel room overlooked a beautiful lily pond. At nights the silence was disturbed only by the peaceful croaking of the frogs. It was hard to believe that with the dawn would come the creaking and grinding of those machines of Armageddon, the tanks, as they plunged and lurched through the beautiful woodland.

At nights, after the sentry had passed and my tent mate had given the "all-clear," I literally went "over the wall," returning by the same route before the first light of dawn. At 6:30 we would "fall in" regardless of rank, for unarmed combat – a mixture of boxing, karate and dirty tricks, where the troops could take a delight in beating up their officers.

Jogging is no longer one of my enthusiasms. Friday Street was several miles away from our camp. Once I overslept. In the early morning light clad in singlet and running shorts, I was running round a corner towards our camp when I ran smack into my new colonel, a very military medical man. He was strolling along, puffing contentedly at his pipe, swinging his walking-stick in the soft light of a summer morning.

Petrified, I smartened my sharp trot to an agitated gallop and thought I might get off with it by giving a smart "eyes right" as I passed him. But he stopped me. "This," I thought despairingly, "is it." But he beamed at me. The pipe was removed from his mouth. He waggled the walking-stick at me.

"I like that!" he barked. "Keen young officer! Extra exercise! Excellent! Get all you can! Don't let me stop you."

So I pounded on, fell into line just in time, and to demonstrate my enthusiasm, attempted to slaughter my surprised and inoffensive opponent.

But foot-drill was something different. The orders that were being barked at me by the R.S.M. heralded the commencement of my private purgatory. It had begun the day after my arrival.

It so happened, contrary to predictions from my brother officers in the home from home I'd left behind me, that I wasn't going anywhere exotic – just up and down the quiet quadrangle of an evacuated boys' school, barked at, every few paces, by this tyrant of a warrant officer. I and my men were there for training, to be moved eventually to a newly-formed armoured division on the northeast coast of England.

Thankfully, I was to be drilled in a spot secluded from view and the ribald comments of the common soldiery: the R.S.M. was bad enough just on his own. He was waiting for me that first morning, watch in hand, a stocky, frozen-faced man in his early thirties. With his drill-stick held rigidly horizontal under his left arm, he swung a salute with his right that would have done credit to the Brigade of Guards. He was not saluting me. He was saluting the King's Commission – and very shortly I'd have given mine away to the first applicant.

"We will commence one hour of instruction in foot-drill," he'd bark, having coldly watched me return his salute. Then filling his lungs to bursting point, and apparently addressing a battalion, he'd start on one lone, inoffensive medical officer.

Each morning, when he finished, to the second, he'd snap into that immaculate salute of his, and wordless, as poker-faced as when he arrived, he'd march off.

It went on for weeks. I didn't like him at the beginning, and I detested him at the end, for he was a humourless martinet. But I should have been grateful. He did two things for me: he gave me a fellow-feeling for the poor old recruit, bashed about and pushed around, and he made me proficient in foot-drill. What was more, I began to like its snap and precision.

Other skills had to be acquired. My company of medical corpsmen, thirty of them, well-trained and drilled though they were in many respects, had to learn these new skills with me. Map reading in the dark has surprises all of its own, especially when, in a rainstorm, one leads one's happy little band in the opposite direction to tomorrow's breakfast. Mobile warfare necessitates the use of vehicles which have to be driven and manoeuvred, sometimes in the dark and at considerable speed. Rivers, which definitely had not been clearly delineated on the map issued to me, had a particular, and fatal, fascination for the vehicles of my little convoy. As the months went by, strange though it sometimes seemed, we became professionals, until eventually, in the dark of winter we could do forced marches and turn up, more or less on time, ready for action, and not infrequently, at the correct rendezvous.

However, we doctors still looked after the medical needs of our comrades. One morning when, as duty officer for the day, I was asked to see Sapper Tomkins, Royal Engineers, I breezily sailed into the medical inspection room, ready to deal with another case of minor illness.

There was nothing about the sapper or his complaint to make me feel concern. Most of our men were youngsters. My sergeant was an elderly gentleman of twenty-eight. I was next in line for an old-age pension and the whole section was younger still. I was surprised to find a patient in his early forties: he was a long term regular, just home with a draft from India. He felt he had "flu," he said. He was "all aches and pains" and had an awful headache. He'd not felt well for a couple of days. That morning he'd felt worse, and had decided to seek medical advice.

I examined him carefully enough. He did have a fever; a high one in fact, but I could find no reason for it. Obviously he was no complainer. Because of that raised temperature and the weakness he complained of, I admitted him to the sick bay for observation. Admitting people for observation has saved my skin – and my patients' – on many an occasion, especially when years later as a G.P. in Canada, I could take people in to my own hospital beds. Appendices that might have been dismissed as trifling stomach ache have "ripened" under the watchful eyes of nursing and medical staff, to be dealt with before complications arise. People with vague but suspicious chest pain or "indigestion," who might just be in the early stages of heart attacks, could be watched and treated with emergency equipment at hand.

All that was in the future, however, as I sent the sapper to bed. He was happy enough to go. I carried on with my duties, but lightheartedly, for Janet, having managed to get a weekend off from her job as medical officer in one of Glasgow's infectious diseases hospitals, was coming to see me. She would arrive that very afternoon.

With luck I had found her accommodation. That seaside resort was a dismal shadow of its former cheerful self. The beaches were deserted but for selected areas where the troops might bathe in summer or do physical training in winter.

The great North Sea rollers were as beautiful, as graceful; or as menacing as ever as they swept down upon the sand, disintegrating into the breakers that thrust upon the land. Now they swept down, not upon innocent family parties, but upon barbed-wire entanglements, half-hidden in the sand. The watchers on the cliffs no longer turned their carefree, idle glances at the diving seabirds. They were men in long drab coats, the colour of the land around them, steel-helmetted, with rifles slung, pacing deliberately, looking out to sea.

Most of the hotels were closed or occupied by troops. The ancient cobbled streets echoed to the crash and clatter of hob-nailed boots. Along what had once been a carefree promenade, the heavy coastal guns lowered menacingly over the North Sea, and tanks, armoured vehicles and trucks, hundreds of them, lined the streets. Anti-aircraft guns, permanently manned, stood ready to give supporting fire to the merchant navy con-voys as they passed close in. Army wives did not go there for the social season. In many ways their visits were not encour-aged, but whenever Janet could save a few pounds from her pay she would come to see me.

On this visit she was to find herself involved in an unusual case. I met her at the station, saw her to her lodgings, and reported back to the sick bay. An anxious looking Staff-Ser-geant Jones was waiting for me.

"Sapper Tomkins, sir – have you made a diagnosis?"

"No, staff, I haven't. He hardly has any physical signs."

"He's got plenty now!"

"What do you mean?"

"Come and have a look. You'll need a mask and gown, sir. I have them ready."

I looked at Jones questioningly but donned the gown as I was bid, and accompanied him to the patient's bedside. Sapper Tomkins lay in bed, ominously quiet and disinterested. His temperature had shot up; his headache was intense; his supper lay by the bed, untouched. Within the last few hours he'd broken out in a rash.

Watery blobs festooned his face. The staff-sergeant helped the patient take off his pyjama jacket. His chest was clear of any rash, but my colleague almost casually lifted the man's arms for my inspection. The blisters were there as well.

Giving me a significant look, the N.C.O. replaced the bed-clothes and followed me to the office. "Any idea what that is, sir?"

I didn't answer, whether from ignorance or fear it would be difficult to say, but the staff-sergeant didn't wait for my reply. "It's smallpox. I did my spell in India. I've seen lots of it – and that's it."

Aghast at the enormity of the possibilities that now faced us, I could only nod. Jones was a good man. He'd been in the R.A.M.C. for years, was a fully trained male nurse, and I respected his opinion.

"But staff! He's just back from India. He's been vaccinated umpteen times probably. Where's his A64?"

Jones produced the small health and immunization record every soldier must carry. Tomkins, according to the book, had been vaccinated a number of times.

Relieved, I handed back the book, but Jones wasn't satisfied. "Old soldiers dodge the column. He could have faked the M.O.'s signature, or slipped a few rupees to a medical orderly to get it stamped. Sir, on this you can't take a chance."

He was right, Tomkins maintained he'd been vaccinated. Even at that, I suppose his recorded "reactions of immunity" could have been incorrectly, if honestly, recorded. Smallpox is one of the most dreaded of all infectious diseases. Successful vaccination confers immunity, but in countries like India it has been a scourge for centuries. In Britain until the nineteenth century its record was equally evil. Between 1793 and 1802, 36 percent of the deaths of Glasgow children were due to smallpox – at a time when half the children born there didn't live to see their tenth birthday.

Simply to be somewhere in the general vicinity of a smallpox case is enough to become infected and in the unvaccinated it can kill, horribly. Smallpox has almost been eliminated as a threat from the face of this earth. This is a tremendous achievement for humanity, but if eternal vigilance is the price of civil freedom it is also the price of freedom from this dreadful scourge.

During the Second World War a ship from the Far East, carrying a sick seaman, docked at Glasgow. Tragically, because the man was seen by an acknowledged expert, the case was diagnosed as chicken-pox – a minor but not dissimilar illness. Only when the seaman became deathly ill was the diagnosis corrected. By that time doctors, nurses and hospital staff were infected, and a number died. Troops were forbidden to travel to, or through the city, so serious were the possibilities of spread.

The responsibility for Tomkins and for immediate action was now mine. I believed the staff-sergeant. I had never seen a case, but the clinical picture was well known to me – "flu" for a few days, headache, fever, and then those watery blobs, typically on the face and extremities.

I reported the case, and my suspicions. If I'd dropped a bomb I couldn't have had more effect. Here we were, thousands of highly-trained men, and this wretched M.O. has to report that he thinks he has a case of smallpox on his hands.

Orders were given that Tomkins was to be transferred forthwith to the nearest infectious diseases hospital. "Not on your life," said the superintendent of that institution, firmly. "It's an army case and the army knows what to do with it, too. This is a civilian hospital."

I was to be quarantined. Jones was to be quarantined. Tomkins' draft was to be quarantined, and so was everybody else within shouting distance. Then leave for the whole brigade was stopped and I, the innocent victim of circumstances, became a pariah – not because I might be carrying the plague, but because I'd stopped the chaps going to see their girls.

Nobody else volunteered to give a second opinion on the case. Opinions were offered, among them, that I'd better be right. If I wasn't, it was suggested by my betters I'd very shortly be leaving my little command for another one – a latrine detail in darkest Africa.

The one person I wasn't quarantined from was Janet. She listened to my story, then said, "let me see him!" I wasn't having that, but as the medical officer from one of Glasgow's "fever" hospitals pointed out: "I see more awful infections in one day than you'll see in a year."

By this time Jones had phoned me. He'd found a small, half-empty hospital, qualified under the regulations, that was willing to take our patient. The elderly medical superintendent, who had worked in India as a medical missionary, saw Tomkins with me, and shook his head. "I'm afraid you may be right. It looks very like it to me."

Janet, at the superintendent's invitation, gowned and masked, interviewed the sapper, by now a very ill man. She couldn't be sure. What impressed her was Tomkins' record of vaccination. She had to leave the next morning, but suggested that I put my patient on to full doses of sulphonamide. The antibiotics were still years away. Some bacteria, she said, were beginning to behave very peculiarly. Sulphonamide was worth a try.

By now Tomkins was worse than ever. His fever had reached an almost astronomical level and as he became delirious, I became worried to death. The War Office had been told and tomorrow morning the great Sir Knolly Pratt, its civilian consultant in tropical diseases, would arrive to see Tomkins. Till then I must content myself. I only hoped he'd last till then.

For the next twenty-four hours I led a lonely life. Armoured brigades are tightly knit communities. Word gets around. Tramping along the pavement I saw before me a troop of cavaliers, drawn up in parade order. I would have to pass in front of it. The old cavalry regiments mounted in their steel chargers had become known to the more common, if no less licentious soldiery, as the cavaliers. Their troop commander, a man I knew, an individual who had accepted my hospitality and my liquor, saw me coming. Promptly he called his men-at-arms to attention, and marched them three paces back from the pavement. As I smartened my pace past them, he bowed me on my way, nose held daintily twixt finger and thumb, a gesture that would have appealed to his aristocratic forebears.

That afternoon passed into night. To lessen the chance of spread of the infection, I was to be in sole charge. My patient's condition steadily deteriorated. Medical textbooks weren't plentiful in my surroundings but I devoured what few there were.

My kindly ally, the superintendent, gave me all the advice he could and went home. If Tomkins' condition terrified me, so did the matron. There weren't any congenial little nursing committees in her hospital. Miss Giles didn't need them. The place shone like a mirror. She was an elderly battleaxe, her uniform as stiff and starched as the rest of her. Her mere appearance in a corridor was enough to send nurses scurrying into the nearest room, and I'd have done the same if I could. She took a special dislike to my hobnail boots on her floors. They were, however, the only ones I had, and the day for barefoot doctors had not yet arrived.

That night seemed interminable. My patient's fever was still rising. He was raving. I sat beside him most of the night or occasionally dozed in the next room. Eventually he slept. Dawn came at last. Whatever I might say about Miss Giles, she brought me bacon and eggs herself. She wouldn't let any of the nurses near Tomkins. She dealt with him, with her terrifyingly capable efficiency.

I was comforted by the knowledge that Sir Knolly was somewhere between London and me, but when I went in to see my patient, he knew me, for the first time in twenty-four hours. His temperature was dropping. He had even toyed with his breakfast. His face and wrists were an awful mess, red, swollen, and covered with crusting excrescences, and some blobs had appeared on his body, but he no longer looked as if he might die. The sulphonamide, I thought, had done some pretty dramatic work.

The next few hours seemed an eternity and the future of my military career darkened as Tomkins' prognosis brightened.

Finally an enormous American car drew up at the hospital main door and Sir Knolly descended, and with him his retinue of three.

The great Sir Knolly was breezy and affable. A man of about sixty, he was a short chap of my own height, stockily built, with heavy gray eyebrows and piercing blue eyes. His second-in-command was in his fifties: he made up for his chief's lack of stature, standing head and shoulders above him, thin, spare, and taciturn. The other two were, I presumed, residents. About my own age, their condescension suggested that army M.O.'s were among the lowest known forms of medical life.

Miss Giles was on the hospital steps to meet them. Himmler himself would have edged away from that dame, but not Sir Knolly. He had her sized up at one glance. He positively oiled his way across to her, shook her hand effusively, and commented on the immaculate exterior of the hospital.

"And now, dear lady, let me have *your* opinion of the case," he said, taking her elbow gently. It was practically love at first sight. Miss Giles simply dissolved and became an elderly version of a simpering schoolgirl. Her new personality was as nauseating as the old one was frightening, but before I could ponder the matter we had arrived at Tomkins' door.

Gowns and masks were ready. I had told the sapper that a specialist was coming to see him. I hadn't reckoned on four. As we filed in, all six of us, I thought my patient was about to expire – of fright. Only his head was visible. He had a long beak-like nose and as we crowded into the room that nose kept swinging from one to the other of us like a scarlet weathervane, his eyes popping with apprehension.

Sir Knolly examined him, finished his work and nodded to his sub-chief, who took over. Tomkins watched every move as if he were about to be disembowelled. Sir Knolly washed his hands, picked up my carefully written notes, his eyebrows signalling his concentration. He pointed to the notes, then to me. I nodded, signifying that the notes were mine. He nodded. Not a word had been spoken.

The sub-chief examined him all over again; then he nodded to the senior resident, who produced culture tubes and swabs and vials, and an array of needles that had my patient grasping the bedclothes in his agitation.

Still not a word. Sir Knolly had retreated from the hand-basin and gone into a state of meditation. His sub-chief had washed his hands and had accepted a towel handed out reverently by Miss Giles. The resident who wasn't working was surveying me with the arrogance of an English version of a young Greek god.

Finally it was over, and Sir Knolly and his second-in-command retreated to a private sanctum.

Sir Knolly and his confidante returned eventually. Miss Giles poured tea with prim propriety, and then, tea over, Sir Knolly reached for his coat and indicated that the consultation was over. He had grasped the door handle and was on his way out, when suddenly he turned and said, "Well, s'not smallpox!"

He was halfway through the door when I summoned up my courage from the soles of my feet.

"Sir!"

He turned. Those eyebrows shook and quivered as his eyes met mine. "Well?"

"Sir, I am the medical officer responsible for all this. The brigade has had all leave stopped. I must make a report to my A.D.M.S."

He looked at me questioningly. I'm convinced that by telepathy, or maybe experience, he could see that latrine detail I'd been promised, as clearly as me. "Sir. If it's not smallpox, sir, what is it?"

"Ah, yes," said the great man, "Well, as a matter of fact, I rather wish you hadn't asked me that question. To be honest with you m'boy – damned if I know. Good morning to you."

The mystery was never solved, but Tomkins recovered and I retained my command.

Chapter
Seventeen

After leaving hospital work, Janet continued to practise and she was always busy. Overworked doctors eagerly sought her help.

In 1943, Catriona was born. Loyalty to a tired physician kept Janet working almost to the end of her pregnancy and she did not have an easy time. When she returned to Scotland she did so with the intention of finding a resident post in hospital. Doctors were in very great demand, and as a ''temporary single parent'' with a nursemaid to look after the little one, the idea seemed feasible. But Scottish tradition disapproved.

When she did find such a post, it was in England. She became resident doctor to a private hospital in Lincolnshire. The chief attraction of the position was the suite of rooms provided for the doctor on the top floor of the building.

The job was no sinecure. There were still air-raids, and the V One rockets had made their nerve-wracking appearance. The medical superintendent, who was the only other resident physician, did not believe in women physicians, including those with babies, being shown any special consideration.

During air-raids, Janet was expected to patrol the wards. She had done that many a time these past few years. But this was different. Leaving her apartment and locking the door behind her, she would make her way down flights of darkened stairs, and with the dimmed light of an electric torch to guide her, begin her rounds.

Doors were locked and unlocked for her as she went from ward to ward, calming patients and consulting with nurses. She was now a doctor in a mental hospital.

A young woman whose husband was overseas became Catriona's nanny, but soon the girl was peremptorily directed to work in a factory. Apparently untrained labour was more important to the war effort then the badly needed skills of a well-trained physician.

Janet stood up to the repeated bullying of bureaucracy, but the situation had become all but unendurable when some enlightened official relented and waived rigid regulations. Mary stayed with Catriona and Janet in Lincoln until the end of the war, a devoted nanny and companion. And to her work in infectious diseases and anaesthetics, Janet added experience in psychiatry, a subject she still finds fascinating.

When the war ended I was stationed at a large staff headquarters, carrying out adminstrative and medical duties. Demobilization was not far off.

I wasn't interested in becoming a specialist. I enjoyed dealing with people on an everyday basis, and I wanted to make a home with Janet and our loving, lively little bundle of a daughter.

I remembered how Professor Glen spoke so warmly of his days as a G.P. And general practice appealed to both of us. Janet was an experienced anaesthetist but she had a broad interest in medicine in both its physical and psychological aspects, and she had no intention of giving that up.

We pored over the "Practices for Sale" columns in medical journals, phoning one another when some advertisement appealed. We had to limit our ambitions, for like most of our generation, we had no savings. Wartime expenses had seen to that. That didn't matter. We were twenty-nine and had a sense of future while so many of our friends faced a world of broken dreams and tragic memories.

Most of the practices advertised were beyond our means, but one day, there it was – "Small practice for sale, capable of development. Nos. 535 and 537, Anlaby Rd., Hull. Suitable office and living accommodation *for rent*."

We wrote to the advertiser, a veteran deafened by gunfire and unable to practise. His patients had mostly gone elsewhere, but he knew a number would return, and was sure we could "pull the practice up again."

The atlas showed Hull, on the north shore of the Humber estuary, to have about a quarter of a million people in and around it. It was the third largest seaport in England, lying as close to the North Sea as to the Yorkshire dales. As a soldier I had slept in many a dale's field and had never lost my feeling for the beauty of those bare hills and valleys.

Hull appealed to us for a number of reasons. Since Janet was working as a doctor in a private mental hospital in Lincoln, not very far from the estuary's south shore, Hull would be easy to visit. We liked the country – but above all the price of the practice was right! A visit of inspection would be relatively easy to arrange. Leaving Catriona with friends, we met for the momentous expedition. This really got under way, we felt, when we boarded the ferry at New Holland for the trip across the Humber.

The estuary is wide, almost like the open sea, and we had time to reflect on the fresh, salt sea air, the great dome of sky above us, before we disembarked at Hull's Victoria Pier and hailed a taxi.

In the centre of the city, we were appalled to find great areas simply reduced to rubble. Floors hung drunkenly, ceilings and roofs open to the sky. Here was what had once been a bedroom, the bed still lying, forlorn and rusted, against a wall. There was what must have been a cheerful sitting room. Now the wallpaper, drenched by past rains, hung in strips. That kind of scene was repeated over and over again. Whole blocks were mere facades, with windows, or what had once been windows, boarded up. Basements lay open to the sky, their floors littered with rubble. Nothing lay behind those walls but ruins.

Parts of the city centre were devastated; acres of ground that once supported thriving shops and offices lay in ruins. The rubble had been cleared off the streets but small mountains of bricks and masonry testified to the savagery of the bombing. Thankfully, wherever there was an open space the fireweed had taken over. The wild flowers made a blaze of colour that relieved the general scene of desolation. I remembered those wartime news broadcasts – "A northeast coastal town was bombed." It was often Hull.

The taxi driver easily read our thoughts. "Jerry gave this place a real packet. We had big raids and little ones. And they went on all the time. It was easy for 'em to sneak in over the coast and get away. And then they were always after the shipping. Lost thousands, killed in raids."

We moved along Anlaby Road and were deposited at No.535. Even among those dilapidated empty houses with their glassless windows boarded up, No. 535 looked outstandingly shabby. But we were no longer in an area of heavy bomb damage such as we had seen in the city centre. Nevertheless we eyed one another uneasily as we walked towards the front door. We knew the place had lain empty for six years and we knew, or thought we knew, what six years of neglect could mean.

The small front garden had six years' growth of weeds in it, and the decorative effect wasn't improved by a lavatory pan, an old stove and barrow-loads of rubble. The dirt on the inside of the windows was almost as thick as it was on the outside. We scrubbed away at the glass to remove enough dirt so that we could look in. Standing knee-deep in weeds and stale grass, we could only gape at the scene before us.

The house was being used as an air-raid storage depot. It had been damaged by bombs. Drain pipes leaned precariously away from the building. Loose tiles lay on the roof. Sandbags piled as high as a man occupied the whole of one front room, while in the other a gaping hole showed in the ceiling and the fireplace leaned drunkenly off the wall. The whole place was filthy.

We went to 537, the "residence" next door. It was worse. It was a three-storey red brick building with the front door opening directly on to the pavement. Floor boards were filthy and broken, ceilings sagged, huge strips of damp wallpaper hung from the walls. The yard was one huge rubbish dump. As high as a single storey house, a miniature mountain of masonry, bricks, wood, clothing, paper, toilet bowls, metal pipes and rusting stoves occupied the space: the summit above my head was topped by a metal bath leaning drunkenly over me.

Aghast, I stepped back, and stared, unbelieving, at my wife. She was in paroxysms of mirth.

"My God!" I cried, "I don't believe it!"

I closed the wooden gate behind me, shutting out the sight, but however appalled I was not defeated.

"Janet," I said grimly, "there's another man in Hull who wants to sell his practice. Let's ring *him*."

When I phoned Dr. Frank Micks, a rich Irish voice answered.

"Sure, I'll be delighted to see ye. Don't budge, now will ye, and I'll be right with ye."

Dr. Micks was a tall man, over six feet, alert, erect, burly and cheerful. About sixty, he wore tweeds, a leather coat and a very ancient tweed hat festooned with wet and dry trout flies. Lovely things they were – "March Browns," "Greenwell's Glory," "Black Gnat," and "Lock's Fancy" among them; some new and alive looking, others battered and frail and attesting to their successful use in the Yorkshire streams.

Grasping my hand he looked behind us. "Ah!" he said, "ye've had a bit of a fright have ye? Well, never mind, we'll have supper and a talk. Talkin's one of me hobbies and I'd be lyin' if I didn't tell ye the other's trout fishing."

His car was small and the only unoccupied seat was the driver's. The front passenger seat he courteously cleared for

Janet by heaving a medical case into the back and placing a heap of medical journals and unopened letters on the floor.

"You'll not mind resting your feet on them, doctor?" he asked her. "I'm always meaning to open some mail, but it's all a question of time."

I climbed into the back, where I was surrounded by medical cases, hip waders, fishing rods and creel, as well as a bag of groceries obviously just purchased. There was also a glass-topped box containing more fishing flies. This box was reverently lifted out of my way.

"No woman loves her jewels more than I prize these," commented the doctor. "By the by," he added, "be careful with your feet, doctor. I'd hate ye to break any of the bottles."

On the floor were a number of old medicine bottles containing mysterious fluids varying in colour from amber to dark brown. I took care to avoid them.

"If ye broke them." said our colleague jocularly, "then I'd *niver* test them, would I?"

When he ushered us into an imposing looking house, it was as if the occupants had left for a long holiday. The furniture was covered with white cloth, and the floors were bare. Dr. Micks led us into what had been the drawing room, a large room and no doubt at one time a gracious one, now devoid of furniture, except for one corner.

That corner was quite a sight. It was a well-designed, almost bomb-proof bunker. Great beams supported other beams that held up the ceiling. Sandbags lined the walls. Inside the shelter stood cupboards, a table, chairs and a small bed.

"That's been my home for four years," said Dr. Micks. "And the best lodgings in town! I sent the wife back to Ireland when the bombing became intolerable. We both hated that, but sure I wouldn't leave Hull, for Hull was good to me. The only good thing about her being in Ireland is that she keeps me supplied with certain delicacies, like Irish whisky! Ye'll have a taste yourself with me now?"

The groceries were unloaded. Homemade jam and butter, gifts from his wife, were placed on the bare table. A knife was placed beside the loaf and plates were put on the table. Dinner, said Dr. Micks, would begin as soon as we'd done justice to another glass. And a generous one it was.

"And now," said our host eventually, settling himself in a large chair, "I want to know all about you young people." Legs stretched luxuriously, pipe in one hand and glass in the other, he waited for us to speak. This we did, both of us at once, and it didn't seem to matter. It mattered less as the evening wore on.

The hours passed like lightning and not a word had been said about the purpose of our visit. I reminded our host. Surprised, he looked at us through the haze of tobacco smoke. "Ach! Are ye still worried about that! Sure, I made my mind up two hours ago. I'm not selling ye my practice. I want far too much money for it, and that's a fact."

Crestfallen, I looked at him. He laughed.

"Now I'm going to tell ye what to do. Rent those two houses. I know! I know! They frightened ye half to death. But don't be put off. They need young doctors up there! Ye'll be *needed* – and sure but that's a wonderful thing in this world!"

He looked at us and blew a cloud of smoke towards the ceiling.

"I'll not *let* you young people buy something ye don't need to. Just slap a bit of paint on here and there and you'll be just fine! Besides, I'll speak to the ARP people and get the place cleared up."

I looked at him aghast. Slap a bit of paint on! With the fireplace blown into the middle of the room and the ceilings falling in! He must be mad. The whole thing was crazy! And then I looked at Janet with her dancing eyes.

Micks went on, waving aside the tobacco smoke. "I'm serious. That place used to be a warm home; aye, and the best practice in the city, too. Pullen ran it, then. 'The Baron,' we used to call him, with his liveried chauffeur to take him on his rounds. It'll be the same again. And there's one more thing," he continued. "There's an old doctor lives opposite. He badly needs the kind of help you young people could give him. Hugh Webster – nearly eighty and still in practice. He's a poor man in terms of money, but this city owes him more than he'll ever get credit for. And now, I'm taking ye to your hotel."

There the hall porter greeted our companion with a warmth and respect that would have done credit to royalty itself. "Now James," said the doctor, "see that my young friends here get the best in the house," and he was off.

"He's quite a character," I said to James as he picked up my suitcase.

"Character, sir? Aye, 'e's a character that one! Everybody knows 'im on Hessle Road. Y'know, when t'bombing were bad, 'e'd put that coat an 'at of 'is over 'is pyjamas and just walk along t'road wi' 'is medical bag. Into a burnin' house once. 'E'd just deal wi' casualties, cool as a cucumber. We all knew 'im, ambulance men and firemen. Some'ow when we saw 'owd Micks wi' 'is pyjamas an' that owd 'at an coat of 'is we knew things'd be awright.''

We slept, undisturbed by ''the little people.'' The elves of Ireland had been banished by Dr. Micks' magic potions. We were at breakfast when a large man in tweeds, a leather coat and tweed hat joined us and poured himself a coffee.

''I've just come to see you don't change your minds,'' he said, ''for you'll be happy there and you'll be going where you're needed.''

I didn't see the leprechauns, but they must have been with him. An Irish spell had been cast upon us. We rented Nos. 535 and 537 after all, and they remained our office and home for years.

Chapter Eighteen

At last we had a home. True, it was filthy, battered and infested with mice. They ran over everything, including beds and tables. Undiscovered live wires declared themselves by spitting blue sparks when packing cases were pulled over them. Dust and debris lay everywhere. But it was a home and it was our own. Compared with many of our friends we were fortunate almost beyond belief. In the months ahead many obstacles would be overcome by our determination to establish a decent place in which to live and practise.

But the first of those obstacles was insuperable. Suddenly, apologetically but firmly, I was told that my demobilization was to be delayed. My service, which had been marked more by hard work than hardship, was not yet at an end. Administrative work required my remaining in uniform for a few more months.

We had contracted with the National Health Insurance Committee to begin work on a date coinciding with my release from the Service. Now that that had been postponed, Janet would have to open the practice alone. Furthermore, she had "given notice" and relinquished her comfortable hospital suite. She would have to move into this wreck of a building.

There was no question of restoring the place to its former state of gentility. Air-raid damage throughout the city was so extensive that only the essentials could be attended to. Peeling wallpaper was stripped off and we were left to paint the walls as best we could. But Dr. Micks, true to his word, moved into action.

He urged the air-raid repair people to treat the place as a priority. Rubble disappeared from the yard by the truckload. Heaps of sandbags disappeared from what, almost unbelievably, would become our living rooms. Drooping ceilings were repaired, fireplaces replaced and broken floor boards renewed.

When Janet arrived with Catriona from Lincoln, the place *was* habitable; that is to say, if you could ignore the mice, and the clouds of dust and debris that accompanied the hammering of the workmen. They started at the top of the house and worked their way downwards, so my wife elected to occupy the one liveable place, the attic bedroom, sharing it with our little one.

Late one night when I arrived at the door, the dim street lighting, the steady drizzle of rain and the darkened houses around, added to the foreboding loneliness of the place. There were few passersby. I rang the bell. The sound echoed through the empty house and a light appeared at the window high above me. Then past those stripped walls and down those flights of stairs, as bare and coldly miserable as anything I had seen in the slums of Glasgow, came Janet.

There was another obstacle. We would have to obtain a loan. Mr. Gray, our lawyer, adviser and friend for years to come, arranged for Janet to meet a lady willing to make a loan as an investment. Middle-aged, blunt and unsmiling, our lawyer told Janet that this interview would be merely a preliminary one. I would have to secure the loan at a later date.

Miss Blake had been "Head" of a girls' school. At twenty-nine and an experienced doctor, Janet was suddenly returned to her school-days. Her eyes twinkled as she described the interview: she had felt rather like a schoolgirl again, guilty of some misdemeanor, called before the headmistress. Outwardly composed and dignified, she assured me, inwardly she had bubbled with amusement at the inquisition.

But Miss Blake turned up trumps. She gave Janet the loan

on the spot, saying that her word was all the assurance she needed. As professional women they had recognized and respected one another. She didn't want any man to ratify or secure anything, and Mr. Gray, grumpily complaining of the waywardness of women and their unwillingness to be protected, had to bow before this formidable lady.

Several doctors, calling to leave their visiting cards, commented on Janet's spartan accommodation. Nor was it really acceptable, they hinted, that a woman should be a mother and a practising physician at the same time. These physicians were very conscious of their own and their profession's social position. But we were part of a *new* generation. We went our own way. Comfortable affluence and social acceptability bothered neither of us any more than it bothered many colleagues of our generation.

There were others who opened their homes to Janet, encouraged her, made her feel part of a medical community and helped her through a period that would have daunted many a strong individual.

Then one weekend I came home on leave to a house that had been transformed. True, there was only one comfortable room but floors were scrubbed and spotless. The kitchen was serviceable. A few rugs lay scattered about, little ornaments adorned the mantelpiece in the sitting room, and a carpet, worn but colourful, covered the floor. Best of all, the bare and filthy windows of a few weeks before were gleaming, bright, and tastefully curtained. Catriona played before a cheerful hearth.

I gazed around. "How on earth did you manage all this?" I asked in wonder.

"It wasn't easy," smiled Janet, "but I did have some help. I've engaged a housekeeper, and then I hired a cleaning lady to scrub the place. The curtains," she went on, "are pieces of factory jute, washed and dyed, then sewn into curtain lengths. My uncle sent us an old carpet. And one of the soldiers you knew in the army, Gunner Miller, has found all kinds of stuff for me. The furniture, none of it's new." She had worked wonders. But still there was the matter of mice.

"Oh! The mice!" Smilingly she pointed to a broad-faced, lop-eared ginger tomcat that had entered the room with much dignity. "He's taken care of that problem, he and his lady friend between them. She's even smarter than he is."

I was rapidly coming to the conclusion, as I looked at old Ginger, that if that was so, there was a certain similarity between his domestic situation and my own. Wandering from one bare but spotless room to the next, carrying Catriona, with Janet beside me, I could only marvel at her ingenuity and accomplishment. But then, she had always had the knack of making her hospital quarters, however drab to begin with, little havens of domesticity and I should not have been surprised.

"The practice?" I asked. "How are you managing that?"

"Well," she replied. "It's not very big. I don't even need a secretary. I handle it all myself. The waiting room is quite presentable, and so is one of the consulting rooms. I have this big desk, and the doors are open during the prescribed consulting hours. It's strange," she went on, "how people can associate a house with medical care. You know, it seems there's always been a doctor here. One old gentleman was surprised to see a woman doctor – but do you know what he said? 'This house has always been my doctor and I've always been well treated here, so I'll stay'."

Frank Micks had been right; we were to be given a chance. New patients gave us a trial, and old ones drifted back.

It had all been a revelation to me. True, the windows didn't all fit properly. Some opened too easily and some didn't open at all. The cold east wind found its way into the house, but as we sat and sipped a precious glass of sherry that night, Janet told me that Mr. Taylor was coming to meet me in the morning.

"He's such a nice man," she said. "Older than us a bit, but it was all very amusing how it happened. There I was, sitting in my white coat, looking very professional, when I heard the surgery door open. So I went out to greet our first patient. I ushered him into the consulting room and took his name and address, and that seemed about as far as I could get. But he was quite charming and we talked about the weather and Hull and all kinds of things, until finally I thought it was time I got down to business. So I asked him what was the matter with him."

She sipped at her sherry and chuckled as she recalled the interview. "Well," she went on, "he seemed quite taken aback, and politely said he'd rather discuss *that* with the doctor." "But," I said, "I *am* the doctor." She paused. "His face was a perfect study. Then he looked at me and laughed. 'Oh, my God!' he cried, 'I thought *you* were the secretary!'"

Janet laughed. "We've become great friends. He says he's not having any other doctor except yourself and he's coming in the morning to meet you."

Mr. Taylor came as he had promised. He was older than

us all right, about ten years. Tall, dark and handsome, he simply beamed at Janet as she introduced me. He smiled at me, shook hands, and said, "I think we'll get on very well together. I said to myself when I first walked into this office, 'with his taste in secretaries, I'm bound to like this doctor!' "

Chapter Nineteen

We had been married for five years but had never had a home or much time together. We had to find one another again. Above all, we had an infant, the very centre of our existence, who needed security. She was puzzled by this strange interloper called "daddy" who visited for the occasional day or two, competed for *her* mummy's attention, then vanished again. Now that I was out of the army I had to win Catriona's confidence and love.

Rapidly, with the return of people to the city, the practice grew. We had to organize, arrange our respective responsibilities. Janet continued to see patients each day, but she also decided that her responsibilities as a wife and homemaker were paramount. I held consulting sessions each day and did the house calls.

The whole tradition of medicine is one of hard, unremitting work, and I fell into the trap. Yet, despite all the evidence that such a way of life can lead to ill-health and marriage breakdown, doctors continue, on the whole, to overwork.

Children, confronted by a tired physician for a parent, can be deprived of affection, and that has long-term effects, none of them good.

Janet saw the danger. She urged upon me the idea of taking a weekly "half day" when the three of us could explore the countryside or travel to the beaches only thirty miles away. Occasionally, she said, we should go out to dinner together, or to the repertory theatre. Sometimes we must get away from our work and learn all over again how to talk to one another.

It was, and is, excellent advice. But then, coming home meant coming back to emergency calls. There was no emergency room at the hospital for general use. We G.P.'s were responsible for our patients. It was my custom to ask the cinema or theatre managers to notify me of any emergency calls. One chap was most obliging. My name, scrawled across the hero's face just as he was about to get the girl, didn't improve the audience's sense of high drama. We slunk out of the cinema, and I determined to "do something about it."

Next morning I phoned my nearest medical neighbour, only a few hundred yards away on the busy street. Norman Rymer, middle-aged and bespectacled, greeted me affably when I called on him but my suggestion that we "stand in" for one another once a week was not welcomed. "Oh! I've worked on my own for thirty years and now isn't the time to change. Perhaps I'm too set in my ways," he said apologetically but firmly.

That was that. I walked home rebuffed and discouraged. As I opened the front door Janet placed the telephone receiver on its side and came towards me. "It's a lady," she said. "I don't know who she is, but she demands to speak to you. She has," she added in a whisper, "a *very* commanding voice." Puzzled, I picked up the receiver.

"It's *Mrs*. Rymer here," said the voice. "Just come right back and talk to my husband – he's prepared to listen."

So, the "Syndicate" was born. In Great Britain, partnerships and group practices were outnumbered by doctors practising on their own. The North American-style clinic, where doctors in various branches of medicine work together, was virtually unknown. And "solo practice" was a hard struggle – a struggle to remain competent, with little or no time off, and few holidays. Surely there was a better way to practise and live.

Norman and I had no formal agreement. We covered each other's practice for one half-day per week and on alternate Sundays. Within five months Douglas Ferens had joined us, followed by "Ozzie" Prosser, Adam Boyne and Geoff Snowden. We stopped at that, never going beyond the original practices, though as associates joined our practices they became members. Between us we could handle emergency calls in our sector of the city. Too many participants would have made the scheme unwieldly.

We organized: one night's emergency duty and one Sunday on duty in five. A full day's work on Saturday was the rule.

Most of us held Saturday night "surgeries" and we still, all of us, worked on Sunday mornings, which was typical of the lives of general practitioners in industrial areas of Britain.

Still, what an advance our scheme was! We had three weeks' holiday per year, but we went further. If a doctor was sick, the others would handle his practice for a month, then review the situation. Janet, in those far-off days of male chauvinism, was excused by my colleagues from all emergency work, but she was an honorary and popular member of the male enclave. One important stipulation was that each man would be responsible for his own maternity patients; such was their sense of personal commitment.

We held monthly meetings at the Medical Society's club house, and there we arranged the next month's duty roster. But the highlights of the evening followed. Informally lounging in the armchairs before the fire, we held our clinical sessions. Case histories were presented and discussed. These occasions were instructive, thought-provoking, and many of the cases unusual or puzzling.

But at 10:00 P.M. promptly the meeting was closed and the bar opened. The Medical Society, perpetually short of cash, with due formality and tongues firmly in cheek, passed an annual vote of thanks to the Syndicate for its generous financial support. What it had in mind was the healthy state of the bar fund.

We became friends as well as close colleagues – men who had previously hardly known one another. Our houses became quiet havens where we'd share a pre-dinner cocktail or a Sunday morning sherry. There was many an informal consultation over a difficult or puzzling case. We learned from one another and were the envy of many less fortunate practitioners.

Above all, we trusted one another to look after our patients, and the patients accepted and appreciated the service we offered. No emergency or night call went unanswered. For nine years, or more for all I know, not a penny changed hands. And that's not a bad effort for a mixed bag of Scots and Yorkshiremen!

As a young doctor I was fortunate to have such colleagues. They were strong men, individualists to the core. They were different, too; humorous, witty, reflective or sardonic, they varied from the short and burly to the tall and handsome. But in one thing they were united – a dedication to their profession and patients.

The National Health Service was almost upon us. With it

would come many changes in our way of life as general practitioners. We did not foresee those changes when we formed the Syndicate. But demands for our services would increase. There would, in many cases, be insidious deterioration in that tenuous, nebulous but important relationship of goodwill that existed between doctor and patient. Sheer pressure would force many of us to substitute hurried work for efficient personal care.

The Syndicate was our bulwark against the wearing effects of stress and overwork. And as one of the group said, "It'll postpone my coronary for a few years!"

Chapter Twenty

The average general practitioner prescribes twenty to thirty different drugs. With over 36,000 chemical compounds to choose from, it seems a small number to rely on, and might imply a less than adequate knowledge of pharmacology.

I'm not so sure. If the G.P. knows his drugs as well as he should know his or her patients, then perhaps the latter are fortunate in their choice of a doctor. Few drugs are safe. Penicillin kills people every year because of chemical sensitivity. It can also, by over use or abuse, damage a person's natural immunity to disease. Even the lowly pain killers, bought over a druggist's counter, can cause severe reaction, and I have seen people become blue in the face, gasping for air from sensitivity to them.

Physicians should not prescribe drugs casually, any more than surgeons should operate casually, even on "minor" conditions. The G.P. should know when not to use a drug, and should be quick to recognize its side effects, just as the effects of a drug on a patient's body chemistry should be known to the prescriber. When a doctor takes a few minutes to describe to his patients any complications that may arise, however beneficial the drug may be, it forewarns the patient and shortens or thwarts the side effects. A new drug should be used only after a careful study of authoritative literature. And even then things can go wrong.

Of course, conservatism can go too far. Dr. Hugh Webster, who lived in Hull across the street from Janet and me, was a socialist, a member of the *Fabian Society*, which included Webster's old adversary, Bertrand Russell and other intellectuals such as George Bernard Shaw and the elite Bloomsbury Group. Although his practice had shrunk over the years, he still saw a few people every day. His "consulting rooms" occupied most of the lower floor of the house.

I hadn't had time to call on him as Frank Micks had suggested, and our meeting, when it came, wasn't altogether propitious. When I answered the telephone one afternoon it was Miss Webster, Hugh's daughter, a lady in her fifties, who wanted to speak to me. Hugh's wife had been dead for many years, and to Miss Webster had fallen the lot of "taking care of father" – not the easiest task in this world.

"Father's ill, doctor, and has asked to see you. I think," she added diffidently, "he might have pneumonia."

It was 1946 and we were still seeing mostly the classical type of lobar pneumonia; the early cough, chest pain, pleurisy, rising fever and respiratory distress. All this was accompanied by equally standard physical signs of consolidation of one or more lobes of the lung. The infection would proceed to "the crisis" in about a week, then cure itself – or kill the patient.

Pneumonia was a common and very serious complication of often minor respiratory infections. It used to be caused by a relatively small variety of known bacteria, but today it is the result of infection by a host of infective organisms including the viruses. Even its symptoms and signs have changed.

As I walked across the road to Dr. Webster's place, I wasn't thinking about the history of medicine. I was recalling that my colleague was nearly eighty, that pneumonia was still called "the old man's friend." Miss Webster, a competent businesslike woman, met me at the door and took me upstairs to her father's bedroom.

It was a sparsely furnished home and as I walked through the narrow hall I noticed on the coat hangers a well-worn greatcoat and two hats – a bowler, green with age, and an ancient straw boater. Summer began on June 1 for Dr. Webster. The straw boater was donned for house calls, and discarded in October, to be replaced by the bowler. Beside them, propped against the wall, was the doctor's bicycle. Old, heavy and so high that it must have been difficult to mount, it was his conveyance when he went on house calls.

His bedroom was as spartan as the rest of the place. Bare, polished floor boards were graced by a threadbare bedside mat. An old sea chest standing at the window comprised his wardrobe, and a simple cupboard, mirrorless, completed the furniture. The patient lay in a metal hospital bed. There was no fire in the grate to warm the room physically or spiritually.

"Here's the doctor to see you, father," announced Miss Webster.

"M'm," was the grunted response as the patient's eyes met mine.

He was a striking looking old man, and at one time he had been a handsome one. There wasn't an ounce of superfluous flesh on him. With his mane of light gray hair, piercing blue eyes and aquiline nose he looked like an ancient Viking – with temper to match.

"Well," he said, "I've got pneumonia. Aren't you going to examine me?"

"Yes, doctor."

His face was flushed, pulse racing and his temperature dangerously high. He had pneumonia all right, the classical kind, and I told him so.

"Well, what d'you propose to do about it?"

"I'd suggest giving you penicillin by injection every four hours...." I began.

He exploded, "Penicillin! Penicillin! I'll have none of your new-fangled damned nonsense in this house. Girl, fetch me my paregoric!"

"No, father."

"What d'you mean, 'no, father'! Do as you're bid, woman."

"No, father, I won't. The doctor will tell you what to do."

I came to the rescue with my best, my most soothing bedside manner. I suggested a compromise: that the paregoric be incorporated into the treatment with penicillin. Bedside manners aren't well accepted by a certain type of Yorkshireman – Hugh Webster's kind.

"Don't give me that malarkey. I know when I'm being worked on. What does this damned stuff do to you anyway?"

"It'll cure *you*!"

"I won't have it and that's final. And don't push me into any hospital, either. That's an order. Just fetch me my paregoric, young man."

"Doctor..." I pleaded.

"Don't 'doctor' me. Show him the dispensary, girl."

So I made him up his paregoric. It's a camphorated tincture of opium, soothing, but like all of them, not harmless. In Hugh's case it would sedate his cough, and prevent him from coughing up sputum, and coughing up sputum is what used to save lives. In fact, his paregoric could speed him on his way to his Viking "Valhalla."

So I left. At the front door I said, "There's nothing we can do, Miss Webster. If he refuses treatment he refuses it. This paregoric stuff is useless."

"I know doctor, but you don't know father. He's as stubborn as a mule."

I walked across the road, and had a sherry. Maybe, I thought, Frank Micks could deal with him, and after supper I was on the verge of phoning him when the telephone rang. It was Miss Webster. Could I come over again. Dr. Webster was delirious. Over I went.

"Now," said Miss Webster, "he's quite out of his mind, and I am in charge of my father. I give you full permission to proceed with penicillin treatment if you think it will save him. He's in no fit state to argue with anyone."

For the next three days Hugh Webster raved. He said something about some barquentine sailing out of Whitby. Maybe he'd sailed on her. He came from that part of Yorkshire. His daughter, the same breed as himself, wouldn't have a nurse. She and a friend took turns in nursing him, and every four hours, night and day, I injected 40,000 units of penicillin. On the morning of the fourth day, a smiling yet apprehensive Miss Webster met me at the door.

"He's better," she whispered, "even ate some breakfast. But he's not in the best of humour."

I nodded, and climbed the stairs. Dr. Webster was very much alive – weak, but alive, and as "ornery" as ever.

"I told you not to use that damned stuff," he whispered. (If he could have roared he would.) "I forbade it, damn you."

"Father," said his daughter in tones of outrage. "Instead of swearing at the doctor you should have been thanking him for saving your life. Now you just thank him!" Hugh glared at her then at me.

"Thank you," he said. Then to his daughter – "And now I don't have to say it again, do I?" He turned over on his side, and pulled the blankets over his head.

"You're not finished," I warned him, "not for another

couple of days at least." There was a muffled grunt from under the bedclothes. I pulled them back, and a poor, withered, dehydrated old backside came into view. In went the needle. "Ouch," he rasped. "Does it have to sting like that?"

"It's a salt solution," I said cheerily. "One every four hours for the next three days."

So Hugh recovered. I met Miss Webster one morning and she said her father was holding his first surgery that afternoon. At three o'clock my office phone rang.

"Webster here," said the voice.

"Oh hullo, doctor," I began. "I hope you're feeling better..."

"I don't want to waste time," he replied. "I have a man here with a septic toe. Now in my opinion, penicillin would be the treatment of choice, and how would you prescribe penicillin for a septic toe?"

So I told him. Half an hour went by. The phone rang.

"Now," said Dr. Webster, "I've got a patient here with lymphangitis and in my opinion penicillin would be..."

"Doctor," I interrupted, "how would you like me to come over this evening and we could talk about penicillin?"

While a new chapter was opening in our own lives, Hugh Webster was discovering an unopened page in the old book of his life. For years he had practised medicine alone. He shunned medical meetings. He was, he believed, too old. Most of his friends had gone. His wife was long dead. The political comrades of his hot-headed youth had gone. Some had accepted honours or achieved wealth. The world had not embraced the Brotherhood of Man, even though his belief in that remained, if bitterly. As a doctor he had been content for years to apply old cures and ways.

Suddenly he became a student again. He read of new developments and applied them in his little practice. He argued their pros and cons with the same conviction and vehemence he applied to politics.

At nearly eighty, Dr. Webster had entered the era of modern medicine.

Chapter
Twenty-One

At one time most British babies were born at home. Doctors who delivered them were privileged individuals. For a little time they were almost a part of the family, and in the years to come, often a relationship developed that would grow in terms of mutual trust and respect.

A baby's arrival was almost always a momentous event for the family. Everyone was involved. Sometimes, of course, the other children in the family were parcelled out to relatives and friends during the labour, but sometimes they stayed at home, keeping out of sight, as quiet as mice, wondering if nurse was bringing a baby brother – or would it be a sister?

Father was usually stationed in the kitchen where his duties consisted of boiling kettle after kettle of water, some of which was used for medical purposes, some for the very necessary cups of tea. On the other hand, often he sat with his wife for periods, comforting her, until it was time to be banished to another room. To absent oneself from the delivery of baby and afterbirth was considered the discreet thing to do, though occasionally the midwife (who usually orchestrated these occasions), would allow him to attend the delivery, even assist in some minor way.

We were fortunate to have in general practice a number of physicians with their specialty qualifications in obstetrics and gynaecology, among them Dr. Frank Micks. In 1948, with the inception of the National Health Service, these doctors would be forced to choose between becoming full-time consultants or remaining in general practice. Those who chose the latter course, found themselves barred from hospital work. It was to prove a hard decision for many physicians who had given their communities good service both as G.P.s and as specialists.

But home deliveries were not always straightforward, joyful occasions. Emergencies sometimes occurred without warning or apparent reason, and when they did, it was often with frightening speed. Catastrophes were not unknown.

Sudden, unexplained bleeding before, during, or after delivery was only one type of accident. The unborn child's heart could suddenly, for a variety of unsuspected reasons, cease to beat. After delivery, a baby might not breathe properly – or at all. Despite careful pre-natal examinations, babies did arrive in unexpected ways, pushing a little fist or a foot into the world instead of the expected head. Or what had been thought to be a presenting head turned out to be a little bottom – sometimes a difficult, dangerous matter to deal with. Then there was the possibility of post-partum haemorrhage, maternal bleeding after delivery. This is a rare, but dreaded complication of childbirth. Careful history-taking and pre-natal examination is tremendously important as a preventative measure, but death from massive haemorrhage can still occur within minutes.

When such complications occurred – and they always seemed to happen in homes far from the nearest telephone and an SOS to the flying squad – then simple skills were no longer enough. Both doctor and midwife would face heart-racing stress as they tried to prevent catastrophe.

However, all my experience in this field was still to come, as one afternoon, sitting at my desk making a few notes, I wondered if I'd ever be competent. Obstetrics interested me. True, I had taken advantage of the invitations given me by Frank Micks and his crony, Dr. Gavin Brown. I had made it my business to attend rounds at the Women's Hospital where Janet was now a sessional anaesthetist. I had read, listened and watched for months. I had done a few deliveries, but my technical skills were still minimal.

The waiting room was empty. Suddenly, there was a gentle tapping on my door, followed by, "Are you in, now?" in a pleasant Irish accent. It was our friend and benefactor, Dr. Micks. His tweed hat was deposited on my desk, the leather coat thrown over the examination couch. Frank made himself comfortable. He was an infrequent but welcome visitor. This, however, was not to be one of his usual little special occasions, and he came straight to the point.

"I've sold my practice. I'll be leaving for Ireland within the month, just as soon as all my business is dealt with."

He smiled as I stared at him in dismay.

"Frank, I had no idea you were this close to leaving."

"Sure, if ye'll remember, I was trying to sell the practice when I first met you. I don't see why you're surprised!"

He was right, and yet as the months had gone by and Frank continued to practise it seemed as if he might go on forever. He knocked the still smouldering contents of his pipe into the ashtray on the desk, laid down the pipe, fished in the pocket of his tweed jacket and produced a large notebook which he laid beside the ashtray.

"There are some trout streams south of Dublin that have needed my attention for a long time," he grinned. "Now, the man who's bought the practice won't be doing obstetrics. This notebook contains the names of all my domiciliary deliveries for the next six months, and I want you to do them." I stared at him, aghast. "Frank, I can't do that! You're a specialist. That's what these women have booked — a specialist, not a nincompoop like me."

"I wouldn't be giving my list to a nincompoop. You'll learn, gain experience as you go. You've learned quite a bit already. Besides, these are all normal cases. A lot of them I've delivered before. I've given the doubtful ones to Gavin to look after, and," he added with a grin, "he says he'll look after you as well."

I sat and stared at the notebook. It held me in a kind of apprehensive horror.

"Frank, I can't do it. I did no maternity for six years — and the ones I did before that would turn your hair white if I told you about them. No! I can't do it. These people will expect a specialist, not the likes of me."

"No, they won't. I've told them you'll take care of them. And if you don't," he added, "sure but I'll come back and haunt you!"

The notebook was slowly being pushed across the desk. I watched its progress towards me with about the same fascination as if it had been a cobra.

"Frank, I can't. It's terribly kind of you, but I'm not competent to take your list."

"Get on with you. Besides, I'm depending on you!"

I determined that he must see my point. "I'm not competent to deal with emergencies. I haven't a clue."

"We're not talking about emergencies. We're talking about normal cases!"

"But if there was a simple emergency, just the possibility of a forceps delivery for instance, do you know what I'd do?"

"No, what?"

"Nothing. Sit on my backside and think — and wait for something to happen!"

Dr. Micks had risen to his feet. He reached for his coat and hat.

"By God," he said, "I'm not too sure but that statement doesn't make you one of the safest men in town."

And he was gone – leaving me holding, not just the baby, but fifty of them!

Chapter
Twenty-two

It wasn't long before Dr. Webster abandoned his bicycle. He acquired a chauffeur. Me. For I had acquired my dream car – a fast low-slung roadster. In Wass, over six years before, I had begun my career on a bicycle. I reverted to that when I was demobilized. It didn't do me any harm to trundle along to house calls. New cars were almost unobtainable, even for "priority" people like doctors, and I decided to wait for a car in which I would take pride. Second-hand cars were usually in poor shape.

Dr. Webster's few routine house calls, usually to old patients, were easily handled. He'd "save" them until I could take him. I'd drive him to his destination, drop him off, and travel on to one of my own visits. On my way back, I'd pick him up, patiently waiting for me in the shelter of a doorway, or I'd finish my visit to find him sitting in my car, usually rolling a cigarette. Smoking homemade "fags" was his only extravagance.

He was as much my student as I was his. I talked about modern treatment in medicine. He talked about Yorkshire, especially the Yorkshire of his young days when, appalled at the living conditions of working people, he had become a socialist. He had known Bertrand Russell, had campaigned and worked with him, didn't like him, and dismissed him as "an arrogant and immoral aristocrat." Hugh was an agnostic, moralist and humanist.

In his fight for socialism he had spoken at street corner meetings, opposed the policies of his own profession, and had, in turn, been rejected by many of his colleagues. But the voters of Hull had made him an alderman of the city in his young days, and in old age he had been honoured by the Socialist International.

He must have been one of the last of a kind, for as a youth, he told me, he had been apprenticed to a "penny doctor" who for that small sum from each individual per week had dispensed medical care. Later he had studied for five years at Edinburgh University qualifying in 1892 as a Licentiate of the Royal Colleges of Physicians and Surgeons of Edinburgh and of the Faculty of Physicians and Surgeons of Glasgow. Thereafter he devoted most of his life as a doctor and a man to improving living conditions for working people in his city.

The important thing, he told me, was that even as an apprentice he must on all occasions wear a black top coat and top hat. The shirt underneath might be patched, the cuffs frayed, but the uniform was essential. It was part of the mystique of its time. Top hat and coat may not have been too far removed from the witch doctor's switch and face mask, and in those far-off days, when drugs were few and relatively useless, they may even have had therapeutic value!

He'd sometimes sardonically say that he was bewildered by his friendship with a Tory like me. But then, since Janet's views coincided with his own, perhaps our relationship was bearable. Janet's uncle, Geordie Buchanan, at one time the youngest member of parliament in Britain, and with the largest majority recorded, was our frequent visitor. Over the years the flamboyancy of his rebellious youth had departed and Geordie had achieved a certain respectability. So had James Maxton, his friend and colleague in the Independent Labour Party, that tiny group of Scots known as the "Clydeside Rebels." Sometimes they were called the "Clydeside Reds!"

The only thing that was red about Geordie was his mop of hair, tumbling over his forehead and emphasizing the mischievous twinkle that seemed always to be present in his eyes. George Buchanan, the Right Honourable Member of Parliament for the Gorbals of Glasgow, one of the toughest and poorest areas of Britain, would have understood my friend Hugh Webster. But I question if the two would have liked one another.

Geordie, as he was affectionately (or otherwise) known to thousands of Glaswegians, was a big man, bulky, untidily dressed. He had a constant smear of cigarette ash on his waistcoat, a mouth that laughed as easily as his eyes twinkled, and a tolerance for all the weaknesses of mankind. Hugh, on the other hand, was lean, austere and fiercely political in an unforgiving kind of way. The one thing they had in common was a love of cigarettes. I hardly ever saw either of them without one dangling from their lips.

They never met. Perhaps I felt it best they shouldn't, for where the coming of the golden age of socialism was concerned, Hugh was not a humorist. Geordie, equally dedicated in his beliefs, had a wonderful sense of fun, while Hugh's sallies of wit were sardonic rather than mischievous.

Within a year of the war's end it was obvious that the government was going to institute a compulsory National Health Service. It is often implied that this measure was forced upon a reluctant and reactionary medical profession. It is not generally known that almost half of the thousands of British doctors canvassed voted in favour of such a scheme. Janet and I openly supported the idea. Not only would good medical care be given to all, but *properly organized* it would mean, for those of us in general practice, raised standards of work, a breakaway from outdated methods.

A public meeting was held in Hull. The guest of honour was Aneurin Bevan, Minister of Health, and the man who brought the National Health Service to fruition. As a woman of conviction and her uncle's niece, Janet sat with the platform party and spoke in favour of this great social measure. She was the young idealist. Beside her sat the old Fabian socialist, Hugh Webster. I did not attend. I didn't like Mr. Bevan's attitude, and although I have always believed in some kind of health insurance, I didn't believe in having it stuffed down my throat. Mr. Bevan's attitude to doctors was not conciliatory.

When I returned from a late call I found my two revolutionaries having tea together. The meeting was over. Afterwards they heard Mr. Bevan tell officials of the Labour Party that in the coming Health Service, local administrative committees must be "packed with our people." Janet was dismayed and Hugh was seething.

"I know men of goodwill in this city," he growled, "on the other side of the political fence from me, who've given a lifetime of unpaid work to improving health care for working people. And now, their reward? To be dismissed!"

Still, we felt, mistakes were inevitable. With time they would be corrected. We saw a great future ahead for general practice.

Geordie Buchanan became a cabinet minister in the Labour government, and a privy councillor. He was a politician, but above all he was a parliamentarian. As a young man he had been a vehement, fiery speaker and an acknowledged champion of the rights of working people. He was still that, and his belief in the need for a National Health Service was unshakable, but he listened with tolerance and understanding to our criticisms of the political manoeuverings of his government and the medical politicians. Tolerance and understanding, however, are poor companions in a power play, and no one knew that better than "Nye" Bevan.

Once I suddenly said, "Geordie, who is our greatest living parliamentarian?"

His reply dumbfounded me in its immediacy. "Anthony Eden."

"Geordie, that's an astounding tribute from a life-long Labour man."

"Not at all. Eden, you see, is utterly incorruptible. 'He never did aught,' " he quoted, " 'but he did it for England.' "

We walked along in silence.

"You're friendly with Churchill," I said. "Tell me about him."

"I was waiting for that," he replied with that puckish grin of his. "Everybody wants to know about Churchill. Well, I'll tell you. He's a great man all right, and this country, aye, the world, owes much to him."

"How did you get to know him? Churchill never struck me as the sort with the common touch – or much time for Labour men."

"We were never close, but we knew one another all right. We played cards together every day for months on end. I'd been thrown out by my crowd, and Winston had been thrown out by his lot. Nobody'd speak to him, and none of my crowd'd speak to me. It was long before the war. So we played cards in the members' room. Everybody, from both sides, was angry at us. For verra different reasons, you understand," he finished, nodding significantly.

He laughed. "It was na' funny at the time. But, aye, I could say I know Winston Churchill."

He walked on, and suddenly he stopped.

"The greatest living Englishman, that's Churchill all right. But Winston's trouble is that he missed his century. Man," he concluded with reminiscent glee, "but he'd have made the ideal captain of a pirate ship."

In addition to their agreement about things political Geordie and Janet shared other traits, including a willingness to try the unorthodox and a blissful disregard for what others might think of their actions. It was results that counted.

I had to be out of town one night. All contingencies had been covered. Janet had arranged for her friend, Mrs. Allen, to stay overnight with her, and one of my colleagues was on call. Outside the rain was pouring. Janet and her friend were listening to a late radio programme when there was a thunderous knocking at the front door.

It was Mr. Elder, one of our patients. His bicycle propped against the door, he stood in the downpour, agitated. His mother, a lady in her late seventies, had suddenly gone berserk. Would the doctor please come at once?

Our colleague on emergency call lived a few miles away, and Janet decided that she would answer this call herself. I had taken the car, and no taxi was available. Mr. Elder's agitation increased.

"Things are desperate up there, doctor. Mother is shouting and carrying on. Half the neighbourhood's out on the street listening to her. They think she's being murdered."

The Elders lived in Albert Avenue, perhaps a mile away. Janet looked at the bicycle.

"Could you give me a lift on the crossbar?"

Mr. Elder was sure he could, and Janet went to the surgery to get her medical case. Unfortunately, she found that I had taken not only the keys to the car, but the keys to the surgery as well. Not to be thwarted, Janet said to our patient, "There's a little window at the back of the surgery. You might be able to open it with a jimmy and squeeze through. If you could do that, you could unlock the door from inside and let me in."

Mr. Elder was happy to cooperate. The window was levered open, Mr. Elder vanished inside, and very shortly, Janet was in the office. Snatching up her medical case and securing it in front of her, she perched herself on the crossbar of Mr. Elder's bicycle and they wobbled their way up Albert Avenue.

The scene was exactly as had been described by our patient. Janet had dealt with this kind of emergency many a time as a doctor in a mental hospital. Having got rid of most of the spectators, she gave the old lady a strong sedative injection, then sat by her patient for ten or fifteen minutes, by which time the injection had worked like magic, and the old lady fell fast asleep.

A very grateful son took Janet home the same way as they had come. At the end of the wobbly trip he shook her hand.

"Doctor," he said, "I've done two things tonight I never dreamed I'd ever do in my life. I've broken into the doctor's office, and I've carried her to an emergency on the crossbar of my bike!"

Chapter Twenty-three

"From Hull, Hell and Halifax, Good Lord deliver us." That was part of the beggar's prayer of nearly five hundred years ago. It was not an unreasonable plea. Hell can speak for itself. In Halifax, the stealing of a piece of cloth meant instant execution by beheading. Hull's reputation for hospitality to gentlemen of the road was equally unwelcoming.

Even by Yorkshire standards, Hullensians throughout the centuries have been regarded as a tough lot. Of course, many Hullensians have told me, they hardly consider themselves to be Yorkshiremen at all. After all, they'll point out, Hull, or the city of Kingston-upon-Hull, to give it its proper title, was until recent years not only a city but a county unto itself.

As early as the twelfth century it exported wool, and today, almost eight centuries later, more wool leaves Hull for overseas than from any other English port. By the middle of the fourteenth century it was a walled and fortified town. A hundred years before that, the king had given it the right to hold markets. The open-air market continues now much as it did in medieval times, with itinerant merchants selling their wares from the shelter of their open-air stalls.

Towering above the market place are the great gray walls of Holy Trinity Church, the largest parish church in England. Sir William de la Pole lies buried within its fourteenth century walls. William de la Pole was a commoner who became a merchant prince, so wealthy that he could finance the king's schemes abroad. He was one of the founders of the city, and the city has not forgotten him, for his statue still faces the Humber that brought him wealth and fame. Not far away stands another statue, that of King William the Third. This one seems a little out of place. They have dressed King William as a Roman emperor and he sits astride a gilded horse. He has mastered an art that many a politician would envy. He is riding the horse without any visible stirrups. Just as they have for centuries, people still throng around the market looking for bargains, antiques, rare first editions, clothes, shoes, and all the miscellany of material that makes the English open-air market places so colourful.

A short walk away, through narrow lanes, lie the wharves of the river Hull. It supports mostly river traffic now – Hull barges, loading their cargoes just as they did centuries ago, for the slow journey up to the centre of England.

In this part of the old town even the names conjure up thoughts of vanished times: Whitefriargate, Blackfriargate and that lane so beautifully called "The Land of Green Ginger." These are thriving business places today, but a few blocks away the Humber flows as relentlessly, and as dangerously, as it had done throughout the ages.

Under blue skies the estuary, with its tang of salt air, looks deceptively gentle. It is only in fog and rain that the silt is obvious and the waters show their swift, silent menace. Then the ferry from New Holland and the south shore over two miles away, looms through the mist, curving wide against the current, churning its way towards Victoria Pier, its wake more brown and gray than white.

There are miles of docks. One of them still abuts the city pavement and it was a common sight to see the bows of moored trawlers high above passers-by. Just across the way, in the centre of a busy modern traffic circle, stands a statue of the lady who epitomizes Hull's past glories, Queen Victoria.

The statue must have been placed there in more leisured times. To reach it now can sometimes mean risking life and limb. Still, it is a risk worth taking, indeed sometimes essential. There she sits, impassively erect, looking straight ahead. This is just as well, for if the statue recalls the great days of imperial glory, its function demonstrates the practical attitude of largely non-conformist Hull. Underneath it are several of the city's public lavatories.

Non-conformist tradition is strong, even today. They closed the city gates against King Charles I and his army, and the Royalists turned away. They still show that toughness. During the Second World War, Hull suffered more physical damage than did Coventry.

It has a long history of culture and libertarianism. Andrew Marvell, the Restoration poet, politician and satirist, was born here. William Wilberforce, member of parliament for Hull, fought his dogged and often lonely struggle against slavery from this city. Today, it has its university, college of art, nautical and technical colleges, and perhaps it is slowly becoming a regional capital. When the Humber bridge, an enormous single span structure, the greatest of its type in the world, is completed, the city's comparative isolation will end. The south of England will be within easy reach.

The city lies on flat ground. The surrounding country can be beautiful, but Hull itself is not a beautiful city. But then, it is not an ordinary one, either. The sea is too close for that. Spurn Point, twenty miles down river, boasts one of the few full-time lifeboat crews in England, and these men earn their keep. Hull accepts its past more than it reveres it. In some respects it seems to conceal its past, almost deliberately; for only the old city remains to remind us of times gone by.

One evening, as I stood by a dockside, a sea-going tug casually edged its way from the quay. The last mooring rope was nonchalantly dropped into the dark, oil-scummed water, as the powerful engines whispered into life. A man on the quayside shouted to a crewman.

"Where are yer off to, Bert?"

"Valparaiso, Bill, see yer in three months."

Hull is one of Britain's gateways to the oceans of the world, and the past is the past.

I was on my way to Ferriby, a pleasantly wooded village a few miles out of the city. Dr. Webster dearly loved a run in my car and I took him with me I commented on the attractiveness of his city.

"Take the streets," I said, "wide, airy. Now somebody had some foresight when they built them like that."

"Aye," said Hugh, clamping his straw boater firmly on his head, then rolling a cigarette.

"Take Boothferry Road, for instance," I went on, "the road we're on now; a divided highway, years ahead of its time."

"Aye," he said. "We'll soon be at the city limits, then step on the accelerator and see what she'll do."

"Look," I said to my friend, who didn't seem to be listening to me, "I'm talking about the foresight somebody showed in developing these roads."

"Yes, we're nearly there. Do you think she'll do a hundred?"

"Hugh!" But Hugh was busy lighting his cigarette.

"I *was* listening," he said, when the smoke announced his success. "Y'see, you'll have to give *me* some of the credit for all this. Many years ago, I was an alderman of this city. I told them to make these roads wide, to leave that lane up the centre there. 'For mark my words' I said to them, 'We'll live to see the day when horse-drawn tram cars go all the way out to Ferriby.' And that," he said, sardonically, "is what the gift of foresight can do for you."

His cigarette had gone out. He was rummaging in his pocket for matches, and finally found one. "And now," said my ancient road-hog, puffing contentedly, "put your foot down!"

Chapter Twenty-four

I received my medical education at the end of an era. Queen Victoria was a memory to older people but her influence, like that of John Knox, remained. When I was a student there was no formal discussion of the problems related to sexual behaviour.

These problems can lead to unhappiness, broken homes, and other tragedies. When I first attempted to help people in their difficulties I wryly reminded myself of the author who likened his literary critics to legless men teaching someone to ride a bicycle. I was a product of my upbringing.

Sexual impotence in the male is a problem that requires much understanding, and while the majority of cases are psychological in origin, various diseases can cause it. Some patients can be cured by the understanding advice of their family doctors, while others require the help of skilled and interested psychiatrists. Some, it seems, are beyond help.

There is often a deep-rooted mental cause for the complaint. As an example, in one case in which I was interested, a nagging, contemptuous wife reduced her husband to total impotence by deriding his sexual ability. His later friendship with a divorcee cured him. She gave him understanding, flattered him, and in six months achieved more than any pyschiatrist could hope to.

Mr. Bert Brackley displayed his medical card, sat in the chair beside my desk, and came straight to the point. "Doc, I'm impotent, can't get on the prod at all. Can you help me?"

I'd been in Hull for two years. This was Mr. Brackley's first appearance. He was an insignificant looking man, wearing his 'demob suit,' one of those creations handed out to every departing serviceman. Some suits were blue and some were gray. Brackley was wearing one of the gray jobs with the double-breasted cut and dark stripes intended to give them that 'executive look.'

Mr. Brackley's suit, however, was worn and creased and any appearance of the budding business man had vanished, emphasized by the stains that discoloured the jacket. He seemed to be in his late-fifties. He needed a haircut. The hair at the back of his neck was white and straggled untidily over the collar of his soiled white shirt. He had a long thin nose on which the veins were beginning to show, and his face was unhealthily flushed. His skinny fingers drummed a tattoo on the desk top as he watched me.

"Well, d'you think you can help me?"

"Mr. Brackley, the first thing to do is to take a history, then make sure you're not suffering from some disease that could cause this – diabetes, for example."

He began in a flat, unemotional voice. "There's not much to tell. I'm forty, single, and I live with my sister. She's an invalid; spent years in the sanitorium. I help support her. I've never had problems with women before – you can always get one when you need one." He said it off-handedly, implying that he had never been over-particular and my ex-service mind slipped into gear.

"Have you ever had V.D.?"

He half smiled. "I'm not a fool, I've taken care of that. No, I've never had V.D."

"Have you ever thought of getting married?"

He looked at me, momentarily stoney-face, hesitated, then said "Aye, once. It's a long time ago. But she saw more in another chap than she saw in me, and that was that. There's never been anybody else for me. When I need a woman I find one.'' Behind this hard face there lay sensitivity, loyalty, longing, deep hurt.

''What do you do for a living?'' He looked as if he might be a storeman, a clerk on the docks, perhaps, I thought as I waited for an answer.

''I'm an electrical engineer to trade. I left school at fourteen and served my apprenticeship.''

''I see. I notice you're wearing a demob suit. Where did you serve?''

''The navy.'' The answer was non-committal. The half of Hull had been in the navy and I waited for some elaboration.

''You've left the navy a long way behind *you*,'' I thought as I looked at him in his soiled clothes.

''You want the details, doc?''

''It might help.''

He looked at me thoughtfully. ''Maybe. I was a bomb-disposal officer.''

Struck dumb, I looked at him. If he saw my astonishment he took no notice of it. This nondescript creature a bomb-disposal expert? An officer of the Royal Navy! He seemed to sense my thoughts.

''Lieutenant commander when I got out. Promotion was fast in that job.'' He said it unsmilingly, then went on, ''Maybe it *is* important, doc. You see, I'm drinking, heavily. Could that have something to do with it?''

''A great deal, Mr. Brackley. Alcohol can cause this kind of thing.''

He nodded. ''I thought as much. I'm not drinking on the job – not yet, but I just spend my nights getting drunk. I can't keep away from the stuff.''

He looked at me, wondering, I think, what was going on in my mind.

''I had a feeling for those bloody mines, doc, a kind of instinct maybe. And then, gradually I got the feeling that my luck had run out. Have you ever had that? That's when I started. Mind you, I'd always enjoyed my liquor. But if I took a tot of rum before I started de-fusing something, I felt better and my wits seemed sharper. It was always in my own quarters, and I don't think any of my crew knew. They depended on me and,'' said this man of forty who looked more like sixty, ''I never let 'em down either.''

It was tragic. His tragedy had perhaps begun long ago when ''she saw more in another chap than she did in me.'' The problem was an immense one for me and I was determined to do all I could, for he refused to see a psychiatrist.

"They can't help me. I suppose it's mostly alcohol. I'm steeped in it. You know, doc, I'm living in a world I don't belong to anymore. I've no roots since I left the service. There isn't a place for the likes of me. I just don't fit anywhere."

There was reaction here, and depression, though he wouldn't admit it. One day he appeared in the office unexpectedly.

"God, doc, you've got to help me now. I'm in awful trouble."

"What's happened?"

"I've been charged with indecent exposure. I'm damned lucky I'm not charged with attempted rape. If this gets out I'm done for."

"*Did* you try to rape somebody?" It was quite possible that he had desperately tried to prove his manhood and warily I took note of his answer.

"Don't be bloody silly, man. In any case I was too drunk to do it! Doc, I was in a strange pub out at Willerby. My bladder was bursting. I missed my way to the loo and found myself outside in the back lane. That's where it happened."

"Go on."

"I thought I'd never stop; the relief was wonderful. It was dark. I couldn't see anybody and I didn't think anybody could see me. Then I realized there were these young tarts standing not far away laughing. I got abusive. I'll admit to that, but I never laid a hand on them. One of them ran off and by God, she came back with a policeman. It happened so fast I hardly had time to button up my pants. That's it."

It wasn't a convincing story and I saw trouble ahead. "That's the truth?" I queried.

"I was as tight as a tick, but I swear I meant no harm and they're lying if they say I threatened them. I swore at them, and they deserved it. I just wanted to be left in peace. But they've landed me in a hell of a packet. I could lose my job. My lawyer says it would help if you'd appear in court on my behalf and tell them about the impotence."

True, a statement from me might save the day, and his job. He pleaded with me to appear. He didn't need to. How many men owed their lives to this prematurely aged, disreputable looking man? I thought of how a year or two before I would have gladly saluted him, knowing he had the kind of cold courage I never had. I'd have appeared on his behalf before the devil himself, let alone Hull's stipendiary magistrate.

It was my first appearance in court. A stipendiary magistrate is a full-time judge of the Lower Courts, and Hull's MacDonald had the reputation of running a business-like establishment. Our case was held 'in camera' in view of the awful revelations that might come to light. I arrived early at the courthouse. A large oak-lined room was to be the scene of the trial. The magistrate's bench was empty and I had time to look around.

Brackley's three accusers were easily identified. With their giggling heads together, they were not an impressive trio. They looked about seventeen and 'tarts' was, I felt, an apt description. Brackley's lawyer warned me that the prosecuting counsel would try to discredit my evidence.

My patient had pulled himself together for the day, and I could see what he might have looked like a year or so before. With his hair cut, and wearing a well-pressed suit, his face gave an impression of resolution, and God knows he must have possessed plenty of that at one time.

The court was called to order, and the stipendiary took the bench. There was none of the awe-inspiring solemnity of the high courts. This place was all business. He had seen a lot of life, had the stipendiary, and it showed in his lively, intelligent eyes. An elderly, spare-built man, he nodded to the lawyers as he settled himself on the bench.

I gave my evidence to the lawyer for the defence and was then left to the tender mercies of counsel for the prosecution.

"You are, you say, in practice in the city of Hull?"

"Yes, sir."

"Aren't you a very *young* man to have your own practice?"

"Possibly, sir."

Now, I didn't look my thirty years, not by a long way, so, forewarned by Brackley's lawyer I listened intently as counsel for the prosecution condescendingly said, "A *very* young man. I put it to you, doctor, a somewhat *inexperienced* young man?"

Diffidently, I questioned the validity of that statement.

"Let me put it to you that you have had very little experience of sailors and, Your Honour (with a smirk toward the Bench) we *all* know what sailors *are*!"

I was silent.

"I put it to you, doctor, that you have had little experience of sailors?"

I was forced to agree.

"Your Honour, I think we can dismiss the evidence of this

young physician as a well-meaning if misguided attempt to help the accused. He has just admitted that he knows nothing of this kind of individual.'' He sat down.

"I didn't say that,'' I protested.

Turning to the Bench, I said, "with all due respect, Your Honour, I served for six years in the army. I don't know much about sailors but I can't believe they're all that different from soldiers!'' The magistrate's face registered amusement.

"You're a Scot, of course?''

"Yes, sir.''

"And a Highlander, naturally?''

"No sir, a Lowlander.''

"Ah, that's a pity. I'm a Highlander myself. A MacDonald, you know.''

With a smile and a shrug of his shoulders, he turned to a frustrated counsel for the prosecution.

"Lowlander or not it'll do, Mr. Switch. His evidence will do!''

But it was Brackley's lawyer who brought the case to a successful conclusion. He had the accusers brought in one by one. Facing them was a large blackboard. On it was a diagram of the lane with measurements marked. Each accuser was asked the same questions.

Had they seen the accused very clearly?

Yes, they had.

Did they carry flashlights?

No, they hadn't.

Could they describe the accused's behaviour in detail?

It puzzled the defence that they had seen Mr. Brackley at all. The girls pointed confidently to what appeared to be a street lamp indicated on the blackboard.

"But,'' said the lawyer, "there is no street lamp in the lane, nor is there any other means of lighting.''

The third lady to testify countered this by saying she had seen the threatening monster by the light of the moon. But alas, there had been no moon that night: the lawyer produced a calendar to prove his point.

The case was dismissed. The girls may have thought they could have a lark with a man they dismissed as a figure of fun and contempt.

Brackley may have been pathetic. But he *was* a hero. The war, however, was over. He had become an anachronism. I have often wondered how many of the Brackleys of this world slipped into depression, alcoholism, lonely anonymity.

Emily Dickinson wrote:

> It feels a shame to be alive,
> When men — so brave — are dead

To that I would humbly add:

> Or broken and despised.

Chapter
Twenty-five

Hull was still struggling back to some kind of normality. Even though "t'lads" had long come home, the mental and material destitution of war lay all around. Acres of bomb-blasted brick and concrete had been at least tidied up so that crazily leaning floors and walls would not fall on passersby. Pits in the ground where land mines had fallen, left huge acres of broken concrete. Exposed earth and building foundations were becoming overgrown, thankfully, by the reds and purples of a wild flower appropriately called "fireweed." Rows of burned-out homes and remnants of curtains flopping out of long glassless windows were among the sights that people met daily on their way to work as they tried to return to the ways of a peacetime that for most of them seemed a lifetime away and, for some, an eternity.

The mental scars of these six years began to show themselves to the medical profession in a multitude of ways, though "stress" was not yet recognized by all physicians as a causative factor in a whole range of illnesses. Even today, we are just beginning to probe this field; but general practitioners may have been among the first to suspect that illness could be caused by unresolved grief and unhappiness.

It became commonplace for them to comment on the numbers of patients who complained of unusual symptoms, and the amount of sedatives they prescribed in daily practice.

Medical training today has to some extent developed an

emphasis on the psycho-sociological aspects of illness, but at that time, as doctors became more overworked, they began to rely increasingly on the fairly well-controlled use of sedatives such as phenobarbitone. Tranquillizers, with their advantages and drawbacks, had not yet been developed. Because of his workload, the average doctor in general practice could seldom spend more than a few minutes with each patient. As a result, people overburdened by past strains and anxieties or by grief, or by tensions associated with all the aftermath of war, had to pull themselves together by their own strength of will, or with the help of some basic counselling from family physicians largely untrained to give it; or retreat mentally within their shells, all too often developing intractable and often puzzling symptoms of illness in the process.

Men who had withstood the worst the enemy could throw at them might develop complaints for which there would be no physical explanation, but with luck and reassurance after careful examination the weird symptomatology would gradually fade away. Housewives, far too long alone in one of the most bombed cities in England, were especially victims. Sometimes their complaints were mainly physical. Perhaps they had given part of their rations to the children, and consequently had become anaemic, suffering from some mild "sub-clinical" deficiency condition that complicated matters.

Curing the obvious anaemia might satisfy physicians, who assumed that the physical signs and symptoms having been dealt with, the psychological ones would follow. But the human mind is infinitely complex, and this optimism was not always justified, if the deep turmoil within the patient's mind had not been helped. Sedatives, despite their often mildly depressing side effects, had at least a calming effect, and they were a boon in the treatment of many cases, provided people did not come to rely on them too much.

We are no different today. The stresses are different. The use of modern "tranquillizers" has proved to be a mixed blessing, but their prolonged use is no substitute for careful history-taking and examination. One of the doctor's most important duties is to listen, to watch, to assess the nuances of expression in a story and then to analyze scientifically the physical condition.

But at that time I was too busy just doing my work to devote much time to the academic side of medicine. When Mrs. Teale came into my office I waved her into the chair beside my desk. She had flaxen hair and gray-blue eyes, and her high cheekbones suggested something Scandinavian in her background. She was a most attractive thirty-year-old, though today her face didn't light up in its usual responsive fashion. Perhaps her smile had recently been too easy. It may have been "the smiling face of depression," but I was not to know that then, although I had looked after her for a year or so. She was an infrequent visitor to my office, but I had dealt with several episodes of respiratory infections, routine matters that necessitated several house calls.

She was apologetic as she began to give me her "history of present illness," the first step towards diagnosis, and often one of the most important.

The Teales lived in a comfortable, if small, terrace house and when I first met them, her husband had recently come home after long service in the tropics. He had been through the mill, had served his country well in appalling circumstances, and she beamed with pride as she introduced me to him. Their house had been untouched by bombs and showed evidence of all the care that a woman could lavish on it. All her savings during these cruel years had gone to building a nest egg and improving the little house.

A cheerful carpet covered the floor of their comfortable sitting room, and bright prints, chosen with care and good taste, decorated the walls that Catherine had so painstakingly painted. It was not a millionaire's home but it was a home fit for a hero to come back to, and for Catherine Teale her Jim was a hero: her pride in him, in her home, in her ability to make up to her husband something for the lost years, was obvious in her every expression and gesture.

So when Catherine sat in the chair beside my desk, I was prepared to spend a little time chatting with a young woman who could talk about the latest art exhibition, or tell me about a new phonograph recording.

"Now then, Catherine, what's brought you in? On a night like this I thought you'd be home listening to a record and watching Jim down a pint of ale!"

She half-smiled at my cheerful sally.

"Oh, I wish I knew what it was. I just don't feel all that well these days. I've been sleeping badly; I'm tired in the morning and I'm sure people at work notice it. I'm not really ill, you know, just constantly tired. Perhaps something to help me sleep, or a tonic or something..." she ended, on a note of apology.

This wasn't like Mrs. Teale, but a dozen possibilities came

to mind — some simple, some ominous. But there was one happy possibility. She was thirty and childless.

"What about it, Catherine? Periods normal? No possibility that you're in the early stages of pregnancy? That makes a lot of people feel tired, you know."

"No, I'm not pregnant. I'm sure of that."

Well that was that. It would have been a happy spot diagnosis, but I passed it over, and listened to her story of increasing tiredness over the past few months. She gave me no clue as to its cause, and so I arranged to examine her in the next few days, for it was obvious, judging by the scuffling of feet in the passageway, that the waiting room was full to overflowing, not so much with the sick, as with people requiring "clearance certificates" to go back to work on Monday morning after a bout of flu. I had better get on with my Saturday night chores.

When I examined her a few days later I was no further on. Our simple laboratory tests showed no sign of anaemia; there was no indication of either diabetes or any urinary problems. I went over her thoroughly: system by system her findings were normal, and while I was no Harley Street specialist, I prided myself that I knew my medicine, that I had kept up to date. Furthermore, my wife was a doctor with several years of hospital training behind her and she intended to see to it that I did keep up to date.

Leaving Catherine to dress behind the screen, I puzzled over the symptoms. Headaches, almost constant tiredness, loss of weight, mild lower abdominal discomfort that fitted no specific pattern, and finally insomnia. We still saw a fair amount of tuberculosis which could present itself insidiously, accompanied by symptoms that didn't quite fit into any medical jigsaw, and so I paid particular attention to her chest, listening carefully at the apices of her lungs for any tell-tale whispers.

I sat in my chair, doodling with my pen while she finished dressing. Then I asked Janet to come in from her office next door and gave her a resume of my findings.

She listened silently.

"Keep an eye on her. Make sure she comes back in another week or so; perhaps a mild sedative, some vitamins for now," and with a wave she was off to her own consulting room.

"Catherine," I said, "it's another of these mysteries. Certainly, I can't find a thing to account for your story, but we'll arrange an X-ray, though your chest sounds as clear as a bell. A year ago I'd have said it was a reaction to the war, or something of the sort. It could still be, too. Experiences, you know, lie deep in our subconscious minds, stored away like phonograph records we can take out and play. Maybe it's something like that with you – a kind of delayed action."

She nodded, that quiet smile again.

"I'm going to give you a mild sedative at nights for a bit," I went on. "But I have another prescription for you. Make Jim take you out, just once a week. Shopping, dinner out, fresh air. Take walks together. Try to recapture the days before the war when you were courting. Six years away – and you were only kids when you were married. Why, you hardly knew one another."

And then I added, "That's not really my prescription, Catherine. It's my wife's. Janet and I could easily have lost touch with one another, but she makes me take her out once a week for dinner and a show, and it's working for us. Try it."

I saw her several times shortly after that: she was uncomplaining but no better. She refused my suggestion that I should refer her for another opinion. And then, almost three months later, she appeared in my office again, her eyes lacking lustre, her careful coiffure gone. So was any pretence. She wept.

"I think I'm desperate," she whispered as she sat down, fingers constantly intertwining on her lap, the raincoat wet and unheeded still unbuttoned.

"It's Jim, isn't it?" I asked. "I suspected something a month or two ago, but you two always seemed so happy together. I couldn't bring myself to think of anything between you. What is it, another woman?"

She shook her head.

"No, not that. I know it's not that."

"You're happy with him? Catherine, you so obviously love him!"

"Oh yes. I love him. You know, I waited six years for him. I had plenty of opportunities. You know what I mean, doctor. But I never once looked at another man. Not once. All I wanted was him home. Even if he'd been blinded like Bill Herron, or his legs gone, I'd just have loved him all the more. He went through hell, you know."

I nodded. She struggled to regain control of her emotions.

Sometimes silence is the best policy. I moved over to the window, looked out at the busy street and waited for her to regain her composure.

"You see, I know it's not another woman. I've followed

him. He's never seen me. He just goes to the pub, the same corner night after night. Just sits there alone, drinking.''

"I see!"

"No, that's not it. A pint or two will do him all night. He never did drink much, you know. Even now, after all he's been through, he still doesn't take much. Nowadays he just comes home, quiet, goes to bed. He never touches me. That's really it, doctor. I couldn't bring myself to talk about it.''

"Is he impotent?"

"I think I'm repulsive to him,'' she exclaimed. "He can't stand to be near me anymore. I disgust him.''

I was astounded.

"You!" I looked at her attractive, intelligent face. "You couldn't disgust anyone, ever, Catherine! Don't talk nonsense.''

She sighed deeply. "Things were all right for nearly a year. We couldn't have been happier. He told me about his years away; then one night I told him about myself. You know I was a secretary during the war. But there was something else. It was the first big raid on Hull. Hundreds of people were killed. Burned alive. Buried. Torn to bits. Drowned, some of them. Buildings collapsed, fires all over the city. But I went to work the next morning; most people did.''

She stared at the wall behind me, dry-eyed, conjuring up her nightmare.

"That morning the air-raid warden came to the office. There were a dozen or so of us girls. He wanted volunteers, he said. They were desperate for help. He told us it would be awful. It was to work in the morgue office, to help identify the dead. None of us wanted to go. I'd never seen a dead person. But he pleaded with us.

"I was twenty-three then, the oldest girl in the office. I felt I should set an example, so I went. It was terrible.'' She continued calmly. "I was sick, time and time again. There were – bodies, heads, arms and legs. I don't know how I got the strength to see that day through, but I did. We all helped one another.''

She paused, drained of emotion.

"Then after the next raid, they came for me again; and the next, and the one after that. In the end it was almost a kind of job. I even was good at it.''

She looked directly at me.

"You see that's where I went wrong: I told Jim it was a job

in the end, and *that I was good at it!* He's never touched me since."

I walked around and put my hand on her shoulder.

"Catherine, war is a brutal, terrible business. It scars all of us in some way and your emotional scars are dreadful. Perhaps, though, your husband's are worse."

She nodded.

"Let me talk to him," I pleaded. "Maybe get him into the hands of a skilled psychiatrist; he has to get all this off his chest."

I saw him a couple of times but it was useless. He refused to see a psychiatrist and he obviously regarded me as an interloper. Their relationship deteriorated month by month. Catherine, I could see, was nearing the end of her strength.

It was not an easy decision, or easy advice to give, but when she came in for that last visit, my mind was made up.

"Clear out," I said, "It's over with. Clear out – completely! Not just out of your home, or this city, but out of England. Catherine, there are places where the sun shines and skies are blue, and you don't have to go to work every morning past shells of buildings that remind you of a hell. Leave here. You've got no parents, no brothers, no sisters. Go away. Start afresh."

She stared at me, aghast.

"I've never even been to London in my life! But I know you're right. We're only torturing one another. What a fool I was to tell him I was good at it!"

"Catherine," I comforted her, "Jim may not see it that way, but his wife is a heroine."

"No." And those gray-blue eyes met mine steadily as she shook her head. "In his mind he's married to a morgue attendant."

Chapter
Twenty-six

"Pain," said Buddha, "is the outcome of sin." He had more in common with John Knox than I'd have thought. Knox, that figure of repressive righteousness so typical of Scotland's brand of Protestantism, believed in Calvin's theory of original sin. Adam, Eve and that apple had placed a heavy burden on all mankind. We are born in sin. Sex in Scotland, however pleasurable, however loving, even in wedlock, to many is perhaps just a little sinful. If, therefore, pain is the outcome of sin, and sex is sin, then the natural outcome of that sin, having a baby, should be painful.

Besides, doesn't it say in the Book of Genesis, "In pain, ye shall bring forth children?" The logic is irrefutable – if you have that kind of mind. But I like to think that our techniques, if not always our philosophy, have progressed quite a bit since the days of the Old Testament prophets.

Having a baby today isn't the risky or painful business it sometimes was even just forty years ago when I was a young doctor. Infant and maternal mortality figures have improved vastly over the decades. The science of genetics has reached the stage where couples can be warned of the possibility of abnormalities in their offspring. Haematology, the scientific study of the blood, has done much to prevent infant and maternal mortality. These are only two examples of the progress we have made in medical science affecting obstetrics.

For many years I have forbidden my nursing colleagues to use the word pain with reference to childbirth, or in the presence of a woman in labour. Pain cannot be altogether banished from the process of having a baby, but it can be greatly alleviated – and not necessarily by overloading patients with drugs. It can be alleviated by education, explanation, exercise, relaxation and encouragement. Tell a woman that when the pains are coming every five minutes she'll be close to having her baby, and I will almost guarantee that she will have pain; such is the power of suggestion, coming especially from a figure as authoritative as a doctor. Nowadays it's more usual to speak of "contractions" rather than "pains."

Of course, the careful use of drugs is an essential part of

obstetrical practice, but while drugs are often necessary, and may complement the other techniques of pre-natal education, they cannot supplant them.

So when Frank Micks left me his list, he left me the beginning of what would become a busy obstetrical practice. The mid-wives, taking their cue from my Irish colleague, began to call me to see their patients in the district, mostly for the minor complications that arose. I had not yet had to deal with any major complications and I still had not applied forceps unsupervised in a home.

Perhaps the most common reason for a midwife to call in a doctor would be an obstructed delivery requiring the use of forceps. The baby's head would have progressed through the pelvic birth canal into the lower birth space, the perineum, and from there, for a variety of reasons, it would refuse to budge. The mother's efforts to expel it would be unavailing; she would soon become worn out, over-anxious, and a candidate for trouble if help was not forthcoming.

The usual form of help was use of obstetrical forceps by the doctor. There was usually little time to be wasted, for the baby, too, could be in distress. A quick examination of the mother and the baby's heart would be made, an immediate anaesthetic given, usually by the doctor with the nurse assisting. With the patient anaesthetized, the doctor would quickly don gown, mask and sterile gloves, carry out an examination of the pelvis to make sure of the baby's position, and if conditions were favourable, obstetrical forceps would be used. Usually, without too much trouble, another member of our species would be eased, or drawn, into the world. This procedure is sometimes known as an instrumental delivery. With reasonable skill, this is not usually a difficult operation but is not free of risks to mother or baby and certainly it is not to be embarked upon lightly.

Frank had impressed on us the importance of regular examinations of our maternity patients. Such examinations usually detected complications at an early stage. They also established a personal relationship between patient and doctor and that, said Frank, was most important. So we set aside an afternoon for our baby clinic. It was interesting, useful work, but still that "Sword of Damocles," my first forceps delivery in a home, unsupervised, hung over my head.

Mrs. Stainsbury was having her first baby. She had attended our little clinic, was in excellent health, and went into labour one morning exactly on time. All went well. The early stages of labour were perhaps a little slow, but while nurse busied herself with her preparations, during the day, I dropped into the cheerful little terrace house occasionally as my rounds permitted to see how things were going. Neither nurse nor I could see any signs of trouble. Then the labour began in earnest and seemed to be progressing uneventfully.

Uneventfully, that is to say, until later that afternoon Mr. Stainsbury arrived at our door on his bicycle and announced that nurse would be obliged if I would call around to see my patient. Hoping that the happy event was drawing closer, I hitched my medical case to the back of my bicycle, which I sometimes used, and made my way to Sandringham Avenue.

But nurse was not her usual cheery self. She met me in the narrow passageway and whispered, "She's going to need forceps, doctor. Her pains are getting her nowhere, and they're becoming weaker. She's been pushing for the best part of an hour and she's getting tired. Oddly enough, the head is quite low in the pelvis, and I've been waiting for it to appear any minute. Perhaps," she added, "the baby has big shoulders, or the cord is round its neck, for everything seems normal enough."

"The baby's heart?" I asked.

"Oh, just fine. It's never altered."

"No signs of distress?"

"None at all. She's just tired, but she'll never have that baby without help."

Nurse was an excellent midwife, kindly, calm and capable, and she was experienced. I had often remembered and had cause to value Dr. Micks' only half-jocular remark about the value of observing and thinking in such circumstances. Soon it was obvious that nurse was right. A forceps delivery was required.

It was now or, perhaps, never, for me, and I have known doctors adopt exactly that attitude. One failed forceps delivery has discouraged more than one doctor from maternity work. I explained the situation to my patient, who agreed that she was becoming tired, and felt she was making no headway, but she was quite confident and obviously not on the point of exhaustion.

"I'll give you another fifteen minutes," I told her as cheerfully as I could, and bicycled to No. 537, there to confer with Janet.

"This is it." I said. "If I don't do it now I never will."

"Let me come with you," said Janet, "I'll give Mrs. Stainbury the anaesthetic, and you apply forceps. We'll do it together."

And do it together we did. Janet put our patient to sleep. Mrs. Stainsbury even smiled at my wife, and said that with two doctors and all this attention she was getting there just wasn't a thing could go wrong, was there now?

I stood by, gowned and gloved, and waited for the signal from my wife. When she nodded at me, I examined the pelvis. Everything was normal. Blade one was inserted, blade two followed. Grimly, I locked them in position, waited for a moment, then pulled, gently at first. There was no response. I pulled again, a little harder. Our patient lay breathing easily and Janet nodded at me encouragingly.

Tensing my forearm muscles, I pulled again, more vigorously still, seeing to it that the blades followed the natural curve of the pelvis, thus diminishing the possiblility of bruising or tearing the tissues. The baby's head still did not budge. How I longed for Frank Micks to be by my side.

"She's just fine," Janet said, encouragingly. "Don't try to rush anything. Take your time."

Even by comparison with the scores of such deliveries that followed, it was not easy and I felt the sweat gather on my forehead as I brought my arm and shoulder muscles into play. But almost imperceptibly, the baby moved and with a sudden rush the whole thing was over. The head appeared, the blades were off, cast aside, and I was edging and pulling into the world a little chap, with shoulders like a prize fighter. To my immense relief, he immediately yelled his protest at this unceremonious arrival. Mrs. Stainsbury, more perhaps by good luck than by good management, had delivered without even a vaginal laceration. It was a little triumph in my career, one of those challenges that must be met or lost forever.

Janet had removed the airway tube from our patient's mouth, and soon she was stirring, then awake, a little dazed at first, before eagerly, lovingly, she stretched her arms toward her little one.

"All in good time," said nurse, cheerfully, as she reached for the binders and pins and all the paraphernalia of her profession. "All in good time. By the way he's howling now, you'll be wanting to give him back tomorrow."

But she was smiling as she said it, and so was our patient. As she replaced anaesthetic bottles in her case, Janet was smiling too, partly out of happiness for the Stainsburys, partly perhaps out of secret amusement at the changing expressions she had seen on my face: anxiety, fear, determination, relief, pleasure and – it must be admitted – a little pomposity. After all, it's not every day you tackle your first domiciliary forceps delivery.

But then, I gained experience and soon I'd go out on my cases just like my colleagues, leaving my anaesthetist fast asleep in her bed unless I needed her, but on my return there was always the same sleepy question, "Boy or girl?"

There was at least one recorded instance where the obstetrician, before turning over to sleep like a lamb replied, "Golly, I forgot to look."

Chapter
Twenty-seven

"A thousand pounds?" repeated the bank manager, settling himself in his leather chair and doodling on the green blotter in front of him. "Quite a sum of money."

If there was a glint of amusement in his eyes, none showed in his voice as he pulled the desk pad over towards him.

"And to invest it?"

"Right!" I replied.

Janet and I had never saved a thousand pounds before. Nor did either of us have the least idea about investments. But someone had told me I was foolish to keep our savings in the bank collecting a modicum of interest when they could be doing something both productive and profitable. Not for nothing am I a child of my race. The idea struck me as eminently sensible. And so there I was in my bank manager's oak-lined office, ensconced in an imposing chair, to discuss the matter.

Stocks, bonds, real estate, and the long columns of quotations in the business pages of the newspapers were a strange, incomprehensible and hitherto unattainable world to me. I needed advice. So does every young doctor, and later on in life, by organizing lectures and short courses for those of them who wished to participate, I made it my business to see that my residents were shown at least the basic facts of intelligent investment and savings. These were given by experts in the field. Mendacious though it may seem to have a teacher of medicine lay emphasis on such matters to young physicians whose interest should be in healing of the sick, divorced from pecuniary thoughts, I never regretted it. My only regret is that I did not involve their wives in our courses, for they need the instruction more, and for a number of reasons, not the least being to keep their spouses on an even keel. Many physicians, strange to say, considering their work, seem to believe in personal immortality and infallibility. And yet their wives do become widows, are often quite ignorant of financial matters, and at a time when they are lost and alone, often utterly vulnerable, they may make disastrous financial decisions.

When most doctors finally emerge from their residency programmes, having been paid just enough to live on, and become licensed to practise, they are approaching thirty. Usually they are married, sometimes with children, and almost always heavily in debt. They will work, statistically, somewhere over sixty hours a week until the age of forty-eight, during which time the males will be subject to heart attacks at double the rate of the rest of the adult male population, and by the age of fifty-five in terms of ability to work long hours they are "over the hill." Generally speaking, their "productivity" begins to wind down. Their really productive life span is one of under thirty years and in this time they must amass their savings for later years. Governments are not really kindly uncles. If, because of inept personal management as well as high taxation and inflation, doctors are badly off or insolvent, there is little they can do about it. However, all that was to be something for the future.

My friend looked at me across the desk.

"A thousand pounds. Stocks?"

"Stocks?" I repeated, questioningly.

"That's right. Some very sound ones on the market these days." He looked at me quizzically, for we were now friends.

"D'you really know what common stocks are, as compared with preferred ones, or debentures?"

I admitted I had the belief that buying common stocks meant buying a small share of a firm's capital, in a sense becoming a minor partner. I also remembered what had happened to my father's savings in the thirties and was not impressed.

"Bonds? Very safe if you get the right bond," he said.

"Very uninteresting, too, and taxation makes them less so. That right?"

He ignored my remark.

"Investments depend on one's personality to a great extent. Some people need security, and should go for that, while others want the risk of speculative investment as opposed to the relative security of high grade stocks. It's all a matter of taste and, as well, the ability to make an unemotional analysis of facts and possibilities."

Finally, having decided that Marks and Spencer and Standard Oil of New Jersey were just a little frail to be entrusted with our thousand pounds, my friend leaned back in his chair, tilted it slightly towards the wall behind him, put his hands in front of him, fingertip to fingertip, lifted his face to the heavens, or at least to the fluorescent light in the ceiling, went into a state of deep meditation, righted the chair and looked at me in that portentous way that bank managers and doctors share.

"I may have just the thing for you," he mused. "Different from the usual kind of investment, but interesting – ah! very interesting. You would be in control of your savings, have a great deal of influence as to future success, as far as that is possible, of course."

"Of course. Excellent."

"Also, give you another interest, something else to think about."

Considering that I was working about twelve hours a day and seemed to spend most of my waking hours thinking as well as slogging away at my routine work, I was somewhat sceptical of the benefits of another interest. He went on.

"I have a young customer who is going into business on his own. Needs some capital. Would admit a suitable investor as a full partner."

"What kind of business?"

Apparently he hadn't heard me.

"A very capable young man. Previously the manager of a dairy store. Very progressive. Good ideas. Feels he could do well in his new line of endeavour, given enough capital to acquire the necessary stock."

"I thought we'd just decided that stocks weren't my thing?"

"Stock, doctor," he corrected me. "Not stocks. It's a pig farm."

"Pig farm!"

Previously lounging comfortably in the easy chair that banks

141

provide for customers who reach the manager's sanctum sanctorum, I sat bolt upright as if somebody had put a needle in my spine.

"Pig farm! I don't know one end of a pig from the other!"

"It's amazing how quickly you'll learn that," he replied. "Of course, its a gamble to some extent, as you must know, but many a business man has interests away from his main source of income. Why shouldn't you? You're just beginning to earn. You'd earn more. This would be an outlet for you. A very interesting one. You'll need a partnership agreement, of course. Need to meet your potential partner, size him up, that sort of thing. We trust him; always been a steady customer of the bank. Young fellow with initiative. The kind we need to encourage in this country. Think about it."

"I'm not a business man. I'm a doctor."

"Ah, but you should also take an interest in business. That's the trouble with you professional men. You despise business. After all, you are just beginning to earn your life's savings. Who do you think is going to look after your money if you don't? Think about it," he repeated.

Janet had spent most of the war years as a hospital physician earning a pittance. I often said I wooed and won her because I rescued her from the dreadful hospital food of wartime and fed her in decent restaurants. She was happy to have the smallest luxuries. She had told me to invest the money as I thought best and besides, she was in London visiting her aunt and uncle.

A pig farm, I rationalized, might be very interesting. True, I was somewhat less than knowledgeable in the subject, but visions of country life, the gentleman farmer, arose in my mind.

"I'll do it!"

"Think about it first," said my friend, a little more cautiously, it seemed. "Won't your wife want to know about this?"

"I have been given *carte blanche*," said I, with emphasis.

My prospective partner was within call and came around. He was a chap of about my own age, a tall, dark, good-looking fellow. But what was more important, bright. He sat in the remaining chair quivering like a whippet at a gate, full of aims and ideas. I liked him. His ideas seemed sound and he had had four or five years of managerial experience in a fair-sized shop where the bookkeeping had been his responsibility. We shook hands on the deal.

There was only one small snag. Until a month or so ago he hadn't known anything about pigs either!

I then went to see my old friend and lawyer, Ernest Gray. Mr. Gray, old enough to be my father, had looked after our affairs since we had set up in practice, vetted us for a loan from one of his clients, been like a father to both of us and had always given us sound advice. A Yorkshireman through and through, he was never one to mince matters.

As he listened to my story, he had moved over to his office window and stood looking out at the busy narrow street below. He heard me out, silent. Then he turned to me.

"You're a fool," he declared. "You mean to say you've committed every penny you have to something as speculative, as risky, as a pig farm? If I were your wife I'd shoot you, and then I'd go around and shoot your banker for ever mentioning the subject."

"It was my decision," I protested.

"Your decision be damned. Do you know the worst business men, the worst plungers in creation? Doctors. Terrible! Educated men, too. Well, if you're committed, I'll do my best to protect your interests in the matter."

Somewhere at the back of my mind is the old saying that the doctor who treats himself has a fool for a patient. Ah, well...

I phoned Janet that night at her uncle's Baker Street flat. But now, reflections and misgivings had descended upon me, and when I heard that cheerful voice at the other end it seemed advisable to lead up gradually to the subject of our investment rather than blurt it out and with what might be considered unseemly haste.

"Would you mind getting on with it," the voice at the other end said in that half-Highland lilt. "What *did* you do with the money?"

"Put it in a pig farm."

The only words that came over the line were, "Oh crumbs!"

Chapter
Twenty-eight

Janet returned from London the next day. Apart from telling me she didn't intend to set foot on the place, that I needn't rationalize the matter, and that when our savings were gone the failure was not to be projected on to her with the argument that it had all been done for her financial well-being, she said very little.

Our investment consisted of somewhere around an acre and a half of land, an elderly house occupied by Jack, and his wife and family, a row of sturdy concrete pig styes, and a collection of huts that had been constructed by someone with all the architectural skills of a drunken trawlerman. The surrounding land, flat as a pancake, had a remarkable capacity for becoming water-logged.

We owned about fifty pigs: pigs of all kinds, part this and part that, "large whites," part saddlebacks, part Tamworths and something else. Not one of them of any real quality, but all in hearty good health as far as I could see.

My apprenticeship began almost immediately. Jack phoned to say that a farmer in the dales had a litter to sell at a reasonable price. He felt it would be interesting for me to on the trip; I would learn the ropes a bit. I finished my rounds early that day and with a few hours to go before the evening surgery I drove out to pick up my associate.

My black Citroen roadster, spotlessly shining and low-slung, with its red leather upholstery, was a dream to look at. So, I thought, was I, in my immaculate, double-breasted blue suit and light gray homburg hat. But it gradually dawned on me that Jack, from under his cloth cap, was eyeing my ensemble with less than admiration. The rain had poured for days, but it had stopped, and a trip into the country was just the thing.

"Jeez, doc, but you look funny in that get-up."

"What d'ye mean – funny? I dress like this every day."

"Aye, maybe y'do, but ye don't go buyin' pigs oop in t' dales every day." He gave a raucous guffaw and lapsed into silence, broken only by the occasional titter and an incredulous shake of the head as he looked sideways at me in my elegance.

"You'll see," was his cryptic reply to my indignant protest at this unseemly amusement.

Eventually, having left the highway and lurched and bumped across roads that were no longer coping with the rainfall and had become mires of sodden earth, he told me to draw up at the next gate.

Dismayed, I surveyed my beloved car, windows obscured by a coating of filthy rainwater, the windshield thick in glutinous mud that had been stirred into an almost solid cake by the wipers.

The farm road, ending at a cottage a quarter of a mile up the hillside, was impassable. Floods of water cascaded under the five-barred gate and the rutted road was a bog.

Indignantly, I cried, "Do we have to walk up there?" To which my associate, with all the smugness that knee-high rubber boots could confer, merely replied, "Come on, doc, no time to waste," and began trudging his way through the muck.

My investment was beginning to look sour, but I followed him, my shoes and socks immediately engulfed in slime, my beautifully pressed trousers the colour, shape and consistency of the mud around us. As a potential part-time gentleman farmer, I felt this was most inappropriate and when my Homburg hat was flipped off by a sudden gust of wind my discomfort became acute.

"Now," said Jack, sludging comfortably along slightly in front of me, quite ignoring my distress, "this is where you begin to learn the pig business. This owd gaffer says 'e wants three quid a pig. 'E knows, an' I know, they're not worth that. I'll start at two pun twelve an' six; 'e'll act oop, and after an argument we'll settle at two pounds fifteen. 'E knows right now that's about it, but 'e'll argue for t'sake of arguing. But silver'll change hands around two pounds fifteen, you mark my words. Now, doc, *just keep quiet*. Let me do the talkin' – and for God's sake, don't tell 'im 'is animals look good or the price'll go up before you can bat y'r eyelid."

I assured him of my total cooperation. I was beaten. It had all been too much for me, and as for Janet's face when I got home, I preferred not to think about that at all.

The pig yard was a square of heaped-up mud, a few miserable tufts of earth topped by dirty grass, unsavoury islands in a sea of filth, all of it surrounded by a waist-high wall of stone and cement. I ploughed my way towards it; Jack, the essence of confident comfort in his dungarees and rubber boots, ahead of me, already greeting the farmer.

"Day Gaffer. Bit wet."

The new arrival, an irascible-looking elderly gentleman attired in a pair of incredibly loose trousers that might have fitted him had he been fifty pounds heavier, merely grunted. A soiled and battered bowler hat was clamped on his head and he kept adjusting his braces, though his trousers, dragging at the seat as if he kept a five-pound weight permanently there, were held in place to some degree by a pair of ancient army puttees wound untidily round his lower legs, and fastened down somewhere over boots thick with black gumbo.

" 'E yer pal?'' he nodded in my direction, ignoring Jack's outstretched hand.

He eyed me up and down, a sour, unwelcoming stare, but he led us over to the wall while he vanished into the stye and chased the piglets out for our inspection. They were as filthy as the rest of the place, but they were fat and frisky and obviously Jack was satisfied.

"Three pun' a piece," Gaffer said.

"Two pun' twelve an six. Take it or leave it. That's my offer," replied Jack.

The bargaining started and soon Jack was finding the competition tougher than he had expected. One little brute had momentarily pulled its snout out of the mud to inhale, and was standing still for a split second. Jack saw his opportunity. "Look at that one there," he cried indignantly. "Proper poorly it is. I just don't see where y'get yer two pun seventeen an six from, Gaffer. Do you, mister?''

I had been listening carefully and was astounded that Jack was now appealing to me. If it had come to this pass I was determined to play my part to the full. I leaned over the wall, prodded one of the dirty little things in the back just the way I'd seen my associate do it five minutes before, and announced my verdict.

"I would personally suggest two pounds ten shillings each and leave it at that.''

Mildly I looked around. I thought that was rather good, but to my astonishment Jack looked alarmed and I thought the old boy was about to have an apoplectic fit.

"An 'oo the bloddy 'ell asked thee to open thy mouth?'' he roared. "An' 'oo is 'e anyway?'' he snarled at Jack, "an' wot the 'ell does 'e know about pigs?''

"Oh, 'es a pig man aright, mister," replied my associate soothingly. "In a big way, too, just bought a lot 'o pigs," he added with a snicker.

I retired from the argument. I had shot my bolt, but taken

aback, the farmer was not yet recovered enough for further bargaining. The shock of my assault had unnerved him.

" 'E don't look like a bloody pig man t'me," he grumbled, before proceeding, but he was in disorderly retreat. The end was in sight.

Two pounds fifteen and sixpence. They shook hands and the silver half-crown changed owners as custom prescribed.

Jack and I began our trudge through the mud again and half way to the gate an ancient farm truck driven by our friend overtook us. Splashing us generously *en passant*, it did not offer to stop, but when we reached the road it was drawn up behind my Citroen, filthy beyond belief, like its owner. Our friend was prowling round it.

"See y', Gaffer," nodded my partner, settling comfortably on to the red hide seat and dragging half the Dale in with him.

"I'll fetch 'em tomorrow. Get'er going', doc," he hissed in an aside. But I couldn't oblige without running over the Gaffer. He had got round to my side and was tapping on the window, which I could do little but open.

A fierce old face, unshaven for days, crowned by a greasy, generations'-old bowler hat, was thrust close to my nose.

"An as for thee, young man," it snarled, "I still don't think thou 'rt any bloody pig man."

Chapter
Twenty-nine

"It's your partner," said Janet drily, "on the phone."

Considering that *she* already was my partner in more ways than one, and that I consistently referred to Jack as "my associate," I felt it would have been kinder, more considerate, less acidic, for her to have used the latter term, but she would persist. A month or two had elapsed since our investment in the pig business.

"Yes, Jack?"

"Oh, jeez, doc, you'd better come out."

"What's up?"

"They're ill. Two styes. All the same. You'll see. It'll spread. Always does."

It was a Saturday afternoon. Normally at that time on that day Janet and I and our little one would go into town for a relaxed stroll around the stores looking at the goodies we might (until very recently) have bought. Or I might have been hiking around the dales with my good friend, Ernie Fenton. Unfortunately we business men and agricultural types were at the mercy of ill-understood forces, I had told an unsympathetic Janet. My visions of gentleman-farming were being replaced by the reality of dungarees and wellington boots Jack kept for me in one of the outhouses. In half an hour I presented myself at the farm, all acre and a half of it. It was a moody Jack who met me.

"Come and have a look, doc."

Pulling on my work clothes and stuffing my feet into the rubber boots, I followed him up the path. He swung the upper half of a stye door open.

"See for yourself."

My heart sank as I looked. There they were, a dozen or so young pigs, standing listlessly in the middle of the concrete floor, tails uncurled and drooping, their food untouched.

At the next stye, the same sight met my eyes. Animals that a few days before had frisked and snorted with all the virility of youth, pushing one another out of the way to get at their food, hardly moved as we watched them.

"Diamonds," said Jack gloomily. "They'll most likely all get it. An' then, doc," he added comfortingly, "there goes your investment."

"Diamonds?" I replied. "There has to be a medical name for this. Is it common? How does it affect them?"

"It's common enough. They lose weight. Get the skitters. Don't eat. And if they pull through it they're ill for weeks. Those," he added "that don't get over it, die. They call it 'diamonds' hereabouts because they break out into kind of blotches."

With my heart sinking into my wellingtons, I said, "Let's have another look, really close up."

As cheerful as a couple of unemployed undertakers, we tramped into the styes. Normally their inhabitants would have charged away from us but they didn't as much as grunt at our arrival, and it was easy to catch them one by one and hold them despite their feeble protests while I carried out an examination.

"Jack," I said when I was through, "to you this is 'diamonds'. To me, it's an acute infection with a skin rash. Now I'm no vet, but I think we're dealing with something like erysipelas. I'll take a bet on it, and if a human had it I'd give big doses of penicillin by injection for several days. And I'd give penicillin to these animals right now, and to the ones in the neighbouring styes, for I'm sure they're already infected."

My companion brightened.

"It's worth a go, doc. Can you get penicillin for pigs?"

"I don't know anything about penicillin for pigs, but I can get penicillin. Penicillin's penicillin! I'll be back." And I was off to the nearest druggist, calculating how much of the antibiotic I would need for two dozen hefty young hogs. The druggist knew me. He was a bit of a humorist was Bill Green and, as he produced syringes and a selection of needles as thick as bayonets, he kept up a running commentary on the natural proclivity in interest of some medical men he knew. Like Queen Victoria, I was not amused.

Meanwhile, Jack was waiting and on my return we set to work with all speed. We went into the styes, and while Jack grabbed the patients by their tails I administered the life-saving drug. With grunts and squealed protests our charges acknowledged our activities and there was, for the first time that day, some movement. Unfortunately in more ways than one: Jack showed all the latent talents of a ballet dancer as he adeptly manoeuvred piggy posteriors and his legs simultaneously.

"Give me him, that one there."

"Him there? You've done him!"

"No, I haven't. I've done that one there."

Little pigs, if you've ever noticed, bear the most remarkable resemblance to one another. We stopped, drew ourselves erect, looked around. Two dozen piggy eyes watched us with stolid caution. My associate was, and still is, I am sure, a man of quick intellect and great resource. He raised his hand.

"Paint, doc. Paint their backsides the minute you inject them."

It was sheer genius and the job was quickly done. By the next afternoon the patients were doing as well as could be expected and the contacts in the neighbouring styes showed no signs of sickening. It was at this point that I advised a step we never had cause to regret, my medical background underwriting my pigmanship.

"If this infection is as virulent as this, we should set about building quarantine styes. If a stye gets sick, move all of them, and the neighbours on either side, into the observation wards.

Later on we did adopt that policy and I'm convinced it worked for us – combined with speed and meticulous attention to detail, such as scrupulous cleanliness and the care of food.

However, by the third afternoon recovery appeared certain and when I arrived Jack was accompanied by Len Wilkes, another pig farmer. He had heard of my triumph and had come to worship at the shrine of technology. The trouble was that the patients had truly recovered and far from showing any gratitude, the very sight of me coming into their abode, syringe held ready for action, was enough to set up a grunting, squealing stampede. They would bunch up in a corner, climb on to one another's backs, break up like a rugby scrum at our approach and take off for the opposite corner to repeat the procedure there. Pigs are quite intelligent animals, and in moments of stress, surprisingly mobile.

Jack grabbed one of them by its now well-curled tail, but a second, heading for the open range so to speak, took Jack's legs from underneath him and landed the firm's senior partner on his rear end on the concrete floor, which, not to put too fine a point on the matter, could have been cleaner.

Why was it necessary to continue with the injections? The reason is simple. One must *kill* infection, not half-kill it. Germs have their immunities too, and one of our growing troubles is the increasing resistance of bacteria to antibiotics, caused by insufficient therapy. So the job had to be done once again. Our guest seemed overcome by happiness at the cure we were effecting, judging by his mirth, but we prevailed upon him to assist us in our endeavours. I gathered from Jack that if he didn't, his masculinity might forever be in question!

All was well. The next time I saw our patients they were grubbing into the trough, all of them except one – and the only reason for that was that pigs are smart, too. They can simultaneously eat like hogs and manoeuvre their backsides to keep their kith and kin away from their fair share of the food.

I am a general practioner. I have never had any great ambition to reach for the pinnacles of my profession and be a consultant or a specialist. But though I did not know it at the time I was fast on my way to becoming a consultant after all – in the pig business!

Chapter
Thirty

"Could you call round and see my husband?" asked young Nancy Cornish. "He's running a fever and coughing. I know it's probably nothing, but it's been going on for several days, and it's not like Jim to stay in bed."

Indeed it wasn't. I couldn't recall that Jim Cornish had ever consulted me, but I remembered him well. I had delivered their baby a year or so before, and Jim had been a tower of strength to his wife. He had brought nurse and me endless cups of tea as we waited in their pleasant little home. He was our orderly for the occasion and during his duties always found time to sit by his wife's side and hold her hand, or make remarks that had nurse smiling behind her mask. After Master Cornish had arrived and was being "done" by my colleague, the district midwife, before being placed in Nancy's welcoming arms, Jim confessed that once or twice he'd been scared. He and I were standing in the kitchen enjoying a glass of sherry, congratulating each other on being two excellent fellows.

"But I wasn't going to show it, mind you!" he laughed, as he saw to it that my glass was topped up. He'd been an artillery sergeant in the western desert during the war and had refused a commission because he wanted to stay with the men in his outfit. He was a couple of years older than I, somewhere in his middle thirties, a strapping, handsome fellow, and a nice one.

"Of course I'll come round," I told his wife, "just as soon as the morning surgery is over."

In a couple of hours I stood on their doorstep. Jim was a civil servant, able to live comfortably in a modest way, and their little home, with its well-tended garden, was a model of neatness.

"Really, I don't suppose it's anything." Nancy smiled as she opened the door for me. "I'm a bit ashamed of sending for you at all when you're so busy, but I knew you wouldn't mind."

The upstairs bedroom was a warm, welcoming room, and Jim smiled apologetically at me from the bed.

"Sorry to drag you out like this, doctor. I told Nancy she shouldn't bother. But you know what women are like!"

We two male chauvinists having settled the matter of sexual superiority, I got down to the business of physical examination.

Jim was in no distress. He was breathing easily. His fever was of low degree, and quickly my clinical instinct told me he had an upper respiratory infection, influenzal in type; however debilitated he was now, in a few days he'd be better. All the same, I'd examine his chest.

I listened to his heart and after going over the front of his chest, bade him sit up, so that I might "go over" his back.

It was then, with growing horror, that I saw it, low on his right shoulder, and no larger than a pea, a ragged, black spot.

That cheerful visit had suddenly become the beginning of a months-long nightmare.

"Jim, how long have you had this thing?" I asked as casually as I could.

"Oh, it's just a mole, doctor. Been there for years."

"But surely it has changed a bit. Was it always like this?"

"Well, no. It has grown a bit in the past few months."

"And the colour?"

"It's got a bit darker all right. But it's too small to be anything, surely?"

I nodded, as casually as I could bring myself to do.

"Well, it should come off just as soon as you're up and about, and be sent away for examination. I'll make the arrangements."

His wife was hovering around the bed, and her eyes, no longer smiling, were on my face.

Closing my bag, I made my way downstairs. How lightly I had run up them fifteen minutes before! Jim had a skin cancer. And in my heart I knew he was doomed.

Nancy ushered me to the garden gate, closing the front door behind her.

"There's something wrong, isn't there, doctor? That black mole − it's cancer or something isn't it?"

"I can't be sure," I answered. "Nobody can be sure. It has to be analysed. It might be nothing," I tried to reassure her, "but it simply must be removed and examined by a pathologist. Then we'll know."

Skin cancers vary tremendously in their malignancy. Some, thankfully, probably the ones the G.P. sees most commonly, are hardly malignant at all. Diagnosed early or late, once removed they are finished. Their malignancy is low and restricted to the area of their occurrence. Their secondary spread is late or almost non-existent. Others are deadly. Most moles are harmless naevi, but in cases of the slightest doubt, removal and skilled analysis is imperative.

As I drove away from the Cornish's my thoughts were grim indeed: I had little doubt of the outcome. And a few days after Jim's "mole" had been removed, my worst fears were confirmed.

Hardly a week passed until I saw my second case, a man with cancer of the bowel. He had allowed suspicious rectal bleeding to go unchecked until it was too late. The bowel was resected and the tumour removed, but the surgeon reported extensive secondary spread.

Then the next, and a few weeks later, another – this time a cancer of the liver in one of our favourite patients, a customs officer. He had had a very rough war, indeed, and was only too happy to enjoy his mundane job and the pleasures of his growing library, culled with care and pleasure from second-hand bookstores.

I thought it would never end. It was spring when I first saw Jim Cornish, and winter when it finished. There were six patients at the same time, all bedridden, all suffering from terminal cancer. It is strange how many of us physicians experience "runs" of cases like this. Is it coincidence, or is there an explanation?

In those days, with hospital beds at a premium, people died at home. It was often a terrible time for their relatives. The district nurses were wonderful – cheerful, comforting, concerned women, almost always. But in the end, when tablets and medicine by mouth would no longer help, I had to resort to my nightly "morphine round." Larger and larger doses of pain-killing drugs had to be given by injection.

It was the only way to bring relief to these poor souls, and many a night I had to drag myself out to begin my self-imposed round. It wasn't just the injection, it was the advice and support to lonely, anxious and sometimes despairing people that mattered, the stricken and the watchers alike. Every doctor must surely, first, be a sound and careful clinician, but the family doctor has other duties. For his people he must be something of a listener, an advisor, perhaps even a confessor. There are few analgesics or sedatives for mental pain and despair, but sometimes a kind word, free from judgement or criticism, can help.

But inevitably, my morphine round became shorter, and

how I longed for it to be over. Jim Cornish was the last to go, that handsome face and frame shrinking as the end grew near, those once dancing eyes dim, shrunken and yellow.

Nancy, desperate with grief, pleaded with me to do more to ease his suffering, perhaps more than the law would allow. Her love would have driven her to any action that would have eased or hastened his end. Seeing her grow old in these few months, knowing the depths of her anguish, I have often thought that if justice is blind, the law can be cruel. Thankfully, one night my morphine round was over.

It was close to Christmas and almost a year had passed since I told Catherine Teale to go away, start again someplace where the sun shone.

As I came downstairs one morning the mail cascaded through the letter box and on to the floor. When I picked it up I noticed that one letter bore a postage stamp from the other side of the world.

Inside was a Christmas card. It read: "The prescription worked. Here the sun is shining."

It was signed. "Catherine Teale."

Chapter
Thirty-one

A year or so had passed since our initial investment in the pig business. Jack and I were full of optimism, but it was hard going. Although we bought more pigs, he took from the business a bare living wage and I took nothing.

We read books about pig rearing, and I discovered that the veterinarian and the medical doctor have much in common. The diseases they see aren't all that different, but the vet has to be smarter: his patients can't tell him anything. As I looked at some of our baffling cases, and shook my head over them,

I developed a strong feeling of fellowship for my colleagues in veterinary practice.

However, my reputation as a pig consultant was spreading. My associate was partly responsible for this, for he talked to his friends. My growing reputation amused him. I was called into consultation even by our competition, but I usually refused to cooperate, referring them instead to a duly qualified veterinary surgeon – which I most certainly was not.

My interest in hogs was prompted by a strong instinct for the survival of our investment, and usefully, I had a medical education. Once or twice I relented and gave some general advice; once I even visited an old chap's pig farm. With Yorkshire stubbornness, the owner had never sought the advice of a vet in his life, and swore he never would. Their new-fangled scientific methods were all wrong. I'm still not quite sure why he invited *me*. Still, since his pigs were dying in alarming numbers, something was obviously wrong, and I consented to do a house call, so to speak – or a stye call.

There were, of course, many efficient, excellently run pig farms in the area, and today scientific methods of rearing and feeding the animals are paramount; but thirty years ago some of the older generation used the hit-or-miss methods of their forebears. They might be retired seamen who had bought a few pigs for a hobby. With good luck or management their little business would expand.

This particular old fellow fed his animals on swill and waste food he collected from the back doors of restaurants. So did our little firm, but we inspected it meticulously and boiled it till it was sterile. The trouble with some of the old-timers was their belief in a kind of mythology regarding the raising of animals. Strange concoctions of tar and molasses might be used internally, or externally, for various diseases. I once was told that a peeled raw onion stuffed up some piggy's rear end was a most efficacious remedy for diarrhoea. I'm sure it was. Pushed up far enough it could act like a cork!

On the occasion of my reluctant house call, the (by now) anxious pig farmer led me down a hodge-podge collection of duckboards laid over puddles of water and gluey mud to old wartime huts that had once housed anti-aircraft troops. The door was opened and the ghastly, acrid odour of foul urine drove me back, gasping for fresh air.

Stale urine in pools lay everywhere, spilling out on to the concrete walk laid between the rows of styes, soaking the filthy straw on which lay listless hogs, many of them in the grip of infectious diarrhoea. This was known locally, and expressively, as "the squitters."

I was appalled.

"Let the air out a bit," I pleaded, "then I'll have a look around."

"Let air out?" the old man said with great indignation, "but that smell is part of t' cure, mister!"

"Eh?"

"Aye, that's reet. When they gets t' squitters like this, my owd dad allus let t' pigs lie in their own muck till it was all over. Lyin' in t' muck, see, breathin' in t' chemicals from it, that's what cures 'em. When squitters is all gone I cleans place oop an' it's as neat as a new pin. It's that smell as does the trick. It cleans their lungs out – and you keepin' door open like this is takin' all t' good out of t' cure! My owd dad allus taught me that."

Since my informant was well up in his seventies, presumably his old dad was beyond retribution, but his elderly offspring wasn't. It was a kind of mad reversal of the logic of cause and effect. The few pigs with immunity would survive the epidemic and the place would then be cleaned.

I pleaded with him to shovel the filth out of the premises and destroy it before the authorities got wind (in more ways than one) of his "cure" and urged him to get the immediate advice of a qualified vet. Grumpily telling me that his owd dad knew a thing or two, and without a word of thanks, he bade me a curt good day, leaving me to find my own way off his premises. Thankfully, he didn't offer a farewell handshake.

Our own operation improved month by month. New styes were built, concrete replaced mud flats, and we employed a man who did odd jobs, including collecting waste food from restaurants and surplus fish from trawlers. We inspected and weighed our animals and ran our isolation styes with the efficiency of a health department. I was only a weekend helper but the whole thing was interesting, for pigs are interesting animals.

Mother pigs, just like their human counterparts, can be competent, affectionate parents, or they can be sluts. Unlike their human counterparts, the latter type will sometimes eat their young. They can maintain clean styes or have around them a filthy, uncared-for mess; their young can be well behaved little things, or brats. Pigs can also be quite dangerous. In defence of her young, a sow, weighing perhaps 180 pounds, will charge with tremendous speed and power. Jack's opinion was that an enraged sow could take a man's ankle off at one bite. He may have been right. I had no desire to experiment. When one charged me once, I dived over the stye door like an olympic gymnast and with just as much concentration and speed. Once on the other side I buttressed my shoulder against it as Jack and I struggled to bolt the door before the sow battered it down from her side.

They are also powerful animals. When, one day as I was shovelling gravel, one decided to head for the open range or at least the main road to Hull, its squealing rush took it right past me. Jack was far behind me, but I heard his shovel hit the ground as he threw it down.

"Grab it by the tail and hold on, doc," he yelled. His lean figure took off at a run, gum boots sloshing through the rain puddles.

Running myself, I got alongside my quarry, then behind it, stooped, grabbed the curly tail with both hands, dug my heels into the muddy ground, and yanked backwards. There was a squeal from the pig and a gulp from me. With the speed of lightning, I was face down, hauled along through puddles, muck and bushes by my panic-stricken escapee. The hired help and my business associate were bellowing instructions in the background, but suddenly I saw Jack's speeding figure drawing up on us as he streaked across the ground to cut off the escape route.

"Don't let 'er get the better on ye, doc," he yelled, just before his gum boots skidded in the mud and he carried out a most interesting mid-air manoeuvre. I heard the splash as his descending backside hit the water.

But even runaway pigs come to the end of their strength. The headlong rush slowed and finally came to a grunting halt. I stumbled to my feet, panting. A figure loomed up beside me, almost unrecognizable, put a muck-encased arm fondly around my shoulder and said, "Just like I said, doc, never let them get the better on ye."

Speechless with exhaustion, I could only nod agreement.

Never in my life had I struck a woman. But I am only human. From the depths of my being I summoned up the last reserves of my strength, lifted my gum boot and in football parlance, "planted one" on the lady's backside. She never even budged.

Although the end of my involvement in the pig business was in sight, I still kept on working at our small holding. One morning when the rounds were finished early and the firm's hired man was absent, I dropped in, and Jack gratefully accepted my offer of help. Changing into gum boots and dungarees, I joined him as he cleaned some styes. It was heavy work. With a wheelbarrow between us, I shovelled while Jack raked the muck up and piled it, using a long-handled fork.

"Are you the proprietor?"

I looked up. Standing looking in over the top of the stye door was a man. He was speaking to me, presumably because I was nearest to him. Dressed in a blue suit, wearing a trilby hat, eyes sheltered behind horn-rimmed spectacles, his unsmiling face regarded our endeavours with obvious distaste.

"We're partners. He's the senior man." I nodded towards Jack, who was assiduously forking excrement and straw into a heap.

The "senior man" didn't even stop swinging his fork as he looked up.

"What can I do for you, mister?"

"I," said our visitor, "am from the Ministry of Social Hinsurance, and it has come to our notice that there are certain irregularities being practised here."

"Is that a fact?" said Jack, slopping an extra load on to the barrow. "Such as?"

Producing a notebook, he told us we had not paid certain contributions as required by law. Furthermore, he added severely, correspondence addressed to our firm had gone unanswered.

Jack was beginning to smile. He nodded.

"The law of the land, eh? Well, it's news t' me, gaffer."

"Hignorance of the law," rejoined our bureaucrat severely, "is no excuse."

There was no reply from my companion who resumed his forking, but he favoured me with the suggestion of a wink. Silence descended.

"Have you nothing to say for yourselves?" The tone was peremptory. Jack's smile became angelic, and I knew his temper was at the flash point.

"Yes," he said, "I have."

Suddenly the long fork was balanced against the door. The knife-sharp prongs, the blue-black steel shining where it wasn't dripping with richly excremental fluid, quivered a few inches from our inquisitor's nose. He hastily stepped backwards off the concrete into the mud.

Jack's too precious smile lingered on his face. "Get lost."

The forking was resumed. There was no sign of movement

at the door, and my associate looked up from his work as if mildly surprised.

"You're still there! Look mister, you're trespassin'. This is our property."

"It is my duty..." began the inspector.

"Yes, I know," interrupted my friend, "an' we have work to do. Me an' my mate, knee-deep in muck, work to keep the likes of you in your blue suit bothering the likes of us. Why don't you just do as you're told, mister?"

Suddenly no shadow obscured the watery autumnal sun as it streamed in upon us. Our unwelcome visitor had gone. We had won the skirmish. But, we lost the battle. We paid the fine.

Chapter Thirty-two

Doctors can be called upon to give medical evidence. It can be crucial. But physicians are sometimes unwilling, uncomfortable witnesses. Often they have forgotten their brief training in medical law. And often they haven't kept records as carefully as they might have done.

They may deal competently with emergencies, but forget to make notes of their patient's injuries and the treatment given. Then months later, with uncertain memories to rely on, court appearances can be embarrassing.

But a day in court can be instructing, engrossing, even amusing.

It was a raw morning as we waited in the ancient cloisters of the Assize Court. Around us stood lawyers in dark jackets and striped trousers, counsel for the defence and prosecution of the various cases to be heard that day; barristers from London making their appearance in the provinces, gowned and wigged, clutching their long robes around them, not only for warmth, but to keep their black ceremonial gowns from billowing in the sudden gusts of wind that swept round the great stone pillars of that massive building.

They were familiar with it all – the ceremonial, the techniques of extracting evidence, the idiosyncracies of individual judges. But even they stood there with an air of expectancy, a feeling of "occasion." Then there were groups of men and women, soberly dressed, talking quietly among themselves. For the most part they were to be involved in the coming proceedings – relatives of the accused to be tried that day, witnesses for one side or other. It was a quiet crowd, with uniformed policemen moving about, quietly purposeful.

This was no minor court of law. It was the Court of Assize. Three judges would hold court that day, and for days to come. The cases to be heard were major ones. Today, I was to appear as a medical witness before one of England's great justices. I was apprehensive, yet quivering with anticipation, as I waited. His lordship's reputation had preceded him. He was one of the most formidable of men, I had been told. My every word would be weighed in the balance. Should any be found wanting, incorrect or injudicious, then beware, said counsel in the case, for his lordship would pick up any error like lightning. He did not, I was told, suffer fools, and never mind the "gladly."

The case in which I was involved was nasty enough, and I had been warned that I would be "grilled" by counsel for the defence, but I had, fortunately, kept very full notes from the beginning of the case, and in the previous week I had gone over them a dozen times, checking, and projecting, where I could, the questions I might be asked. As nearly as I could think, I was ready, and had been well briefed by our lawyers. In the end the case was straightforward, and my evidence will never reach the annals of English law, but the first case of the day, also to be heard before the chief judge, was an interesting one, and I sat through it as a spectator.

It involved a burglary in a country house. The thieves had stolen jewels and valuable works of art, but they had been captured, and now stood accused before his lordship.

Order was called, and the court rose while his lordship silently seated himself on the high bench. Prisoners arraigned and the preliminaries completed, witnesses began their procession to the box, nervous, over-awed for the most part; calm and professional in the case of the detectives who had made the arrest. They looked at the defending barristers coolly. Knowing the opposition's game was to get them rattled into making inaccuracies, they refused to become annoyed, even under what seemed to me harsh treatment. After all, like doctors in court, they should deal in matters of fact, so the answers given by the policemen were short, self-assured and accurate.

Then a Mr. Arbinger was called to the stand. He was the game-keeper on the estate, and had given the alarm. He lived in a cottage close to the burgled mansion and his prompt action had alerted the authorities and led to the arrest. In view of the alibi presented by the accused, the time of the break-in must be established as exactly as possible.

Several senior and junior counsel were involved in the case. The policemen had been interrogated with icy exactitude by the senior defence counsel, who now relinquished the questioning of Mr. Arbinger to his junior who, whatever his talents, did not lack for arrogance.

So far the case had proceeded uneventfully. His lordship looked incredibly old, and may well have been, for at that time there was no obligation upon a judge to retire from the bench because of his age. Like an ancient sphinx he sat on the high dais, wrinkled face the colour of old parchment, but with eyes burning with intensity.

Mr. Arbinger was a decent old chap, polite, dressed in his Sunday suit of heavy tweed, the kind of English yeoman who knew his place in this world. He meant to do his duty, come what may. The junior counsel commenced his interrogation. It was at this point I noticed that his lordship, no doubt bored by it all, had gone to sleep.

"Now, my good man," began the barrister condescendingly, "tell the court in your own words how you knew someone was breaking into your master's house."

"Well, it's like this, see," replied the witness, "I'm sittin' at me fire, 'avin me last pipe o' baccy for the night, all peaceable like, sir, an' all of a sudden, Bess – that's me owd dog, sir – Bess begins to stir, an' afore you could say Jack Robinson, she's oop on 'er feet tellin' me there's somebody in the next door."

The barrister's gaze suddenly dropped from the skylight. "No! No! My good man, you cannot say it like that! You must tell the court *in your own words* how *you yourself* realized that someone was breaking into your master's house. Begin again."

"Aw reet sir. Ah'll begin again," said an obviously puzzled 'gamie.' "It's like this, sir. There I am, sittin' at me fire. I don't hear a thing, d'ye see, but Bess – me owd dog, sir, she tells me..."

"Yes! Yes! I know about your dog, man! You must not say it in that way. Tell the court how *you yourself* knew someone was breaking into your master's house! You must *not* say that your dog told you."

The barrister's pomposity had vanished. He was clutching his notes agitatedly and casting apprehensive glances at the sleeping sphinx.

You can push the English yeoman just so far. "Ah'm coomin t'that, young man," said Mr. Arbinger severely. "Ah'm coomin to that. Ah don't see 'ow I can tell ye anythin' wi'out me bringin' me dog into it, for it was me dog as told me. Me dog," he concluded indignantly, "allus tells me everything."

Suddenly I was aware that the sphinx had awakened. Two intense old coal-black eyes set in that incredibly wizened face, were fixed upon that hapless barrister.

"Sir," rasped his lordship, "if you can't do better than that with your witness, why don't you dismiss *him* and *call the dog?*"

Chapter
Thirty-three

Eva Stinson was beautiful in a severe kind of way. She was tall and slender. Her hair, coiled neatly at the back of her neck, only added to the symmetry of her features: the high forehead, straight nose and firm chin. She looked aloof, even cold, but it was the lissome elegance of her walk that made men look at her.

Her father spent his days by the fireside, wheezing away his emphysematous life, taking gulps of air in forlorn attempts to fill his sickly lungs. Her mother, small, bent, looking older than her years and twisted with rheumatism, moving with difficulty and often in pain, did what household work she could. It was hard to believe Eva sprang from such parents.

Perhaps her people had once shown the beauty she portrayed, but that was difficult to imagine now.

Their home, one of a row of back-to-back red brick structures built around the turn of the century, contained two cubby holes called bedrooms, and a space that was livingroom, kitchen and scullery combined. A cold-water tap sprouting out of the bare concrete of the wall overhung a large kitchen sink that was used both for household chores and personal ablutions. Hot water was obtained from a kettle on the kitchen fire. A gas stove, the only modern appliance, was used for cooking.

The few windows looked out upon dingy brick walls. Even the sky was obscured by a conglomeration of gray slated roofs and the dirty chimney pots of neighbouring homes, all much the same as this one. The lavatory, standing in the drab loneliness of the back yard, was shared with the neighbours.

It would be too much to say that my patient made of that squalor a place of light and love. But she kept it scrubbed and spotlessly clean. She wasn't a youngster. She was in her early thirties when I first met her on a visit to her father, whose bronchitis had sent him to bed. She was hanging up washing when I arrived; she left her wash basket in the tiny yard and stood beside me as I examined my patient, pulling the bedclothes up around him when I'd finished. It was obvious that she gave her parents warmth and care, and that they depended on her.

She made a living as a door-to-door saleswoman: lingerie, knick-knacks, that kind of thing. She did some trading in what are called "collectibles" today; little ornamental vases, pieces of pottery, all second-hand. It wasn't much of a living, but it satisfied her, and as she said, she was her own mistress. She was no "dresser." Her clothes were plain, unfashionable, and quite possibly were second-hand.

I often wondered why she wasn't married, but I never asked. There were too many wartime tragedies around us, too many women like this, and I didn't want my curiosity to reopen some old wound. And yet, her face showed a kind of serenity.

The evening surgery was about to begin. The front door had been opened, and I could hear the shuffling of feet in the waiting room. I was leafing through some reports I'd need that night when the insistent ringing of the telephone demanded my attention.

"I'm a friend of Eva Stinson's," said a woman's voice. "If she comes to the surgery could you see her straight away?

It's very urgent.'' Before I could think of a question to ask, the phone at the other end was silent.

Within minutes there was a knock at my office door, and there stood my patient, pale, her face sharp with pain, her fist clenched against her abdomen. One glance was enough to convey the urgency of the situation, and I helped her into the consulting room. She groaned in agony, the sweat standing in clammy beads on her forehead, as I lowered her gently onto the examining couch. It was an acute surgical emergency of some kind, and I asked Janet to join me in consultation. Our patient's temperature was ragingly high, and the merest touch on her abdomen caused acute pain.

"Tell us about it, Miss Stinson."

She looked at us, from one to the other, her lips pressed together. "I had an abortion two days ago. I knew from the beginning it wasn't right. Now I know I'm in terrible trouble. Oh! Dr. Janet, I'm not going to die, am I?'' She clutched Janet's hand, her eyes pleading for reassurance.

We comforted her as best we could. We'd both seen deaths following back-street abortions, and Eva Stinson was dreadfully ill. She had acute, generalized peritonitis or infection of the entire abdominal cavity, and her one hope was skilled, specialized hospital care.

A knitting needle pushed, often blunderingly, past the cervix and into the pregnant womb was the usual method of the local abortionists, whose names I never could discover. Since neither the needle nor the hands that held it were probably very clean, the results of this procedure could be catastrophic. Severe bleeding was only one complication. Pushed too far, the knitting needle could puncture the wall of the uterus, allowing deadly infection to invade the abdominal cavity. The result: acute peritonitis, massive abdominal infection, death. This was the picture that now confronted us.

"You won't tell my parents about this, will you?'' she pleaded as we sent her to the hospital.

Somehow her life was saved, and many weeks later, wan but determined, she was back at work. We heaved a sigh of relief, and asked her to come and talk to us.

She came to the office as we had asked, and Janet talked to her. Usually hospital doctors and nurses could be relied upon to protect the dignity and privacy of their patients. What had been done had been done. Abortion was a police matter, and though most of us would have given a great deal to put a stop to the activities of back-street abortionists, our patients' welfare came first. But in her case somebody had talked, and she was questioned as to her part in an immoral and criminal procedure. Who the questioner was remained uncertain but Miss Stinson's hurt and suspicion were real enough.

Following considerable opposition, a family planning clinic had been established in the city, and my wife urged our patient to attend. Janet was a staff physician at the clinic. Advice on contraception was given without question.

We were not concerned about the morality of someone's sexual behaviour. What concerned us were the catastrophes we had seen following blundering attempts to produce abortion. If Eva Stinson had a lover, possibly some married man, that was her affair. Ours was to see that she was protected. But she did not attend the clinic.

Abortion was a criminal offence, and any doctor involved would be struck from the medical register and imprisoned. We could do nothing for desperate people. Turned away by doctors who were unable, unwilling, or afraid to help, they could only turn to the abortionists.

I was a young man when one morally courageous man defied the law. It took a man of distinction, of unimpeachable reputation, to make a test case, and that man was Dr. Alec Bourne. A London gynaecologist, he decided to carry out a surgical abortion on a young girl, "under the legal age of consent," who had unquestionably become pregnant following rape.

Dr. Bourne invited the police to attend the operation and to arrest him. Bourne was neither imprisoned nor struck from the medical register. It was a brave thing to do at the time. But Dr. Bourne's reputation was unassailable. He had set the stage for a change in the law, a change that came only many years later.

Janet and I did not foresee the wholesale abortion business of today, but we did see tormented women. Legally we could do nothing for them. There were the young, unmarried and desperate. But there were also the married women, often older and in poor health, who faced another pregnancy with despair and sometimes, justifiably, with fear. There were the others, those with heart and other problems, for whom pregnancy could be disastrous. Although abortion was legally permissable in order to save the mother's life, it was sometimes difficult to find a specialist who agreed with the necessity for the operation, or was willing to perform it.

These cases deserved medical and psychological assessment leading to action for or against ending the pregnancy. And that assessment should be based on humane, objective opinion leading to a safe procedure. Women should never have been turned away on a legality or condemned out of hand to seek help from unskilled abortionists.

A year or two had passed since we admitted Eva Stinson to hospital. Still beautiful and composed, still with her swinging, graceful walk, she continued selling things from door to door.

One Saturday night the phone rang. It was a woman's voice. Would one of us go immediately to see Eva Stinson. She was very ill. I lost no time and quickly I climbed the narrow stairs to her bedroom. I even noticed that it was as neat as I would have expected it to be, before my glance fell in utter dismay on to the woman lying almost motionless on the bed.

Deeply jaundiced, she opened her eyes as I lifted her wrist and felt her pulse – a futile gesture if ever there was one.

"There's nothing to be done, doctor. I know this time I'm finished. I should have listened to your wife. I was pregnant again. I took some pills to get rid of it."

"Why didn't you let me know? Send for me sooner?"

There was no reproach in the dull, yellowing eyes that were turned towards me.

"What could you have done?"

It was true. From the beginning we could have done nothing. And now nothing could be done. It was too late. But if we knew what pills she had taken we'd at least know the chemical involved. It was a forlorn hope, but it had to be tried.

"What was in the pills? Who gave them to you? I only want to know what drug was used."

A feeble shake of her head was the only reply. We moved her to hospital. We knew she was dying; she knew it. Perhaps she hadn't had enough money for a second bungling attempt at a surgical abortion. Back-street abortionists didn't come cheaply. So she had taken "pills" – a heavy metal most likely; probably mercury. Her liver was undergoing acute necrosis, literally rotting away.

Mercifully her brain clouded over and semi-consciousness became coma. She died without naming her lover. No one came to see her in her last conscious hours. Her parents, lonely and neglected, lived for a few more years.

She was thirty-five. Society had made Eva Stinson, a very worthwhile person, pay a terrible price for loving someone.

Chapter
Thirty-four

"Could you come down here, doctor? I realize it's very late, but Mr. Calvert is ill, and has gone to his dressing room."

I looked at my watch. It was just after half-past ten, a miserable November night in the early 1950's. My caller was the manager of the local variety theatre, a man who never troubled me unnecessarily.

"What's the matter?" I asked. "Can you give me some idea?"

"When he came in for the first show he wasn't feeling well, so Mrs. Calvert told me. He began to get worse throughout the evening, and he barely managed to get through the second show. The theatre's just about empty now. He's got a fever and he's coughing."

Sensing from past experience that my time would not be wasted, I told the manager I'd be with him shortly. I had answered their emergency calls on a number of occasions and had become a sort of unofficial doctor to the music hall theatre. My patients varied from the young and ambitious, the rising stars, to the old and fallen ones; from the "broke" to the highly successful. They were all interesting and, with a few notable exceptions, fine people. I seldom met disillusionment. Theatricals are a breed of their own, individualists for the most part, retaining, even when old and "over the hill," a zest for their profession. For many of them, money is only an incidental mark of success. Perhaps they seek the end of the rainbow, living for the applause of the audience, and only when that is gone forever will they accept, if not admit, defeat.

Janet, sitting on the hearth rug beside the fire, contentedly doing the day's crossword, looked up at me and smiled. "What was all that about?" she asked. The house was quiet, with little Catriona fast asleep upstairs, and the hearth with its cozy fire beckoned to me; but strength of will prevailed as I donned my raincoat and lifted my emergency bag from the chair beside the telephone.

"I'm off to the theatre to see a Mr. Calvert. He must be a star; he's got a dressing room all to himself!"

"Before you go," said Janet, "can you think of a word beginning with 'h' that signifies exhaustion?" Without hesi-

167

tation I replied 'husband' as I closed the street door behind me.

Who Mr. Calvert was, or what he did, was of little concern to me at that point. The cold, moisture-laden wind was blowing off the river as I drove down Anlaby Road. The neon lights, still ablaze above the theatre door, guided the last of the audience on to the pavement, glistening black and gray under the rain. "John Calvert, America's Master of Mystery," said the lights.

It was just another late night call, something that had to be done before I could return to Janet's company and the warmth of our fireplace. I couldn't have known I was about to enter upon a new dimension in my medical career.

I found the patient, a tall, slim man, sitting by his dressing room table. At that point he did not seem to be any dynamo. But if John Calvert did not catch my eye, his wife did. Anne was a stunner, red-haired, blue-eyed, shapely and beautiful. She greeted me, thanking me for my prompt attention. I smiled at her – that wasn't difficult to do – and then I turned my attention to the patient. He came straight to the point.

"Doc," he said, "I've got pneumonia, and I need a shot of penicillin."

I was a little put out. A medical man's sense of self-worth wasn't helped when *every* Tom, Dick and Harry used the familiar "doc." (Within a few years, and for the next twenty-five, every rancher and farmer for miles around would be calling me "doc," and I came to love the intimacy it meant – but that was later on, and in another culture.) Nor did I like my patients to make their own diagnoses, even if they were sometimes right! Finally, however amicable my relations with Americans had been in the recent world conflagration, I wasn't having any cocksure Yankee telling me how to do my job.

I stared down my Scottish nose at the sufferer. "Mr. Calvert, I'd prefer to make my own diagnosis, if you don't mind. And I do not prescribe penicillin without due cause. Its haphazard use is dangerous."

I made my patient strip to the waist while I examined his chest, first tapping out the various areas to detect the dullness in tone that would indicate underlying consolidation of the lung. So far, so good – nothing. Producing my stethoscope, I listened for the whistles and moist rustling of fluid in the bronchial tubes. Nothing again. The one thing he did have was a raised temperature.

"Probably flu," I said with authority. "I can find no sign of pneumonia. However, till I can check you again and for safety's sake, I intend to put you on sulphonamide." My tone of voice conveyed both certainty and finality. Then, melting under Anne's smiling thanks, I suggested I drive them back to their hotel, and promised to come to see the patient in the morning.

Anne, smiling a little anxiously, opened the door for me the next morning when I arrived, and led me to the patient's bed. I hadn't forgiven him, and was in a mood to be formality itself.

"And," I asked in my best professional manner, "how are you this morning?"

Mr. Calvert eyed me without much enthusiasm. "Not good, doc. This pneumonia's sure getting to me."

"Mr. Calvert," I began, "I told you last night there was no evidence whatsoever of pneumonia..." Silently he raised his hand, uncoiled himself from his bed, walked wearily over to the hand basin, coughed, and spat. He pointed wordlessly to the resulting globule of sputum, thick, bloody, rust red about as sure a sign of pneumonia as a positive X-ray. Silently I observed the phenomenon, then from my 5 foot 7 inches I looked up at his 6 foot 3 inches.

"Doc," he said pleadingly, "now can I have my penicillin?"

He got it, there and then. He'd had pneumonia before, he told me. Doctors, you see, shouldn't begin to examine people until they've asked a few questions, or to quote the textbooks, "taken an adequate history of past as well as present illnesses." This apparently obvious injunction will in the end make for better diagnosis, save time and, sometimes, humiliation. I may have been humbled perhaps, but I laid down the law. He must stay in bed; I'd call every day and arrange for injections of penicillin. I got no further with my lecture.

"You just give me these injections, and leave the rest to me. I'll be at that theatre for the first house tonight." He was pleasant, weary but obdurate. "The show must go on, you know. Tradition, old chap." He even managed a tolerable English accent. "Tradition, that's one of those British strong points. That, and being sure of yourselves. These Britishers, I told Anne last night after you'd gone – boy, when they lay it on the line you sure better listen."

Reflectively, I studied my patient, but his eyes were guileless. "You see," he went on, "I'm the whole show. I own it. Without me there is no show. I'd have to refund tickets. The theatre's fully booked for the week. My people, the chorus and all the rest, would be at a loose end. I've got to make it. You've got to help me."

I owed it to him. That night after the evening surgery, and every night for the rest of the week, I sat in the wings of the theatre. John Calvert had a confirmed pneumonia. Only a few years before, it might have killed him. Now, with the help of penicillin he fought it, against all advice perhaps, but he carried on with his show, two houses each night. Once or twice I thought he might collapse, but he always pulled himself together and, smiling, faced the audiences.

During the half-time break I gave him his prescribed shot of penicillin and checked his heart and chest. Then, with Anne beside me when she wasn't acting as John's charming assistant on stage, I sat in the wings, watching. It was a clever show, and if I learned a few secrets I was sworn never to reveal them. I have never violated that confidence.

He occupied the stage alone for most of the evening. He performed magic, told people their ages, asked them secretly to select a number, multiply it by any other number and then astounded them by giving the correct answer. He had a small Ceylonese elephant which he made disappear before the audiences' eyes. There was a chorus line of pretty, smiling girls. I enjoyed watching them and so did the elephant. That chained rear leg of his began to swing a little higher as the chorus line tripped lightly on to the stage, smilingly in line. When they danced off the stage, still smiling, they had to pass behind him and the last two girls hopped a little higher and a little faster than the rest. He wasn't one of your friendly elephants.

But what most intrigued me was Calvert's skill as a stage hypnotist. At first I thought he must pay people to behave as they did, patting imaginary dogs, swimming madly for an imaginery shore, even developing tremendous, if temporary strength. But he appealed to the audience for volunteers and they responded in droves, some of them my own patients. Two things became obvious to me, John's rapid recovery, and the authenticity of his "hypnotic powers."

Later I found out more about him. Stage hypnotist he may have been, but his method of hypnosis is referred to in *Le Cron's Experimental Hypnosis*, an authoritative and internationally known textbook. Hypnotist, actor, stuntman, flyer, film producer, adventurer, John Calvert was all of these. He once sailed across the Pacific single-handed in a small yacht, and even when picked up adrift with his craft dismasted his resolution was undimmed. He simply believed that willpower could give a man the strength of many.

The Calverts were our guests for a few days of convalescence, bringing with them a little fawn they had found in the African bush, standing beside its dead mother. Bambi was a beautiful thing, tame and gentle. John had a giant memory and my brother, a specialist in psychiatry, also a house guest, was intrigued by his ability to memorize and calculate with almost computer-like rapidity.

It was John's sense of fun that most endeared him to us. Catriona was enchanted as he produced rabbits and endless handkerchiefs from nowhere and made them vanish just as quickly. But perhaps the crowning accomplishment of his local appearance came on that last Saturday night.

He had arranged a reception for local dignitaries in the bar at the back of the theatre, just after the show. He was courtesy personified, but finally said, "Gentlemen, I must go – if you will place your last orders." His guests turned as one to the bar, and John moved down the line shaking hands with each man in turn. I had watched him as, Bambi beside him, he moved along the line.

"I really must go now," he said, "but could somebody tell me the time?"

Twenty-eight men elevated their wrists and twenty-eight voices cried "My watch! It's gone." The confusion was so great they even forgot their beer, something very unusual for Yorkshiremen!

"Well," said John, "I wonder if your watch might be here," and from his pocket produced twenty-eight watches all neatly strung together by their straps.

On that last Saturday night Janet came to see the show. After the show, in the dressing room with Anne as a beaming hostess, hypnosis was the topic of interest.

"John," I laughed, "that show of yours is the cleverest piece of fakery I've ever seen."

"Not fakery, doc. That's a nasty word. It may be illusion, deception perhaps, but the magician takes advantage of what the audience perceives. In a sense I suppose it's fakery but there's nothing of the fake in hypnosis. As a doctor, you should be taking an interest in it." He looked at me and smiled as I registered my doubts. "It's quackery to you doctors, isn't it?"

171

"Well, John, for one thing, I don't suppose it has many medical uses."

Calvert looked at me. "Have you read anything about it?"

I had to confess that my knowledge of the subject was infinitesimal even if my scepticism was considerable. With Anne and Janet listening, he said, "Are you open-minded enough to try it?"

I assented, but Janet challenged him. "I don't believe a word of it, and besides," she laughed, "you'll never put *him* under in a million years." A few minutes later I drifted out of a beautiful trance to Janet's alarmed cries of "Oh! Bring him round, please bring him round!"

Calvert looked at me. "Convinced?" he asked. I nodded, still a little bewildered. He went on, "Before I leave here, I'm going to teach you the techniques of hypnosis. It's perfectly safe in the right hands, and the benefits to your patients will be well worth it – almost endless as you'll discover. Here am I, a stage hypnotist using it just to entertain, and there is your profession refusing even to acknowledge it. Why?"

"John, I don't know. Perhaps it's because my profession wants proof, statistics, something in black and white. After all, patients rely on doctors a great deal, John, not to push unproven cures."

"There's nothing unproven about hypnosis, doc. It's as old as the hills. Study the subject and then you'll find it fascinating."

To the technical skills I had learned over the years I was about to add the art of medical hypnosis. Medically speaking, it was barely respectable. Today it is an accepted part of medical practice, and an important aspect of academic and clinical psychology.

As for myself, hypnosis in its medical application has enriched my work and brought help to many of my patients. I have taught its use to students and doctors from New Zealand to Canada, used it experimentally in university hospitals. It has relieved pain, diminished tension and made childbirth a time of joy, not apprehension.

And all this because one night I missed a diagnosis!

Chapter
Thirty-five

Hypnosis has never been explained. It can only be defined. We do not know how it works. As good a definition as any is that it is a physiological state sometimes, but by no means always, resembling sleep, during which the subject experiences an "increased degree of suggestibility," an increased willingness to accept suggestion.

We have probably all, at one time or another, experienced hypnosis, for it is a natural phenomenon. Sitting by the sea listening to the cadence of the waves washing on to the sands; listening to rhythmic, monotonous sounds, musical or otherwise; driving on a long straight road, perhaps into the sun; all these experiences can produce a state of drowsy wakefulness that verges on a light hypnotic trance. Any disturbance usually dispels the trance.

What makes hypnosis interesting is our ability to achieve trances under the guidance of a hypnotist, as well as to use the phenomenon to achieve some objective. In medical practice, the objective is improved health, mental or physical, and this is what Calvert impressed upon me. In a few days he taught me the basic techniques I might use to induce a "hypnotic trance." With my medical background I would soon learn the theory and its application to medicine. Still sceptical and unsure of myself, I was nonetheless determined to use my new skill when the right opportunity presented itself. I would not have long to wait.

In the meantime I read a great deal. Hypnosis has been used for thousands of years. The chanting of the Druids, millenia ago, round their mist-enfolded temples, could produce "the druidic sleep," during which time sense became distorted and the subjects believed that aeons of time had passed. It has been suggested that some of our ancient mythology originated here. The priest physicians of ancient Egypt were skilled practitioners. American Indian medicine men knew of its uses and use it today in some places, just as do the fakirs, their counterparts in India.

In more modern times it was adopted by doctors as a medical skill. Hypnotism is still sometimes called mesmerism, after Franz Mesmer (1733–1815), who believed there was a force called animal magnetism which pervaded the universe, and rested in himself, giving him great influence over others. He was prominent, indeed, distinguished. Much of his work was original and had scientific validity, but his enshrouding it in mysticism drew upon him the suspicion of the scientific world of his time. A distinguished group, including Benjamin Franklin, concluded that his discoveries were physiological, not mystical, and mesmerism, brought into prominence by Mesmer, was cast into oblivion and disrepute. It was to remain there for over a hundred years.

James Esdaile, an Edinburgh graduate, worked as a surgeon in India in the early nineteenth century. Surgery was a brutal business. Operations were often death warrants. Lister had not yet introduced antisepsis, and operating rooms were filthy. Surgeons worked in old frock coats encrusted with blood from previous operations. Discarded limbs were thrown into a box in the corner of the room, to join the others already there from previous amputations.

Anaesthetics were unknown. Patients were rendered almost comatose by rum and held down by brawny friends while surgeons worked, and the death rate from primary shock and secondary infection was awful. This was the scene in all the great university hospitals of Europe until the middle of the nineteenth century.

Intrigued by the trances he had seen induced by fakirs, Esdaile saw the medical possibilities for hypnosis, among them its potential to render patients unconscious during surgery. He carried out hundreds of operations using hypnosis and his patients had a far lower mortality rate than was being recorded in the best European medical schools. His use of hypnosis greatly reduced the incidence of surgical shock.

Elated, he presented his statistics to the *Edinburgh Medical Journal*. His paper was rejected. He was called a charlatan. Embittered, he returned to India. Thereafter every operation he carried out under hypnosis was witnessed by a magistrate and an officer of the nearest British garrison. His reward continued to be rejection by his Scottish fellow physicians, but the Bengal government was more open-minded: it built a "mesmeric hospital" for this remarkable man.

Only forty years ago hypnotherapy was the subject of scepticism, politely raised eyebrows, or ribald laughter. Today the International Society for Research in Hypnosis is a forum for medical scientists of all kinds. Medical hypnosis has achieved respectability.

By 1950 I had become a reasonably competent G.P. obstetrician. I was considered "safe" by the midwives and my colleagues, who sometimes trusted me to look after their patients and, once or twice, their wives. Some men were brilliant, but I was happy to be "safe." I was accustomed to being on call for the local midwives in cases of emergency.

Most babies were delivered at home, some in private nursing homes, but in the main, only complicated cases were delivered in hospital. Physicians like myself, with an interest in obstetrics, and the local midwives, carried out most routine deliveries. In cases where the baby refused to arrive and needed delivering to a hard world by obstetrical forceps, there was seldom any question of being admitted to hospital. We doctors on "the district obstetrical list" would respond to urgent calls, probably administer a general anaesthetic (for often there was no time to wait for an anaesthetist to get out of bed, dress and drive half-way across town) and then apply forceps. Little hearts can stop beating very quickly when the foetus is distressed. With Janet, a well-trained anaesthetist, to back me up, I was one of the lucky ones.

This system of "domiciliary deliveries" was claimed at the time to be one of the best in the world. Admittedly, when the occasional dire emergency did occur we could call on the flying squad from the nearest obstetrical hospital; nevertheless things could go wrong with frightening speed and the doctor on the spot had to face his responsibilities. Fortunately in most cases there are no complications.

It was a few weeks after the Calverts' visit that I was called to a nursing home in a nearby village. The doctor was out of town and a Mrs. Mainprize, who had just had a baby, seemed to be having a lot of discomfort. Would I come at once?

Where obstetrical calls were concerned I didn't believe in wasting time, and within half an hour I was at the nursing home. It was a cheerful, spotless place, and the midwife who owned it knew her business. For a normal, trouble-free delivery I could think of no better place. Mrs. Mainprize, however, wasn't having a trouble-free time. She had delivered a baby, which, when I arrived, was blissfully snoozing, all crinkled and rather second-hand looking, like many newborn babes. But a quick examination of the mother convinced me that there was, much to matron's consternation, another one to come.

Mrs. Mainprize was twenty-five, a pretty, wispy little thing, and this was her second pregnancy. She had lost her first child at birth two years ago, and for the past month her blood pressure had been higher than normal, though she showed none of the danger signs often associated with this condition. At the same time, this information didn't please me. She had delivered the first of the twins several hours before. She had had little sleep the previous night. I was a stranger to her and quite excusably, she was apprehensive. With insufficient sleep and in discomfort from some cause unknown to her, she was approaching the point of exhaustion. If ever there was a combination of factors almost guaranteed to produce trouble in obstetrics, this was it.

I reassured her, explaining that she should deliver the second baby quite easily; that she must rest and I would help her. Confidence in the doctor, rapport between obstetrician and patient are of great importance. I did not feel I had established either. Why should she, with her first baby lost only a year or so before, trust a strange young man now?

Finishing my examination, I told her as persuasively as I could that she'd be fine, and followed the matron into the corridor.

"Has she had any drugs at all?"

"Well," said matron, "Dr. Beaton always gives 100 mg of demerol once during labour as long as the membranes are intact, and I did that."

"How long ago?"

"It's at least four hours now, sir."

The effects of the drug would soon be over. The trouble is that drugs like demerol depress the infant's capacity to breathe properly, and if there's one thing these little characters need, it's to breathe the moment they arrive.

I have sometimes advocated that the demerol could be given more usefully and a good deal more safely, to expectant fathers. It's an excellent sedative. However, some years ago in the course of my studies I learned of a much smarter hypnotist than myself. Without the requisite diploma, this medicine man in the jungles of the Amazon simplifies and renders safer the whole procedure. No drugs: he simply transfers the mother's labour pains to the father. The mother blissfully sleeps through it all, while dad in his loin cloth rolls on the ground. My Amazonian colleague really *is* an artist.

"We'll wait," I said to matron, "the less of the stuff the better. But she does need rest." We tried a mild sedative: it was useless. The girl was tearful and increasingly restless. I phoned Dr. Gavin Brown. Gavin, in his early sixties, was the senior obstetrician in the city. He was a distinguished consultant, but he was a G.P.'s specialist. Quietly, he listened to my story.

"Listen," he said. 'I'm just going to the hospital to do an emergency Caesar. How worried are you?"

"I'm not so much worried, Gavin, as suspicious. She's too tired out for my liking."

"Is she bleeding?"

"A bit of a trickle at times."

"What about the baby?"

"The foetal heart has never altered, quite regular. It's her exhaustion I don't like and her contractions just don't do a thing." I really wanted just his advice, but it was important. So I gave her one more injection of demerol – a decreased dose – in the hope that she would have less pain and more rest. Gavin said he'd ring me back sometime after his operation, and come if necessary. "Their facilities are good," he said as he rang off.

The demerol, like the sedative, was useless. I was loth to give her anything else and yet her apprehension and exhaustion seemed to be increasing. It was then, for the first time, that I decided to try hypnosis. By now Mrs. Mainprize seemed to have a little confidence in me – an important factor favouring success. I had told her I wouldn't leave her until the baby arrived, and as I sat by her bedside I explained what medical hypnosis was all about, "debunking" the popular mythology.

Telling her it was not one person's dominance over another, but a "team effort" requiring mutual confidence, I asked her if she'd agree to try it. I explained that she would go to sleep for just as long as she herself wanted to, that her mind would be alert and her body rested. She could awaken any time she needed or wanted to, and she would hear every word I said. Hypnosis, I explained, was very normal, and best results were obtained when dealing with normal, intelligent people. What she needed now, I said, was rest, and if we worked together, she could get it.

For several years I had been a student of Dr. Grantly Dick Read's methods of natural childbirth. His book had opened a new world of practice for me, for I saw my patients face childbirth confidently. His methods, however, required time for preparation, and with Mrs. Mainprize I had to achieve results immediately. Her state of mind and her weariness, I felt convinced, could speedily take her on the high road to real trouble, either shock or haemorrhage, both catastrophic events.

I began the simple method of "trance induction" John Calvert had taught me. Astoundingly, it worked. Her restlessness subsided. Soon she was composed, calm, and to the superficial observer, asleep. Testing the depth of her trance,I told her that she was now so relaxed that however much she wanted to, she would be unable to open her eyes. The eyelids flickered and struggled but remained closed, and I said with self-assurance I only half felt, "See! You've done it – totally relaxed." For the first time that morning she smiled in her "sleep" and slowly said she was drifting deeper. Soon I could lift her hand and let it fall, relaxed and limp, on to the bedclothes. She would waken after a time, quite refreshed, I told her, and I sat by her bedside.

An hour passed. Breathing softly, my patient lay apparently asleep. A second hour went by, by which time somebody needed to relax *me*.

"Heavens," I thought, "what if I can't waken her!" I was a victim of all the mythology myself. *"Patient hypnotized, Stays in trance for seven days. Hypnotist unable to rouse her."* I could just see the headlines. "Where," I thought feverishly, "is John Calvert?"

Then, I thought, she may just be asleep. The demerol finally worked, and it's all a piece of nonsense, the whole business. But when I spoke to her, that dreamy voice I later came to recognize as belonging to the hypnotic state assured me she was feeling better.

Soon after that she wakened, told me she felt fine, just as I said she would, and that she believed she was going to get on with the business of having her baby. Within fifteen minutes she had produced her second little one, and was beamingly, if rather surprisedly, surveying them, one in each arm, when a nurse arrived and said there was a call for me.

"I hear ye don't need me any more," said Dr. Brown cheerfully.

"That's right, Gavin, no trouble at all."

"Did you have to do anything?"

"No, nothing," I replied airily, "except relax her by hypnosis." There was a pause at the other end of the line.

"What was that you said?"

"I hypnotized her."

"I thought that was what you said. I'll have to hear more

about this." said my friend. continuing with. "Ah. well. I've often said there's a bit of the witch doctor in most of us," and rang off before I could think of anything to say in reply.

But I had learned the real value of hypnotherapy in one case. I subsequently was to confirm it in many more.

Chapter Thirty-six

We should never deny patients their pain. That is a lesson I have learned over the years. sometimes the hard way.

Pain can be transient and trifling. It can be apparently trivial. yet if continued. ominous. It can be very severe. yet of a passing. simple nature. It can appear without any apparent cause. and go away as mysteriously as it arrived. It can increase in intensity and eventually indicate some underlying lesion. Pain can burn. bore. ache. throb. prick like needles. possibly even itch. It can travel. originating in some focus of inflammation or disease in one part of the body. and be transferred along nerves to cause hurt elsewhere. It can be deep or superficial. acute. subacute or chronic. Pain can be the physical ache of disease or the mental suffering of grief or depression. Its variations seem almost endless.

Some people suffer from pain more than others. We doctors talk about patients having a low or high threshold of tolerance to pain. and this tolerance can be influenced by exhaustion. cold. heat. lack of sleep. climate and perhaps even our cultural background. Perhaps. instead of talking about patients' threshold to pain. we should discuss physicians' low or high understanding of it. for some doctors seem to feel. to know. the depth of their patients' pain and to understand what it is doing to them. Many very competent physicians. on the other hand. remain indifferent to. or unfeeling about the hurt they see reflected in people's faces.

Some things are certain. Pain is immeasurable. It is real only to the sufferer. and only the sufferer can describe it. say how it begins, what seems to cause it, what aggravates it or eases it, and how it affects him or her. Its victims are lucky if they have doctors who will listen, question, and observe first – before they examine, investigate, diagnose and treat, not only the complaint of pain, the symptom, but its cause. For pain and its causes form an endless and fascinating challenge to the physician.

It is not only a diagnostic challenge in today's world of science, where we can work wonders in many illnesses considered untreatable a few decades ago; it is a challenge to the physician as an artist, for we still should speak of the "art and science of medicine." To reassure in cases of simple pain, to treat it in serious cases, to comfort, to give support, happily sometimes to give hope: these are skills for the doctor who is privileged as an artist, as well as a scientist, to care for sick people.

I had delivered Mrs. Bertha Ayres of two of her three children, now three and four years of age, respectively. Mrs. Ayres was a handsome woman in her middle thirties, statuesque rather than beautiful, and she carried herself well, with dignity and self-assurance. Tall for a Yorkshirewoman, a naturally graceful walker, she was slim, inexpensively dressed in excellent taste, and if she was aware of her appearance, she never showed it. Her husband, a factory foreman, was a decent, forbearing kind of chap with little to say for himself, and I often used to think that his wife was the brains and backbone of the family. Perhaps she was bored with the hum-drum existence of a housewife as she saw it. Despite her lack of education beyond grade school she had supervised a number of women at work before she married. She was an intelligent, determined woman, even rather a formidable one.

Sometimes I thought she didn't have too much time for men. If Janet was out of the office she'd go away and come back when she was available. She quite obviously regarded me as a second best and yet, knowing that Janet seldom delivered babies, she tolerated me when she was pregnant. Even so, on the two occasions when I had officiated at the arrival of her offspring, I was told on the second day that I needn't trouble to come back. Nurse would handle the rest.

This dismissal amused Nurse McGrath to no end. "Never mind, doctor, you can't win them all! Off with you now! Sure and I don't know how I'll manage without you, but I'll just have to try."

In eight years Mrs. Ayres had called at the office on only

a few occasions. Usually it was to seek advice about the kiddies. Very decidedly she was *not* one of our "regulars." So one Monday morning when I opened the waiting-room door and called for my first victim of the day I was rather surprised to see her seated nearest to the door.

"Good morning, Mrs. Ayres."

With neither embarrassment nor awkwardness she replied, polite but unsmiling, "I'm waiting to see Dr. Janet, if you please." It was no problem to take the next in line, one Mr. Stanley Nettlebed, give him his monthly "sick certificate" for his chronic emphysema, then Mrs. Ada Tyler for her sleeping pills, and so on down the unchallenging line of a routine Monday morning "surgery."

Mrs. Ayres vanished from my mind until there was a knock on my office door, followed by the appearance of Janet in the doorway.

"Could you spare a moment?" she asked.

Handing a grinning Joe Anstey his "final note" clearing him to return to work, I sauntered after Janet. Her office reflected her personality. In place of my official certificates on the wall she had paintings, and since she herself was rather decorative it was always pleasing to visit her. On this particular morning she was in no mood for idle pleasantries. Mrs. Ayres was sitting in a chair, stripped to the waist, a thermometer in her mouth.

Silently Janet extracted the thermometer and presented it for my inspection. Ninety-nine point two – just above normal; usually I'd have said nothing much to worry about. Janet, on the other hand, wasn't the type to fuss over trifles, so I waited.

"Ninety-nine point two, right?" she asked.

"Yes," I nodded, and Janet went on, "I've checked it twice."

"What's the story?" I asked, still puzzled.

My wife looked at her patient, and began. "I've talked to Mrs. Ayres, and I've told her I want a specialist's opinion. I've told her of the several possibilities I see, and I think we understand one another. Would you agree?" she concluded, looking at her patient, who nodded. Janet continued. "She's had a pain in her neck for just over a week. She's put up with it till now. It's a throbbing, boring pain and it's got so much worse that she could hardly wait until this morning. She just didn't want to bother us at the weekend. Now I'd like you to examine her head and neck."

I began my examination. Her neck movements were guarded

rather than stiff. Any attempt to move the neck caused hurt. That was all I could find. There was some generalized muscle tenderness to the touch, but that's common enough. I looked at my wife. "Palpate the vertebrae one by one," she commanded. That was done, and I could see that our visitor was in some discomfort, but it was only when Janet carefully and firmly put a finger tip on one focal spot that Mrs. Ayres obviously flinched.

"You'd say that was focally tender, wouldn't you?" asked Janet, and in response to my nodded agreement, she went on, "I want this X-rayed – today."

After 1948 and for a decade to come that remark was easier made than fulfilled. With the arrival of the National Health Service, came the officially decreed termination of general practitioners from any participation in hospital work. No doubt many G.P.'s did not want such an involvement, but how does a doctor keep up to date without it? Young physicians looked to the N.H.S. for improvement in the doctor's ability to provide good care, not to see ourselves relegated to giving basic care in what we felt were inadequate conditions. G.P.'s simply could not order X-rays "that day." Only specialists could do that, and to see a specialist one required an appointment. That took time, except in cases of emergency. If the consultant thought an X-ray or laboratory work was necessary he would order it. We family doctors had no such authority. Fortunately in many places G.P.'s and specialists had reasonable working arrangements and in Hull we all got on well together. In that tightly knit medical community we managed to circumvent the already emerging bureaucracy's authoritarianism. I bade Mrs. Ayres a good morning and crossed the corridor to the cubbyhole we called our pharmacy, knowing I'd very shortly have company.

"Well," I asked when Janet appeared, "what on earth was all that about?" I was still puzzled by her obvious sense of urgency.

"What do you think she's got?" Janet asked.

"At this point, I couldn't even hazard a guess. I will agree about getting the X-ray though – but what it might be is beyond me."

"It's an osteomyelitis of the atlas," said my wife.

I stared at her, taken aback by the positive precision of her diagnosis.

"Darling," I protested, "that's a tremendously rare disease! I've never seen a case."

"I know," said Janet grimly, "but I have, and the story, the position, the description of the pain, it's just the same. I want that X-ray, and I want it today."

"You'll have to phone one of the consultants, see if you can persuade somebody to fit her in somehow in one of the outpatient clinics. Getting an X-ray today for a sore neck, don't you think it's going to be difficult?"

"I'll phone Bob Armstrong," said my better half, "he's always cooperative."

Dr. Armstrong was an excellent specialist. We had frequently sought his opinion, and I think it is worth saying that he was both an idealist and a rebel. He was a complex man, burning with anger when he felt that political or bureaucratic obstruction stood in the way of better care. He was, however, a rather rigid, dogmatic man, seeing life very much in terms of black and white. In his forties, he was approaching the peak, perhaps, of his skill.

When Janet phoned him, he agreed to see Mrs. Ayres that day, although he gave Janet a dissertation on the statistical rarity of osteomyelitis of the atlas, which in plain English means an abscess of the bone that mainly supports one's skull. It is a rare but deadly disease, if untreated.

"Statistically, Janet, do you know how rare this is?" and on he went at some length. Statistics, however useful to the statistician, (the community health scientist dealing in impersonal numbers), are not a great help to the general practitioner seeing in the office a fellow human being in trouble. There, they are no substitute for thinking power, clinical acumen or experience.

The X-ray report was negative. Dr. Armstrong thought Mrs. Ayres was a bit hostile, uncooperative. There was no sign on the film of any abscess and Bob's letter, brief and to the point, said so. The inference was that women fussed about things, and women doctors fussed a bit more than their male colleagues. He was very definite. There was no visible X-ray abnormality. The laboratory tests were negative. Therefore nothing was amiss. He questioned if her pain could be as severe as she said it was. It was probably psychological. Did she get on well with her husband?

Janet, unconvinced, kept a close watch on her, treating the pain unsuccessfully with a series of increasingly powerful drugs. Then she called me to see Mrs. Ayres again. The change in her appearance was striking, her colour sallow, the fever persistent. The pain had suddenly become devastating. That strong woman was broken. Tears coursed down her cheeks and low moans of agony broke from her lips.

"She is going to be admitted to hospital for observation immediately," said my wife, reaching for the phone in the privacy of my office while Mrs. Ayres waited next door, "and if Dr. Armstrong won't admit her I'll find somebody who will."

Our colleague angrily protested that he saw no reason for further waste of his time. The woman had been X-rayed only days before.

"Then X-ray again, doctor," demanded my partner.

Reluctantly the surgeon said he'd see Mrs. Ayres if she attended the clinic that afternoon.

"We can't wait that long," argued Janet relentlessly, "She must be seen at once. She must be brought to you by ambulance, and *now*."

The tug-of-war continued, but fuming, our colleague agreed to consider our patient for admission. In a few hours the phone rang. "Your patient has been admitted as an emergency," said a very changed voice at the end of the line. "You were right, Janet. I'm desperately sorry. It *is* an osteomyelitis of the atlas. I'm afraid she's terribly ill. The new X-ray film shows it clearly. We'll do all we possibly can."

Janet listened in silence, then coldly asked, "May I ask if she'll live?"

"I don't know. We'll do all we can. I can't say how utterly sorry I am."

Janet's clinical instinct, her experience of a similar case years before, her awareness of Mrs. Ayres' strength of personality, her opinion as a family doctor, should have been listened to. Since the tests showed no abnormalities, therefore there were none: it is faulty, dangerous logic in the face of continuing symptoms.

That same logic denied the patient her pain – and her chance of life. She died within two weeks.

Such cases, fortunately, are rare. Laboratory investigations are of immense help to the investigator. They are not, however, infallible. A case like this holds lessons for all of us. We retained our trust in Dr. Armstrong, and he always justified it. All doctors have made mistakes and no one is infallible. In that one tragic case a good surgeon had allowed his prejudices to cloud his thinking, his faith in tests, technology and statistics to overwhelm his clinical judgement, and he never forgave himself.

What one of us physicians cannot say, "There, but for the grace of God, go I."

Chapter
Thirty-seven

"A substantial amount of money is involved, doctor." Mr. Friggett, senior member of the firm of Liggett, Liggett and Friggett, sat across the desk from me. The senior partners had long since departed this mortal soil, but Mr. Friggett's name was a household word in many east Yorkshire homes. Pompous and middle-aged, he peered over his specs at me, his hands, fingertip to fingertip, held in front of his nose.

I had been invited to appear at the firm's offices at my convenience. It was a matter of importance, involving a will. It was believed I could help in the case.

"A large sum of money! How large?" I asked. It seemed a fair opening question.

"A quarter of a million pounds, sir."

"Eh!"

A thousand pounds was "a substantial amount of money" to me. A quarter of a million was uncountable riches. Englishmen have a gift for understatement, Yorkshiremen more so than most. Their interest in money, or "brass," as the stuff is disrespectfully called in that part of the world, is a matter of record, and Mr. Friggett's calmness in the face of the facts only kindled my interest.

"Mrs. Hackaway, doctor. You *do* recall the name?"

Indeed I did. She wasn't a patient of mine, but when one of my colleagues, Doug Hearne, was ill, I took over his practice, including Mrs. Hackaway – or perhaps she took me over. I wouldn't say she had brightened my days exactly, but she had certainly enlivened them.

"Yes, indeed. What exactly is involved?"

"Mrs. Hackaway, as you now know, was a wealthy woman. Her original will had placed all her assets at the disposal of her relatives. Indeed it had been taken for granted that the entire estate would be so distributed. One month prior to her death, sir, she changed her will. I might say," he added a little petulantly, "she did not come to this firm. We had acted as solicitors for the late Albert Hackaway for many years. Fortunately," brightening up a little, "her action at that time left us free to act for the Hackaway family in its present dilemma."

"Mr. Friggett," I asked, "what has all this to do with me?"

Mr. Friggett did not take kindly to interruptions. "I will come to the point in due course, if I may," he went on, pulling a file towards him, and looking at me primly. "In changing her will, she excluded her family. It is now this firm's responsibility, on behalf of the family, to contest the second will."

"I see!"

"You, doctor, looked after Mrs. Hackaway for some two months, am I not right?"

"Yes, but I didn't look after her when she died. Dr. Hearne was back at work by then."

"We are aware of that, sir. You, I believe, were in attendance on Mrs. Hackaway from the fifth of July to the first of September of last year. Is that not correct?"

"Yes, I suppose it would be. I couldn't be sure of the dates."

"We, sir, *are* sure. The record is here, together with your account and dates of attendance. You saw Mrs. Hackaway every week, and on certain occasions, twice a week. Would you care to peruse our memoranda?"

No, I wouldn't, and I was becoming out of patience with Mr. Friggett, too. I hadn't kept records of my visits. The records of the case were inside my skull. It began to dawn on me that somebody *had* been keeping records, and if there's one thing a doctor needs when he's called to give evidence in court, it's exact notes. In the absence of not just meticulous records, but of any records at all, I had better be careful with this legal gentleman.

"Mr. Friggett," I said cautiously. "I'm not sure what you want of me, but I cannot vouch for the number of times I saw Mrs. Hackaway. I was helping a sick friend, and I was very busy."

"Quite. Quite, doctor. We realize this. However, you saw Mrs. Hackaway on the fifteenth of August of last year."

"Possibly I did."

"But you did, sir, I assure you. Mrs. Bealing, Mrs. Hackaway's employee and companion for many years, is prepared to testify to that effect."

"All right, I'll accept that. What about it?"

"On the seventeenth of August, doctor, two days after your visit, Mrs. Hackaway changed the terms of her will."

Wondering what on earth was coming next, I waited. Was I on the verge of a law suit accusing me of coercing this old lady to change her will in favour of – whom? I was most uneasy. Doctors are very influential people in cases of this sort.

Mrs. Hackaway was eighty-three. She was tall, withered, raw-boned, and bald. She had a selection of wigs of various shades of orange and red. She wore them tilted over her right eye, and that eye was as wicked as the left one, and just as wandering. For a woman of her mature years, to put it mildly, she had an eye for the men, especially, I had found, for me.

She had brazenly displayed her ancient charms to me on a number of occasions, and had invited me to share the delights of her favours on many more. At these times I would hastily close my medical bag and head for the door. Getting away from a surprisingly strong individual like Mrs. Hackaway while carrying a medical bag and protecting one's vital areas is not easy. Her companion, Mrs. Bealing, fortunately was always close at hand and an anguished call for help would always fetch her.

I remembered Mrs. Hackaway all right. It would be difficult to forget her. I sat and sweated.

"On the seventeenth of August she was seen by a solicitor of this city," sniffed Mr. Friggett, "and named another beneficiary as the recipient of her entire estate."

"Indeed?" I gulped.

"Yes," said Mr. Friggett severely. "The entire estate, to the extent of two hundred and eighty thousand pounds, nineteen shillings and tenpence to be exact, has been left to the North Ayeoby Home for Indigent Cats."

I don't think Mr. Friggett saw much to laugh at in this life, and my mirth did not amuse him. He waited with cold courtesy until I had composed myself.

"Mr. Friggett," I said finally. "What on earth has this to do with me? I never discussed her will with her!"

"I daresay this is true," said Friggett bleakly. He was a lawyer to the bone: he wasn't going to compromise himself by accepting my statement. "But you saw her two days prior to the will being changed, did you not?"

"I've already agreed to that."

"It will be our argument in contesting her most recent will, that on the seventeenth of August, Mrs. Hackaway was *non compos mentis*, doctor – in other words, of unsound mind."

"Yes?"

"We believe you could give evidence that would support that argument."

Memories of that recurrent dash to the door, of desperate attempts to retain my footing at the side of the bed, overwhelmed me.

"Not on your life, Mr. Friggett. I'm not going near any court. Besides, I couldn't say she was *non compos mentis*. She was just an old rascal with advanced sexual appetites."

"Quite." He went back to his file again. "Mrs. Bealing is prepared to state in court that on one occasion after she had, ah – um – extricated you from Mrs. Hackaway's advances, you stated to her as you left the house that her employer was mad as a hatter. If you wish, doctor, I can quote from her statement. It would be difficult under the circumstances to deny the substance of your remarks in court, would it not?"

"I won't testify!"

"Of course, doctor. Have it your own way. If the facts as I have stated are correct, then you can appear as an expert witness, summoned, at, of course, an appropriate fee. On the other hand," he went on blandly, "we can subpoena you to attend. In which case, although the evidence we produce will materially be the same, the fee will be that allowed by the state, considerably less, I do believe." Up went the hands again, fingertip to fingertip. I knew I was done for, and I capitulated.

The tactics of attack were laid before me. Learned counsel, the eminent London barrister, Mr. Trublood-Plews, Q.C., would be coming up from "the City" next week to meet the relevant witnesses. Dr. Hearne had agreed to appear in court, and Mr. Trublood-Plews would have a preliminary meeting with Doug Hearne and myself. Since we were involved in the case under similar circumstances, he would see us together. The case would be heard at the forthcoming Market Weighton Assizes.

The eminent barrister's appearance was as distinguished as

his record. He was a gentleman, courteous, unhurried, and perceptive. He took some time to explain matters to us. Mrs. Hackaway had no immediate relatives. The family consisted of nieces and nephews, which made Mr. Trublood-Plews all the more anxious to consolidate his case. He listened to my story without a smile, nodding occasionally and making notes, and then he turned to Doug.

"And now," he said, "it is, as you can see, imperative that we establish as fact, that at the time of signing the most recent will, Mrs. Hackaway was mentally unfit to make such a decision. If we can prove this to the satisfaction of his lordship, the previous will will be validated, the contested will invalidated, and our clients will have won the day. His lordship," he added, naming a distinguished Assize judge, "is not an easy man to convince, and I should like to make our case a very strong one."

Doug remained silent, pondering the matter.

"You see," went on Mr. Trublood-Plews encouragingly, and without the trace of a smile, "while Mrs. Hackaway's behaviour with your colleague here was, shall we say, bizarre, it was not necessarily that of a person of unsound mind. His lordship," he added, "is of advanced years himself, and I understand he still has an eye for a pretty woman. The thing to do is to avoid creating personal bias."

"Well," replied Doug, "there is one thing. She had become a bit delusional in that last month or two. On several occasions she complained to me that during the day little red men kept running over her bed."

"Capital!" exclaimed Mr. Trublood-Plews. He made a careful note.

"And," added Doug, "she kept telling me they were all socialists."

Mr. Trublood-Plews' pencil stopped in its descent towards his note pad.

"I think," he said, "we should just leave your statement at 'little red men running over her bed.' I would hope, doctor, that you would confine your statement to that point. That will suffice. We should not use the word 'socialist.' It so happens, that his lordship was the defeated Socialist candidate in the recent East Pocklington by-election."

The great day came. It was also, by ill-luck, the first day of our long-arranged holiday. Janet, Catriona and I should have been en route to Scotland. Mr. Trublood-Plews was very cooperative. He would, he said, explain the situation to the judge, and perhaps I could give my evidence early, thus allowing us to be on our way. Not only would Catriona be with us, but we had arranged to pick up two little boys from their boarding school, and deliver them to their parents in Scotland. Rather than lose a day of our holiday, we decided to take a chance on our lawyer's influence with the judge.

It didn't work. His lordship was sympathetic but firm. When I had given my evidence, he wasn't too sure that he should let me go.

"The doctor's evidence is corroborative rather than definitive. At the same time we may need to call him back. Tell him" (as if I were not hanging on to every word) "that he must come back this afternoon."

The afternoon wore on, and a hot and humid one it was. I had the car. Janet had three little people who demanded to be amused. Mountains of ice cream were consumed. Games of spotting objects beginning with the letter "A" were played. These were successful diversions, Janet told me later, for all three children were highly competitive. At the same time the alphabet only has twenty-six letters, and human ingenuity, even my patient wife's, could go only so far. Finally she took them to the municipal art gallery, where the atmosphere was cooler and, amazingly, the children became intrigued by the paintings on view. Janet's sanity was saved.

Meantime, I was detained in a stuffy courtroom, but the evidence was beginning to pile up. Even the most obtuse of judges, I thought, must now be convinced that Mrs. Hackaway had latterly become, to put it mildly, a little peculiar.

Then Mrs. Bealing took the stand. She was a strong and forthright woman. She had at the end become as much a warder as a companion. Her evidence was incontrovertible. Still, counsel wanted to drive home all the points she had made.

"Madam," he said. "You have heard the evidence of the doctors. Dr. Hearne, Mrs. Hackaway's own doctor, has given a very sound opinion. Dr. Gibson has also given evidence. Did you at any time notice anything unusual in your employer's attitude to him?"

"Him!" exclaimed Mrs. Bealing. "I'll tell *you*! All she wanted was him in bed."

My blushes and confusion were lost amid laughter and a bellowed "Silence in court!" At which point his lordship exclaimed, "My goodness! Are you still here, doctor?"

And there was just the trace of a judicial smile on that

dignified face as he added, "At this point, I suggest you proceed immediately to Scotland."

Mrs. Bealing's evidence may have tipped the scales. The cats lost the case.

Chapter
Thirty-eight

"What a ghastly smell," remarked Ellis in the well-modulated accent of the upper-class southerner. A lawyer, he was new to Hull. I was driving towards the suburbs. Ellis sat beside me. Ernest Gray, our family lawyer, sat in the back seat.

It was a gray, listless, windless day and a pall of fog and smog hung over the city. After years of living there I hardly noticed the smell. There was a glut of fish and much of the trawler catch had been consigned for fertilizer: lack of wind plus a fish glut and the smell was the result.

It was Ellis' first experience with it. Ernest Gray, quiet till now, leaned forward. "When that smell is gone forever, Ellis, people like us can start to worry."

For centuries the city and county of Kingston-upon-Hull had depended on the sea for its prosperity. Its great industry, its pride, was deep-sea fishing. When we lived there it boasted the biggest trawler fleet in the world. At one time 270 trawlers sailed from St. Andrew's Dock for the Iceland fishing grounds, the White Sea, Bear Island, Greenland. Twenty-one days at sea, forty-eight hours ashore. That was the trawlerman's life, and a hard, risky one it was – sometimes a short one. Every year or two a ship went down and when it did it was often a case of "lost with all hands." Many a trawlerman never learned to swim – deliberately. What was the point, they'd ask: in Arctic waters the cold would kill inside a minute.

Seven hundred tons weight, 190 feet in length with a 32-foot beam and a crew of twenty-one, that was a typical Hull trawler. Dirty, ravaged by the sea, battered, the paint peeling, thin trails of smoke curling from their stacks, at the end of a voyage they looked raffish, disreputable craft. But they were never ugly, even when they were old. They were built like yachts and their lines were graceful. Their high bows could plunge into waves as high as a mansion and breast them.

Once, in a North Atlantic gale, standing on the heaving deck of a great passenger liner, looking awe-stuck at the huge waves that rolled upon us I saw, a mile or so away, a trace of smoke. For a moment a tiny ship slid up and into view, then vanished as completely as its smoke trail. The seas crashed against the liner, sending it shuddering and rolling. An eternity passed. My anxious eyes searched the raging waste of water. Then there it was again. "Hull trawler," grunted the third officer as he passed. "They can have it too, mate, in this weather." But their reinforced decks and powerful engines made them some of the best-built ships in the world. Their crews swore by them.

The crews were a breed of their own. They were frontiersmen, and sometimes they behaved like it. No elite troops had more pride of place than the deep-sea fishermen or faced their tomorrows more casually. And if the crews were like that, the skippers were a kind of aristocracy.

"Three days and nights before we saw the open sea," said Dan Short, as he sat in my consulting room. "Nowt to do but yer spell on deck, then crawl into t'bunks, an' smoke, an' listen. There we were in t'foces'l wi' nowt but that bow between us an' the ice pack. Up 'd go the bow, then down. *Crunch*. Like a bloody pendulum it was an' just as regular."

He pointed to the pleasant seascape behind me on the wall. He laughed.

"Chap' as painted that never went t' sea in a trawler, doctor, not in winter anyhow. Aye," he went on, "three days an' nights. 'E couldn't turn 'er round, d' ye see. 'Ad to just keep goin' into t' ice pack. Ye could hardly sleep, and t' skipper, ah doan't think 'e slept at all. 'E never left bridge the whole time. But we all trusted t' skipper. Ye've allus got to trust t' skipper – an' the good ones are about best seamen in t' world."

"You've never thought of packing up, Dan?" I asked. "Being a 'deckie' is a young man's job and you're nearing forty."

"Ay, ah've often thought o' it. Nice comfy berth ashore 'd suit me fine at times, like in t' middle o' that trip! But ye see, ah've never done owt else but go to sea. Ah doan't think ah could stand life ashore. An' besides," he added as he made for the door, "I make good money on t' trawlers."

"And spend it too, Dan," I grinned, "if I know anything about you. Well, off you go, and good luck."

Dan Short was pretty typical of his kind. For all the good money they made, most of the crewmen and their families lived on Hessle Road, and many a well-to-do skipper who could have lived in a fashionable suburb refused to leave that long, drab road that paralleled the foreshore, with even a view of that obstructed by factory walls and railway lines. It's not too much to say that the trawling fleet *was* Hessle Road and the neighbouring streets of shabby, red brick, back-to-back houses lining the pavements.

They hadn't always, like Dan Short, made good money. The standard wage in the thirties was one pound nineteen shillings, eleven pence per week – about eight dollars, and many a family was raised on that. But prosperity, especially after the Second World War, brought a change. The older, married man usually lived soberly enough, but the young fellows didn't hoist their kit over their shoulders and walk home after a trip.

Groups of them would scramble on to the dock at the end of a trip, board waiting taxis, and take off. From pub, to party, to pub, that taxi would stay with them for forty-eight hours. They didn't dress in picturesque, functional jerseys like the inshore fishermen of north Yorkshire. They favoured often expensive lounge suits, and pretty rumpled some of them were when their taxi drivers helped heave them aboard at the end of their shore leave. There would be no liquor for three weeks. It was forbidden. Besides, being a "deckie" called for quick wits and reactions.

They were a superstitious lot. It was bad luck to sail on a Friday. No woman ever risked the ship by going to see her man off, nor courted catastrophe by doing the household washing on a Friday. There were all kinds of superstitions, and none of them were the subjects of light-hearted banter.

I liked Ada and Joe Templeton. Janet and I knew them not only as patients, but as friends. Joe reputedly was a "top skipper." They were devoted to one another. Once, when Ada had an acute respiratory infection I did a house call. Joe was home, hovering around his wife, spoiling her to death with his cooking and concern, and Ada was lapping it up. Throwing his arm around her shoulder, he said, "Doc, she's my best pal, so you'll have to look after her when I'm at sea!" That was a privilege and one that Janet and I accepted, and perhaps, cherished.

So one morning when I passed Ada standing on the pavement, I bade her a cheery good day and went on my way. Then a dozen paces on, I stopped. "Why on earth," I thought, "is Ada Templeton standing there like a dummy?"

I turned and looked at her. She looked at me, and very deliberately and slowly her stare shifted from me, swept along the pavement and lighted at her feet. There lay a glove. I walked back, picked it up and handed it to her.

"Thanks," she said, "you're a pet."

"What's the matter? Lumbago? Why didn't you tell me?"

"Lumbago, my foot. It's bad luck to pick up a glove."

"Well, you could have asked me to pick it up."

"That's bad luck, too. It's got to be picked up by somebody who sees it. And it's got to be a man."

"Ada, all that for a glove! How long have you been there?"

"Long enough. And those gloves cost me three pound fifteen shillings at Thornton Varley's last week, so I wasn't leaving!"

You couldn't blame them. Strange things happened. All the Newington trawlers were named after famous authors. Edgar Wallace, however, didn't want any trawler named after him. He was a superstitious man. He was an unlucky man, so he said, but all the same, the trawler *Edgar Wallace* took its place in the Newington fleet. At the end of a voyage, off Prince's Pier, in the midst of dense fog, it hit a sandbar, so easily built up by those silt laden Humber waters. It capsized and within minutes ship and eleven of the crew had gone forever. Superstition? Coincidence? Ill luck?

We were honoured when the Templetons asked us to their twentieth wedding anniversary. We would be the only guests from outside the fishing fraternity, and there would be a hundred or more people there: Joe's crew and their wives, his pals from other ships. It was to be a lively affair.

Indeed, it was. No expense had been spared. Joe and Ada were almost teetotallers but they neither expected nor wanted abstinence from their guests. Joe, like many a good man before him, felt that on this occasion, there should be a slackening of his rigid standards.

The meal had been consumed, and conversation, conducted between tables by men used to competing against Atlantic gales, was at its height when somebody called for speeches.

"Speech, skipper!"

"That's reet lad. On yer feet, Joe!"

"Let's hear from ye, skipper!"

194

Perhaps the skipper had had a nip or two and *was* weaving a little as he rose to his feet. Certainly, he was cheerfully oblivious to the deafening row around him as he commenced his speech.

"Can't hear ye, skipper!"

"Speak oop, lad!"

"Use yer loud hailer, skipper!"

Finally, a stentorian voice bellowing "Silence!" and emphasizing the point by thunderously banging a beer mug on a table, achieved partial success.

"I was just sayin' ... chaps ... fellas," said Joe, "that this is more than our twentieth wedding anniversary. It's Ada's birthday. I married her the day she was twenty. Now that makes her forty today. Right?"

He looked around for confirmation. A roar from his guests assured him the point had been made.

"So!" Joe held up his glass. Politely I held up mine and waited for the toast. "So," he went on, "I'm thinking of trading her in for a couple of twenty-year-olds."

Grinning, he bowed to the uproarious cheers of his guests and sat down, rather heavily, for a sprightly character like Joe.

The ladies present howled for revenge. I remembered that house call a year before and looked at Ada with my Scottish sense of propriety of things. She knew her man. She sat there laughing.

"Response! Response!"

"Ada, have a go at 'im."

Like lightning Ada was on her feet. It was pandemonium. Her words were drowned in a gale of noise. But Joe, an Englishman to the core, believed in fair play. Heavily, he rose to his feet. In a roar that had conquered many a hurricane, he appealed for fair play.

"Silence! Silence! Silence for the lady."

The lady looked upon her beloved. "Joe," she said, "I hate t' tell you, but I don't think you're wired for the job."

Then they embraced, joyfully, before us all.

Chapter
Thirty-nine

Hull Fair, an old tradition and one of England's largest outdoor shows, had begun. The myriad lights, reflected in the night sky, created a glow that could be seen miles away. The hum and whine of mobile generators, blaring music from scores of brass-lunged mechanical bands, the roar of machinery and the thousands of voices combined to make a cacophony that was deafening close by, and a throbbing hum even at a distance.

The fair is held once a year just before the winter winds and rain make open-air events unpleasant or impossible. For days great trailer trucks laden with gear and machinery had rolled into the huge fairground which lay not too far away from our office. The field was a hive of activity. Gaudy structures appeared, housing the bearded lady, the pygmy just brought from the jungles of the Amazon, and all the rest of the oddities that make for side-shows. Trailers, or caravans as they were called, some old and ornate, others new and functional, were backed into their parking places for the next week.

Rollercoasters were erected with the effortless efficiency born of long practice. The "big top" went up for the circus. Elephants were watered, horses exercised, sideshows began to line the gravelled walkway; the final touches were feverishly applied and, to the minute, the fair was on. Hullensians in their thousands flocked to join in the fun.

But for the fair people the excitement of tinsel town is not the reality of their lives. They are hard-working, fast-moving folk, and a wet week with poor attendance is something they all dread.

Each year we saw a few of them as patients. They were not given to visiting doctors for trifles. Like "theatricals," their lives were run on tight and demanding schedules.

A gypsy family became our patients. They were proud and gracious people. Their caravan, huge, old and lined with highly polished mahogany, was comfortable, even luxurious, and their hospitality impeccable. They were well-to-do, and had little time for the tinkers who sometimes passed for true "Romanies."

Inside the caravan, among olive-skinned people with ornate jewellery and strange language, was like being in some far-off mysterious land. My few visits met with a gracious courtesy that warmed me to them and their strange exotic ways. I should add that their immediate, unquestioning and smiling payment of my accounts had the same effect!

Winter was never far off, and for many of them their visit to Hull would be almost the last appearance of the season. Some, those who could afford it, would move to winter quarters. Others would continue to work, operating their lonely roundabouts in dreary, rain-sodden little fairgrounds, gleaning a few hard-earned pounds each week.

It was a Wednesday night and the fair was at its midweek peak when Mr. Merod phoned me. "Can you get to the fair right away, doctor? It's my wife. She's gone into labour a month before time, and the baby's coming awful fast."

Quickly he gave me directions which I scribbled on a note-pad. His caravan was behind Ostler's roundabouts and if I used the Walton Street entrance I couldn't miss it. I headed for the fairgrounds. It wasn't an easy trip. Traffic was heavy and the approaches were packed with cars.

But once in Walton Street, with only yards to go, I had reached an oasis. Not a vehicle was to be seen. A police notice sensibly forbade parking. Only emergency vehicles might stop there.

"Well," I thought, "this is an emergency vehicle all right," and I drew in to the curb, put the car lights out, pulled out my emergency bag, and locked the doors.

" 'Ere! 'ere! 'ere! You can't do that there 'ere! See that notice! 'No parking,' it says. Keep moving." A policeman had suddenly materialized beside me.

"Officer, I'm a doctor..."

"I don't care if you're the lord mayor 'isself. No parking 'ere. That's what it says. Can't yer read? Move on."

"Officer, it's an emergency!"

The average British bobby is a courteous, good-humoured chap. This fellow must have been having trouble with his haemorrhoids. His only response was to raise his arm imperiously in the direction of Albert Avenue a block or two away, and repeat, to the obvious interest of dozens of curious passersby, en route to the fair, "Off with yer. There's parking out there."

"It's packed," I pleaded. "There's not a parking spot for half a mile or more."

It was useless. He wouldn't listen. And suddenly I realized that this frozen-faced, bone-headed bully was enjoying himself, the more so as my discomfiture and my pleading increased.

I took note of his constabulary number, emblazoned in metal on his collar, and at the same time I spotted his St. John's Ambulance Brigade proficiency badge.

"Ah! constable," I said, pointing to his badge, "I see you are No. X93 and I see you're a qualified first-aid man! You're just the very man I need. Now look!" I thrust my scribbled sheet of directions into his hand. "X93, *this is an emergency!* Go at once to this address. I'll obey your instructions and park my car. It'll take me half an hour. You'll have delivered the baby, and tomorrow morning I'll see to it that your action is reported to the chief constable. It'll be a *tremendous* feather in your cap!

In a trice, before either he or I could draw breath, I was in my car and moving along at a good clip. Any shouts were drowned in the general noise of the fairground but strangely enough, X93, helmetless, pounding away some yards behind me, finally gained on me, and a demented banging on the back of the car made me stop.

"Yes, constable. *Now* what have I done?"

His best years were behind him. He was a bit comfortable in the middle, and none too spry. I did not view his distress with sympathy, and I was impatient. He leaned against the car for support. His helmet was somewhere on the road behind him.

"Yes, man, what is it? If anything goes wrong I will hold you responsible. You should be on your way to this case."

"Phew!" he wheezed, "You (puff) leave your car 'ere (puff) I'll (wheeze) see as nobody touches it. Just you do wot you 'ave to, doctor. I'll see to your (puff) car (puff) doctor."

Before he'd finished I was on my way. It was just as well. When I reached the caravan it took me about ten seconds to size up the situation. Mr. Merod was standing by helpless, as his wife agitatedly paced up and down their little trailer. Her flushed face and tight lips gave me all the information I needed. She was in her nightgown and in obvious distress. I wasted no time in idle courtesy.

"How long between contractions?"

"Five minutes."

"First baby?"

"No, third."

Third babies have a habit of arriving in a hurry, and inwardly I drew a sharp breath.

"If anything goes wrong here," I thought, "heaven help us!" There were no facilities, and suddenly Mr. Merod cried, "I've got to go and mind the stall," and vanished.

I have never claimed to be one of the world's fastest thinkers, but self-preservation does make for speed, I've noticed.

"Mrs. Merod, there's a nursing home in Albert Avenue. I have to get you there. It's half a mile from here." She nodded.

"I can have an ambulance here in fifteen minutes. Where's a phone?"

She grabbed my arm. "No ambulance. It'll bring bad luck to the whole fair! Fair people don't have ambulances!"

"By all the saints," I groaned to myself. "I have to deal with trawlermen and their damned superstitions; now it's fair people!" But she was adamant.

"We'll walk! Come on! We'll walk." She pulled on her coat over her nightgown, and dragging me behind her she stumbled down the trailer steps. "We'll make it," she cried. We tripped over guy ropes and we half ran behind that line of caravans until finally we left their quiet and shelter, and plunged into the crowd for those last, terrifying two hundred yards.

The midway was crammed: people were elbow-to-elbow, shouting, shoving and jostling. With my emergency bag in my left hand and my right arm protectively round my patient, I fought every inch of the way.

Several times she stopped in her tracks, threw her arms round me and cried, "Stop! Stop! It's coming again." Then she'd bury her face in my shoulder and moan.

Not often have I been clutched at by passionate women. Mrs. Merod made up for any deficiencies.

Among the interested spectators were some of my patients. It was very difficult to lift my hat to the ladies as they passed, but courtesy demanded that, at least, I try.

And so we stumbled to the exit. My car shot into Albert Avenue, and to the nursing home. Bawling to the surprised staff for a bed, any bed, anywhere, I raced to beat the stork – by ten minutes only.

It was the next morning, on looking into my waiting room, that I spotted Mr. Frano. He was a dignified old chap, the owner of a flea circus. I had met him a year or so before when I looked after his wife during some minor illness.

I liked Mr. Frano. He was a gentleman; polite, appreciative of the little services we provided. He had a great sense of decorum, was wearing his Sunday suit for this visit to the doctor's office, and rose to greet me as I walked towards him, hand outstretched. There were no other patients in the waiting room.

"Mr. Frano! Welcome back to Hull. How are all the fleas this year?"

But his smile in reply was wan and fleeting. "Could you come and see my wife, doctor? She's not at all well."

My flippancy vanished as I looked at his face. I promised a visit in a couple of hours. He gave me the directions, and thanking me, he left.

Mr. Frano was in his seventies, his wife a few years younger. They were childless. In a way they were aristocrats. They could trace their families' lineage for almost two hundred years. They were fair people, not gypsies, Mr. Frano explained.

They had a strength, these quiet, inoffensive people. For all their superstitions, like the trawlermen they had an acceptance of the nature of things, a quiet, abiding philosophy, an understanding of life in its hope and harshness.

Later that morning I made my way to their caravan. The crowds of the night before had vanished, and I only needed to avoid the puddles of rain water and the coloured streamers blown against my legs by the cold east wind.

My patient lay in bed. She was a tiny creature, old, wrinkled, wasted. Within minutes I had found the mass in her upper abdomen, hard, craggy, deadly. She had a stomach cancer.

It was only when she lifted her left arm above the bedclothes that I saw the wasted muscles, the terrible scars running from her left shoulder to the wrist. "What on earth," I asked, "is this?"

"I was a lion tamer once," my patient replied, "and the one I trusted most mauled me when my back was turned."

Mr. Frano came towards me. In his hand he had a photograph. It showed a beautiful girl, poised, whip in hand, the lions behind her. "This," he said, "is Ida." I looked at the photograph, the shapely hips, slim legs, the self-assured poise. I nodded, smiled noncommittally and returned the photograph. This old, dying lady had once been a beauty.

I had her admitted to hospital. There was nothing to do but confirm the diagnosis and ease her pain as best I could. Quietly, I told Mrs. Frano that. It was as if she knew. She began uncomplainingly to slip away, and when the fair was over for another year, the crowds had gone and the caravans rolled away, two lonely trailers were left, sitting there in the cold pre-winter wind.

In one corner was the Merods' trailer. Their baby had developed jaundice and I wouldn't let them go until I was sure the illness was under control. Not far away stood the Franos' old, weathered caravan. Only blowing newspapers and discarded, broken toys remained to remind us of the week that had gone. On the same day that I discharged little Miss Merod, Mrs. Frano, flea circus proprietor and lion tamer, quietly went to meet her Maker.

The Merods were pulling out as I stood with my old patient outside of his trailer. I had called to see him one last time.

"I'm sorry, Mr. Frano. There was nothing anyone could have done. You know that, don't you?"

"I know, doctor." He was as dignified as ever, though the tears, unheeded, rolled down his cheeks. "I loved her, you know. She was a trouper. Wherever I went, she went. She never changed much, to me, that is." He smiled apologetically, but I remembered that old faded photograph, those soft eyes and that slim beauty, and I had no answering smile.

He held out his hand. "Goodbye, sir. I have a feeling I won't come back next year." He was still holding my hand as he looked over my shoulder. "The Merods, doctor, they're driving over this way. I think they want to say goodbye."

I turned. The Merods, though they didn't stop, smiled and waved as they passed.

"Their little one, you delivered it, didn't you?"

"Yes. It's fine now. They're on their way."

"That is life, doctor," said my friend. "A coming and a going. Always, for all of us, a coming and a going. But we must always be on our way."

Chapter
Forty

There were still twelve house calls to make before five o'clock and the start of the evening "surgery." A few minutes before, I had parked my car outside the office and had run in to pick up a specialist's report. The door bell rang and our secretary, Mrs. Hughes, answered it.

"There's a patient to see you," she whispered.

"I'm not in."

"She saw you come in, doctor. And your car's outside."

Exasperated, I looked at my watch. "We open the evening surgery at five. Dammit! I'm in an awful rush. Tell her to come back."

"Yes, doctor. She's a nice little thing and she's worried."

"I'm a nice little thing and *I'm* worried. I'll never get done by five. Blast it."

"Yes, doctor. It will only take a minute, I think, and she's walked all the way from Hessle Road in hopes of getting Dr. Janet or you at home. Shall I put her in the waiting room?"

"Well, all right," I grumbled, "and blast you, too!"

"Yes, doctor," smiled Mrs. Hughes, who wasn't easily put out. "I'll see to that, too."

Eventually I found the report I wanted. I had my own preliminary filing system. Mrs. Hughes once saw me working at it. She said "All hope abandon, ye who enter here," and I thought for a moment she was referring to my office. It was just the preliminary filing system she meant, but her remark was made with feeling.

I met her in the corridor as I crossed to the waiting room. "Who is it?" I whispered, to which she replied, "It's Mrs. Crozier. It's her little girl she wants you to see." I groaned quietly. I might have known. Week in, week out, Mrs. Crozier dragged one or other of her three kids to the office. Sore throats, running noses, infected ears, nothing to any of the complaints, but you could be sure one of her brood would be in the surgery regularly as clockwork. Their oldest had just started school and was dragging home, and handing on, every minor infection he could pick up.

Mrs. Crozier and Shirley were waiting for me. They got a reception as chilly as the weather outside. Coldly I looked down Shirley's throat, inspected her ears for infection and her neck for enlarged glands. Half a generation at that time seemed to be called Shirley in honour of Miss Temple, but this Shirley didn't have any childish glamour about her. She was snuffling and miserable. Still, it could have waited till five o'clock, and I said so.

"I'm sorry," said her mother, "but it all started so sudden-like I got worried, and Alf's due in tonight."

"He's a deckie, isn't he?"

"That's right. I'm real grateful for you seeing us like this."

"Oh well," I said, mollified, "I'll forgive you, this time."

Mrs. Crozier was a wispy, nondescript little woman in her middle thirties. If she wasn't ugly she wasn't pretty. She had no figure to speak of. With that pale, thin face and that aquiline nose, the mousy brown hair that constantly fell untidily across her forehead, she looked permanently worried.

Then one evening I was asked to do a house call. Their newest arrival, eight months old, had a fever, and they gave me that story of cardinal importance in a feverish infant: it was breathing much too rapidly. That can signify an acute chest infection and is not the kind of thing to be casual about.

Their home was a tiny place in a back street off Hessle Road. Outside its walls there was no privacy, no garden. But the house inside was spotless and cheerful and I found a transformed woman waiting. Despite her anxiety about the baby she was radiant with pride as she introduced me to her husband.

"You've never met my Alf, have you, doctor?" The introduction was brief, Alf favouring me with an unsmiling nod as he followed me to the baby's cot, where he stood watchfully as I made my examination.

"Will she be all right?"

"Yes, Mr. Crozier, I think so. There's no real distress. I can't find any sign of pneumonia. But at this age any chest infection is potentially dangerous, so I'll call back tomorrow morning." Then, knowing his wife's capacity for worrying, and knowing, too, how rapidly infections like this can develop, I suggested that they take turns that night in keeping an eye on the baby.

My examination completed, I bade the Croziers goodnight, and made for the door, but Alf forestalled me. Wordlessly he handed me a bottle of beer and motioned me towards the one armchair in the room while his wife and he sat on the couch. It was my first visit to their home, I suddenly thought, and like many house calls it had been a revelation.

Crozier's concern about the baby impressed me, as did his obvious relief when I reassured him. His wife, neatly dressed and smiling happily, was a different person from the strained-looking woman I was accustomed to seeing in my office. As for Crozier, his love for his children was striking. They scrambled all over him, hugged him, and his looks for them needed no interpretation. The boy stood at his knee, running an obviously new toy railway engine up and down his leg, while their eldest, a little girl of eight, stood casually beside him holding his arm.

Since Crozier still hadn't spoken, I opened the conversation. Looking at the toy engine I remarked, "A present, Mr. Crozier?"

It was his wife who answered. "It's always presents, doctor. Every trip. Everytime 'e comes 'ome 'e brings summat. You should just see t' new frock 'e bought me today."

Crozier wasn't one for being "out with the boys," and I said something to that effect. He nodded. "They can have that. I've got all I want. A millionaire couldn't buy what I've got here." I looked at him again. Above average height, with broad shoulders and slim hips, his ruggedly handsome looks were enhanced by the curly hair that fell over his forehead. He sat there with his sleeveless singlet showing the muscles rippling on his tattooed arms, and turning to me, raised his glass. More good looks than the average film star, I thought.

That house call was a practical lesson in what the social scientists call the "socio-psychological aspects of medical practice." I now knew some of the emotions and worries that could affect not just the person who is sick, but the people who are close to illness and may be affected by it; in this case, the Croziers. I had a picture of a family, of warmth and love, and I understood the reasons for Mrs. Crozier's frequent visits to my office: possibly insecure herself, she had no one to turn to when the children were sick, and they were Alf Crozier's most precious possessions. Her husband, with the exception of those two joyous, precious days every few weeks, spent his life hundreds of miles away, on the heaving deck of a trawler. He might as well have been on the moon.

For the first time I felt I had made a contribution, and so I lifted my glass to Alf and enjoyed an evening beer, warmed by the affection I saw around me. Mrs. Crozier was still at times a bit of a pest, and sometimes I almost forgot the resolution of forbearance I had made that night, but I "trained" her. She phoned when she was worried and either Janet or I would put her at her ease. It didn't take much of our time, and she trusted us.

The winter gales were worse than usual that year. My friend Joe Templeton showed me some snapshots he'd taken from the bridge of his trawler. Enormous waves, the wind blowing their crests into spray, bore down upon the deck, thick in ice, as the bow buried itself in the sea.

His photographs were awesome. The superstructure of the trawler was encrusted with ice, and the decks must have been perilously slippery. Joe looked at his photographs, grimly reminiscent.

"Gale Force 10, doc. Not quite a hurricane, but trying hard."

"It looks awful, Joe. What about the crew? Surely they weren't on deck in that?"

"Some had to be. Every fisherman dreads a storm like that. I live with one ear on the weather reports, and keep clear of this sort of thing. But sometimes you get caught, all the same."

"What can you do about it?"

"Well, never get caught beam-on to a gale, for one thing. The wind can blow you over. And then, if your superstructure's heavily iced up, you'll just keep rolling. The ship, a small ship like a trawler, becomes top-heavy. And if that's the case, it'll roll right over, and then that's that," he concluded grimly.

"Isn't there anything you can do?"

"Most of the time we keep the ice down with steam hoses and ice axes, equipment like that. But in the worst kind of storm, the men can't work outside for too long, only minutes at a time; it's so cold."

Enthralled, I listened. Joe Templeton laughed. "I know you're interested, but it's one thing to sit here over a cup of tea and look at these photographs. It's another thing to experience that cold, and that's something I shouldn't think you ever will."

Years later, as a country G.P. on the Canadian prairies with the temperature at thirty below I would know how deadly the cold can be, but at that time I smiled over my tea and agreed with him.

"That spray coming over the bow becomes solid ice on the deck and the superstructure. It forms about as fast as you can get rid of it in really bad weather. Dangerous stuff!"

Finishing my tea, I bade my friend good luck, and continued my rounds.

Winters are a dangerous time for trawlers. Experience, superb seamanship, can mean little in the face ot its savagery. That tragic, often heroic phrase, "lost with all hands," is only too familiar to the people of Hull. In January 1933, the trawlers *Emdon* and *Cape Delgado* were lost with all hands. In February of that same year the *James Long* disappeared with its entire crew. In March the *Lord Daramore* went down. That was a tragic year for trawler folk. Next year the *Loch Ard* was lost, and in 1935 the *Edgar Wallace*. Only six men survived these two tragedies. And so it went on, year after year.

The winter of 1955 was a brutal one. It was January 12, when skipper Coverdale, just turned forty, commanding the *Roderigo*, turned his ship's bows towards Iceland. He had been at sea since he was a boy, and was widely respected as one of Hull's most competent and successful trawler captains. He had served throughout the war as a merchant navy officer. At about the same time, the *Lorella*, commanded by skipper Blackshaw, sailed for the Arctic. Skipper Blackshaw, a quiet, unassuming man, had had his masters' ticket since 1932, and he was an acknowledged expert, with a great deal of experience on the Icelandic fishing grounds. He came of a distinguished family in Hull, his father having held that almost legendary title, Admiral of the Great Northern Fleet.

There were forty men in these two ships. There was a boy of sixteen serving on the *Roderigo* with his cousin, a few years older. It was the first trip at sea for a few, but most had served in the navy during the war, often on minesweepers. The ships were modern, well-equipped, and the crews experienced.

On January 26, off Iceland's North Cape, the storm struck and reached its height. The snow, driven horizontally by the Arctic gale, must have been blinding at times, but at some point they saw coming toward them that dreaded black cloud of Arctic frost. It would freeze on everything in its path, masts, bridge, cables and decks. The wind had reached Force 12, over seventy-five miles per hour, and the temperature was far below zero. To survive on deck for even a few minutes in these mountainous seas under those conditions was well-nigh impossible, yet frantic efforts had to be made with steam hoses and ice axes, to prevent the weight of accumulating ice from capsizing the ships.

The first SOS came from the *Lorella*. "Have been thrown on side, need help quick." To abandon ship was impossible, and the *Lorella* lurched and rolled to its doom, but true to tradition the distress signal was answered. The *Roderigo*, against hopeless odds, turned into the storm, but soon radioed that *it* was in trouble, that it was impossible to abandon ship because of the freezing conditions. Its last message read, ''We are overturning.''

It was the *Lancella* that picked up the first distress signals and passed them on to Hull, a city that waited in hope and dread for further news. No further signals had come from the *Roderigo* or the *Lorella* when the *Lancella* signalled that she had turned into the raging gale and was going to the assistance of her sister ship. Afternoon became night. The fishing community suspected the worst, yet hoped against hope, and dreaded that yet more tragedy lay ahead, for the *Lancella* was out there somewhere, searching however hopeless its task. The pastor of the fisherman's chapel spent the night, as he had done many times before, visiting stricken households, trying to give comfort and a hope he must have known was forlorn.

Day broke and the trawler owners gave the word: the *Lorella* and the *Roderigo* had been lost with all hands. The *Lancella* somehow had survived the night, its search, hopeless probably from the first, abandoned. No power on earth could have saved either the *Lorella* or the *Roderigo*, as with the men below and hatches battened down, they rolled to their end.

It is strange that the *Roderigo* should be named after the Venetian gentleman of Shakespeare's *Othello*, and strange, that in *Othello*, Roderigo should say in his torment, ''I will incontinently drown myself,'' and Iago cry, ''No more of drowning, do you hear!''

Trawler folks are superstitious, but deckies probably don't read much of Shakespeare.

Saddened, that morning, I walked in to take my surgery. A sober-faced Mrs. Hughes confronted me.

''I think you should go and see Mrs. Crozier.''

''What is it this time?''

''Don't you know? They've just released the names, Alf Crozier went down.''

I stared at her aghast. ''Crozier wasn't on either of those trawlers.''

''He was,'' she replied. ''He changed over a few trips ago.''

So I dragged myself down to Hessle Road. Two neighbour ladies in the house silently handed me a cup of tea. Muriel Crozier, apparently oblivious to her surroundings, stood looking into the fireplace. The oldest girl lay face down on the sofa sobbing bitterly, while a little one, silent, confused, tugged unheeded at her mother's skirt.

I stumbled out my condolences. It's a technique I've never mastered.

"How on earth," I thought as I was speaking, "will this poor, inadequate little creature cope with her life from now on?"

"She doesn't hear you, doctor," said one of the ladies. But Muriel Crozier had heard me, and might have read my thoughts, rather than heard my words. She turned to look at me. Her face in its grief had strength, purpose, dignity.

"Aye, I heard you" she said, "and now I've something to do. I've these children to look after for Alf's sake, and I have him to remember."

All I could do was murmur, "You've given a great deal," when she interrupted me.

"Aye, I have an' all. But then, you see, it's only them as *has*, as *can* give."

Chapter
Forty-one

The practice grew and so did Catriona. Demurely uniformed, she attended the High School for Girls at Tranby Croft. "Tranby," as the school was affectionately known to pupils and staff, had an excellent reputation. But its reputation had been somewhat different a few generations before.

It was in one of the rooms of this large mansion that the Prince of Wales, later King Edward VII, became involved in the notorious baccarat game that was a tremendous scandal of Victorian England. Edward's extravagances and mistresses were the talk of high society. Even though he was Prince of Wales, he was terrified of his mother's anger.

Queen Victoria's long reign would continue for more than a decade, when, in 1890, Edward arrived in Hull to attend a Yorkshire race meet. He was to stay with the Wilsons, wealthy ship owners, at Tranby Croft on the outskirts of Hull.

There was, as usual on such occasions, a house party, at

which part of the entertainment arranged for the Prince's pleasure was a baccarat game. His Royal Highness was, if not a notorious gambler, an enthusiastic and dedicated one. A member of the Wilson family became convinced that he had seen a guest, a Guard's officer, and a close friend of the Prince, cheat during the game. He confided the secret to his family. The following day, unsuspectingly watched, the guest appeared to cheat again. The Prince, blissfully unaware of the trouble that was brewing, saw the game through, but the damage had been done.

Accusations were levelled at the offender. He denied them. Stumbling efforts at secrecy failed. Within weeks the gambling scandal at Tranby was public knowledge. Colonel Gordon Cummings, the accused guest, became a social pariah. Some things were just simply *not done*. He sued the Wilsons for defamation of character, and Edward, Prince of Wales, was summoned to give evidence in court as a witness. All very sordid, and a tremendous indignity for the royal family. Queen Victoria was *not* amused.

I daresay in today's permissive society the affair would not raise a great storm, but in 1890 the heavy hand of Victorian propriety lay on the middle and lower orders of society. However innocent the Prince's involvement may have been, the results of the scandal were almost catastrophic. There was a public outcry. Meetings of protest took place throughout the country. The future king of England involved in a disgraceful gambling affair? Hauled into court like a common creature? Dreadful! Prayers for his redemption were offered from many an English pulpit. I have no idea how my moralistic fellow-countrymen reacted, but I can imagine the sermons against royal depravity that thundered from many a Scottish pulpit.

Urged, so I understand, by the Archbishop of Canterbury (whose successors became patrons of the Tranby Croft School for Girls), the Prince wrote to the newspapers. (No doubt it would be to *The Times*.) He expressed his horror, his abject and everlasting detestation of gambling in all its wickedness, urged higher thoughts upon his future subjects, and the day was saved.

Reverently, however ironically, "the baccarat room," stripped of all its former finery was always shown to the parents of prospective pupils, but what ghost, I sometimes wondered, whimsically looked down upon little girls innocently studying the mysteries of simple arithmetic.

I had become active in medical politics and was elected president of the East Yorkshire branch of the British Medical Association, commonly known as the B.M.A. This honour entailed the safekeeping of the chain of office, and wearing it on special occasions. It was quite a beautiful piece of crafts manship. It had been created over many years, when successive presidents added new links to the chain. The links, of white enamel, symbolized the white rose of York and were set in heavy gold. As it lay in its box, lined with purple velvet, it greatly impressed two little girls who, on one occasion, were allowed to fondle it.

Said Catriona proudly to her little friend Carole, "My daddy, you know, is president of the B.M.A." By coinci dence, General Eisenhower had just been elected president of the United States. Hearing this news on the radio, Carole called out to her father in tones of the utmost indignation, "It's no true, Daddy, it's not true, it's *Dr. Gibson* who's president of the U.S.A.!" However humble by comparison my position was, it was an honour and I enjoyed it.

Though we were both busy in the practice, our house was by now a comfortable home where, on the whole, domestic affairs ran smoothly, with the help of a Yorkshire housekeeper and a German maid. Interruptions at any hour of the day or night were frequent and routine.

It was no surprise one evening when I sat reading the day's newspaper, to have my peace disturbed by a loud ringing at the door. When I answered it, I was confronted by a well-dressed, middle-aged gentleman I had never seen before. He appeared agitated and in some distress.

"My name is Soames, doctor. May I come in?"

"Mr. Soames, this is my home, not my consulting room. And," I added, looking pointedly at my watch, "it's almos 10 P.M."

He nodded. "I realize that, but this, sir, is a matter of great importance."

"Oh, well, in that case..." and I ushered him into the sitting room.

"No one is ill, doctor. It's much worse than that."

"Perhaps you wouldn't mind, then, telling me as quickly as possible what this is all about," I said, rather irritably.

"You know Mrs. Dempster, doctor? I understand she's a patient of yours?"

"Yes, I know Mrs. Dempster."

Mrs. Dempster was a lady in her mid-fifties, a mild, self-effacing woman who came to my surgery occasionally for the treatment of minor ailments such as respiratory infections. She worked in one of the stores in town; her husband was an odd-job man. As a matter of fact he had been in and out of the office quite frequently of late. He never seemed to have much wrong with him, but he would always come up with some complaint, however trivial, and would leave, giving me a sour look and the impression that he thought very little either of me or my advice. I knew they had no family and I doubted if their relationship was a close one.

"I'm manager of the store where Mrs. Dempster works," said my visitor, "and I'm in terrible trouble. Mr. Dempster has reported me to my head office. He accuses me of having an affair with his wife. I could lose my job, sir."

Wondering what on earth this had to do with me, I asked cautiously, "*Have* you been having an affair with his wife?"

"Certainly not," cried Mr. Soames indignantly, "I'm a respectable married man!"

"Well then," I replied, "Couldn't all this have waited till tomorrow? And besides, isn't it a lawyer you should be seeing?"

"I've already seen a lawyer, and no sir, it won't wait till tomorrow. There's another man involved. Mr. Dempster says he also has been having an affair with his wife. Depraved sexual orgies, those are the very words he used."

"Then, Mr. Soames," I said impatiently, "*he* should be seeing a lawyer, too."

"Exactly, sir, exactly. And the sooner you do so as well, the better. You are to be reported to the British Medical Association tomorrow. Depraved sexual orgies, that's what he said, sir."

I stared aghast at my visitor. "My God!" I cried. "This is ridiculous! It's unbelievable! It's outrageous."

"I thought," said Mr. Soames rather dryly, "you might take more interest in the matter when you heard the details."

The next day Janet and I had come to view that remark as an understatement. We were about to seek legal counsel when Mr. Dempster solved the problem for all of us. He had been hired to "clean up" his neighbour's garden. He was told he could start as soon as he liked. In the morning when his neighbours woke, their carefully tended lawn looked like a neatly furrowed field. The vegetable plot with its produce had been

211

reduced to a patch of virgin soil; their beloved roses had bee
uprooted, while ornamental shrubs and two precious little tree
lay in a large heap at the bottom of the garden.

Mr. Dempster had taken his instructions literally. He ha
elected to begin his task late that night. Working with maniac
fury throughout the hours of darkness, he had indeed done
"clean up job."

After psychiatric treatment Mr. Dempster recovered fror
his nervous breakdown, Mrs. Dempster retained her husband
Mr. Soames his job, and I my reputation.

In the meantime our home was frequently invaded by friend
and family for varying periods of time. Janet's mother was
regular visitor. Come hell or high water she had to listen ever
day to "Mrs. Dale's Diary," a popular radio series of th
time, following the daily happenings in the life of a doctor'
wife.

One afternoon the phone rang in the hallway. Janet answere
it. At the same moment there was a thunderous knocking a
the front door. I hurried to open it. As I passed Janet she said
"It's Mrs. Collier. She's sure her husband's having a hear
attack."

There was no time to answer. On the doorstep, supporte
by two passersby, was a gray-faced man, his coat torn, bloo
streaming from his forehead, his head and shoulders slumpe
forward.

Almost simultaneously my mother-in-law rushed into th
hall. "Quick!" she called out, "someone switch on the radi
or I'll miss 'Mrs. Dale's Diary!' "

Could we be blamed this once for ignoring her plea? W
thought not.

Chapter
Forty-two

"A North American holiday!" exclaimed Janet. "How will you arrange that?"

Post-war austerity had placed severe restrictions on travel abroad for all but business purposes. Tourists could take only a few dollars with them. But our American friends had offered us hospitality and had made arrangements for expense money. Our fares we could pay in sterling.

In the spring of 1954 we sailed for New York aboard the S.S. *United States*. Our travelling companions were mostly American servicemen returning home with their families, and their friendly ways quickly put us at ease. Catriona, once she had overcome her shyness, was especially popular, and when we docked at New York we had already made friends.

It was at Grand Central Station that Janet said, rather fervently, "I *do* hope Bill's waiting for us at Washington." There was reason for her concern. We had two dollars left between us until we reached the capital.

Bill was waiting at Union Station, and soon we were en route for his home in the suburbs. The gray Atlantic with its cold winds was far behind us. In Washington it was hot and humid. There was bright sunshine with only the occasional thundercloud building in the sky. There was the far-off rumble of thunder, the hot smell of electricity in the air, but all around us there was colour. All three of us were filled with an immediate sense of excitement.

Bill and I were friends. We had met during the war and the Hunts had been our guests in England. My friend was now a staff officer at the Pentagon, but that afternoon, like most of the people around us, he was dressed in casual slacks and a colourful shirt. The easy ways we had encountered on board ship followed us. The Hunts' neighbours, navy or army people, "dropped in" that afternoon, introduced themselves and we found ourselves on first name terms within minutes. It was a refreshing, relaxing experience.

"There are one or two things you've to do," said Bill, as we sipped our coffee. "There's been a phone call for you from Chicago, from the president of the American Medical Association. Now what," he added, "would he want with a G.P. from Hull, England?"

The answer was simple. I was an elected officer of the British Medical Association, considered fairly knowledgeable about professional organization and politics, and the B.M.A. had informed its American counterpart that I would be available for consultation.

I made my phone call. Travel to Chicago was out of the question, but the president arranged for me to meet his friend, Dr. Christianson, in Washington in two days' time.

As I replaced the receiver, Bill said, "Next, you can pick up your car tomorrow, just as soon as you've taken your driver's examination."

"A driving test? Tomorrow?" I gasped, glancing at the continuous stream of traffic outside roaring past on the wrong side of the road. "I'll never be able to sit a driving test by tomorrow!"

"Oh, yes you will. It has to be tomorrow, or a week to-.norrow. And you're short of time to do all you want to. We'll practise tonight. Here are the road regulations. The National Guard handles the written part, the police the driving part. You'll be all right," he added airily.

"Written part, driving test, the police, tomorrow!" I cried in alarm.

But next morning we presented ourselves at the Armory. Bill was in uniform, and the National Guard officer, seeing my friend's insignia of rank, rose hastily from his desk chair.

Without too much being said, it was inferred as from one military man to another that this guest of the United States, a military man at one time himself, deserved a courteous and helpful reception.

Would I like a little time to refresh my memory; asked the examining officer? I would? Fifteen minutes, perhaps? He ushered me into a side room. Questions 1 to 10, 14, 18 to 22, etc. would be of interest, he smilingly told me.

For the first time in my life I passed a written examination, *honoris cum laude*.

"And now," said Bill, as we emerged into the sunlit street, "You've got to convince that character over there you can drive, and he doesn't give one hoot about me."

Bill's car was to be used for the test. Standing beside it, dressed in apocalypsean black was a police officer. His hard, craggy face was expressionless as he watched me, with leaden feet, approach him.

214

"O.K. Let's go," said my examiner, taking the passenger seat.

"Yes, constable."

I was unnerved to begin with, and what followed didn't help.

"Constable," he barked. "My name ain't Constable. I'm Buxton. *Officer* Buxton. Ain't no Constable in our precinct. Let's go."

Hurriedly I put the car into gear, and we moved off – backwards! There was a loud clang as Bill's rear bumper contacted Officer Buxton's patrol car behind us.

"Jeez. Stop!" ordered Officer Buxton. "C'n you drive? You're liable to get a ticket before you get a licence, bud. Lemme out."

Bill, watching from across the street, had raised his hand to his forehead in a most unmilitary gesture, quickly quelled. Officer Buxton re-entered the car.

"You're just lucky bud. No damage. Let's go. See if you can make it this time."

"I really can drive," I told him. "But you see, in British cars the gear boxes face the opposite way."

"You a limey or somp'n?"

"Yes."

"London?" His voice was toneless, disinterested.

"No, Glasgow, Scotland."

"Jeez," said Officer Buxton, with unexpected animation, "a whisky and a chaser!"

Now, Glasgow's drinking habit of a Scotch followed by a chaser of beer, requires initiation, a knowledge of the city, and I looked at the police officer.

"You know Glasgow?"

"Yeah. I was there durin' the war. Some lyin' sonofabitch told me I couldn't get drunk drinkin' them things. Say! But I had more free drinks in that town...."

His face had broken into a hard grin. Suddenly my examination became an extended driving lesson. I was initiated into the mysteries of overhead traffic signals, roundabouts, and made to weave in and out of the city traffic while Officer Buxton expounded on the virtues, or lack of them, that had so endeared Glasgow to him.

I passed the test with flying colours.

I met Dr. Christianson the next day. He was a distinguished surgeon, quietly interrogatory, dignified and sincere. He had worked as a doctor in many out-of-the-way parts of this world, including China and northern India, where he had had to make his way from one village to another over mountain paths, sometimes spending weeks on his lonely rounds.

While Catriona played happily with Butch, Bill's young son, Dr. Christianson took Janet and me to famous hospitals and medical centres. The Bethesda Medical Centre especially intrigued us. Each floor of this new building, a government project, was devoted to research and treatment in a particular specialty. No expense had been spared. The facilities for research and medical care were magnificent. I said so to our guide who, smiling quietly, reminded me that the research workers in Britain, the "back room boys" as he called them, had made immense contributions to medical science.

"Take the sulpha drugs," he said, "or penicillin, to name only two. They're British. Have you ever visited that crowded, shabby little laboratory in London where Fleming developed penicillin? You know, it's not the physical plant that makes a medical centre or a university. It's the quality of the people who work there."

But we had to leave Washington for a week or two. We wanted to see Canada. I had been offered work there. But now I had also been offered work in Washington, an internship, prior to sitting the necessary state examinations.

We drove north to New York state and Connecticut through quietly beautiful towns that preserved the dignity of their colonial past. Anxieties were behind us. Our journey had suddenly become a great adventure. While Janet and I were overwhelmed by the size of the meals in restaurants, Miss Gibson hilariously imitated the New England accents. For an eleven year old it had suddenly become an immensely interesting experience, and our excitement mounted as we drove through Maine and towards the Canadian border. A casual examination of our passports and we were on our way again, this time to Nova Scotia. Here, fir trees and rock replaced the lusher vegetation of New England.

The Royal Navy has left an almost indelible stamp on Halifax, where Cornwallis first established a British garrison in 1749. Only its occasional wooden buildings proclaim it to be North America.

From there we moved west through New Brunswick and Quebec, in which province we spoke our Scottish French to the amused delight of the inhabitants. Toronto, even in 1954,

216

showed all the signs of becoming a great metropolis. Then it was back to Washington.

It had been a whirlwind tour. We had seen something of Canada and the United States. We had met charming and hospitable people, and quite often we had been told that our services as doctors would be welcome in communities which had no medical help. Not once were we made to feel like foreigners. Often we had been warmed by the welcome we received and would receive if we returned as physicians. But we knew where home was. We were going back to England to settle down.

I met Dr. Christianson a couple of times on our return to Washington, and on our last meeting he said,

"I've been thinking a lot. I've been all over the world, and I want *you* to think of something. Last year I visited somewhere I'd never been before, the Canadian Rockies. There are little towns all along the foothills, and many of them don't have doctors. They'd welcome people like you, and they need doctors. You'd be happy there, I'm sure."

But I shook my head. "It has been a wonderful experience, and all three of us have loved every minute of it, but we're going back to England to settle down."

"Well, I wonder," said my new friend. "I wonder. I think you'll be back."

And a few days later, as we stood on the deck of the *Queen Mary*, watching the Manhattan skyline fade into the distance, I, too wondered, and I knew Janet did too.

A century or so ago one Dr. Isaac Letsome wrote:

> When people's ill, they come to I,
> I physics, bleeds and sweats 'em,
> Sometimes they live, sometimes they die,
> What's that to I?

> *I. Letsome*

Frankly I don't believe him, but I do admire his sense of humour. In those far-off days of often tragically short lives and necessarily brutal surgery his jocularity must have been a tremendous asset, perhaps as much to his patients as to himself.

Obviously, general practice has altered a great deal over the years; like everything else it is still changing. So are patterns of disease. But some things have never changed.

217

Hillaire Belloc wrote:

> From quiet homes and first beginning
> Out to the undiscovered ends,
> There's nothing worth the wear of winning
> But laughter and the love of friends.

Since family doctors often follow their patients' lives from first beginning to undiscovered ends, many of us will agree with Belloc. Friendship is a treasure that cannot be bought, and laughter, I am convinced, can sometimes cure. Despite all our advances in scientific knowledge and technology, the basic needs of the human spirit remain.

As for us, our patients continued to keep us worried, puzzled, intrigued, alarmed and sometimes entertained. They swallowed their false teeth, had heart attacks, breakdowns, and babies, mostly it seemed in the middle of the night. They sometimes had babies when they shouldn't, and sometimes they couldn't have them when they should. They sometimes drank too much and they sometimes drank too little, for many an old soul would have benefitted more from a comforting tot of brandy at bedtime than from a less sinful, though prescribed, sleeping pill. We shared the lot of our fellow practitioners, seeing the many faces of life and dealing with people and their problems to the best of our ability.

But then, there's an old saying in Yorkshire that sums it all up. They'll shake their heads and say, "Ee, but tha' knows – there's nowt so queer as fowk."

Or as interesting!

A DOCTOR IN THE WEST
Morris Gibson

'Fortunately for mankind and for literature there are many (doctors) to whom the medical profession is an endlessly unfolding rich panorama to be savoured anew each day. There is the drama, the grief, tragedy and humour of human life and there is also the deep satisfaction which the truly dedicated doctor finds in the practice of his skills, in the exercise of his hard won knowledge.'—*James Herriot*, in his foreword to Morris Gibson's first book, *One Man's Medicine*.

Now, in *A Doctor in the West*, we find Drs Morris and Janet Gibson and their daughter, Catriona, at the point of leaving Hull, Yorkshire, to make their home in the Alberta foothills town of Okotoks. Setting up medical practice in this tiny town and adjusting to a new and very different way of life provide both amusing and amazing situations for the Gibsons and the community they've come to serve.

In Morris Gibson, we have a dedicated physician who is also a gifted storyteller, one whose love for humankind makes him only that much more aware of its oddities and frailities. Humour and heartbreak are here in his descriptions of medical practice in Okotoks and so is the loving portrayal of a western Canadian town and its people that should assume its place as a classic of the genre.

Now available in trade paperback...

THE GHOST WALKER
R.D. Lawrence

In the fall of 1972, the author built a small cabin in the heart of British Columbia's Selkirk Mountains from which to observe the cougar—one of North America's most elusive big game animals. For ten months, the author neither saw nor spoke with another human being, as he tracked the cougar, even accompanying it as it stalked its prey.

By the time Lawrence left the wilderness, he had not only learned a great deal about how the cougar lives in its natural state, but he had won the trust of two members of the species. More than the tale of a special relationship between a man and a wild animal, however, this is also the story of Lawrence's survival alone in a perilous and unforgiving wilderness.

A Totem Book

Now available in trade paperback...

THE ZOO THAT NEVER WAS
R.D. Lawrence

The author and his wife did not plan to become keepers of a wild menagerie when they bought their 350-acre Ontario farm. But, in the absence of an alternative haven for sick and wounded wild animals, they found their home becoming a 'zoo', as they took in and cared for a variety of creatures. Their first wards were a pair of baby raccoons found starving by the side of the road. They were joined by others: Penny, a skunk; Manx, a lynx; a pair of otters; a porcupine; and many more. The most endearing and troublesome member of the zoo was Snuffles, a baby bear cub raised in the Lawrence home. This is a story filled with scientific lore, as well as humour, warmth and adventure.

A Totem Book

Now available in trade paperback...

MY FIRST FORTY YEARS
Placido Domingo
Foreword by Harvey Sachs

Here is the life story of one of the world's greatest
and most popular opera singers. Now in his early
forties, Domingo gives us a totally personal book: a
buoyant account of his development as an artist, as
well as a wide range of his ideas and opinions on
everything from zarzuela singing to digital recording.

He tells the story of his family—his parents, successful singers both in Spain, where he was born,
and in Mexico, where he spent his youth; his
marriage at age sixteen and fatherhood at seventeen (which explains his premature grand-
fatherhood); and his extraordinarily happy and
productive second marriage.

He talks about his most demanding roles and those
for which he's most well-known—in *Otello* and *The
Tales of Hoffmann*. He also talks about the singers
he's performed with (from Tebaldi, Sutherland, and
Caballe to John Denver and Miss Piggy) and about
the great opera houses where he's performed.

A Totem Book

THE NIGHT THE GODS SMILED
Eric Wright

It is a particularly puzzling murder case that Inspector Charlie Salter of the Metropolitan Toronto Police is assigned to solve: Professor David Summers of Douglas College has been found dead in his Montreal hotel room while attending a conference. The only tangible clues are a lipstick-marked glass and the whisky bottle that was used to crush Summer's skull. Two clues so banal that they present a challenge in themselves.

From four of the late professor's academic colleagues who were also at the Montreal conference he had been attending, and with the aid of one of that city's detectives, 'Onree' O'Brien, Salter must try to piece together the pattern of the victim's last hours.

Charlie Salter is a most engaging detective character. Real promotion within the Force has eluded him thus far—a compliment, it might be said, to his personal originality. A philosopher-cop of sorts, he is very much his own man and frequently the despair of his wife. Mystery fans will be delighted to learn that there are more Charlie Salter stories to come.

A Totem Book